AF449123

Man of Quality,
Man of Letters

The Bucknell Studies in Eighteenth-Century Literature and Culture

General Editor: Greg Clingham, *Bucknell University*
Advisory Board: Paul K. Alkon, *University of Southern California*
Chloe Chard, *Independent Scholar*
Clement Hawes, *The Pennsylvania State University*
Robert Markley, *University of Illinois at Urbana-Champaign*
Jessica Munns, *University of Denver*
Cedric D. Reverand II, *University of Wyoming*
Janet Todd, *University of Aberdeen*

The Bucknell Studies in Eighteenth-Century Literature and Culture aims to publish challenging, new eighteenth-century scholarship. Of particular interest is critical, historical, and interdisciplinary work that is interestingly and intelligently theorized, and that broadens and refines the conception of the field. At the same time, the series remains open to all theoretical perspectives and different kinds of scholarship. While the focus of the series is the literature, history, arts, and culture (including art, architecture, music, travel, and history of science, medicine , and law) of the long eighteenth century in Britain and Europe, the series is also interested in scholarship that establishes relationships with other geographies, literature, and cultures for the period 1660–1830.

Recent Titles in This Series

Katherine West Scheil, *The Taste of the Town:*
Shakespearian Comedy and the Early Eighteenth-Century Theater
Phillip Smallwood, ed., *Johnson Re-Visioned: Looking Before and After*
Peter Walmsley, *Locke's Essay and the Rhetoric of Science*
Lisa Wood, *Modes of Discipline:*
Women, Conservatism, and the Novel after the French Revolution
Mark Blackwell, ed., *The Secret Life of Things:*
Animals, Objects, and It-Narratives in Eighteenth-Century England
Chris Mounsey and Caroline Gonda, eds., *Queer People:*
Negotiations and Expressions of Homosexuality, 1700–1800
Susan Manning and Peter France, *Enlightenment and Emancipation*
Evan Gottlieb, *Feeling British:*
Sympathy and National Identity in Scottish and English Writing, 1707–1832
Roland Racevskis, *Tragic Passages: Jean Racine's Art of the Threshold*
Lesley H. Walker, *A Mother's Love:*
Crafting Feminine Virtue in Enlightenment France
Rori Bloom, *Man of Quality, Man of Letters:*
The Abbé Prévost Between Novel and Newspaper
Barton Swaim, *Scottish Men of Letters and the New Public Sphere, 1802–1834*
Anthony Krupp, *Reason's Children: Childhood in Early Modern Philosophy*
David Collings, *Monstrous Society:*
Reciprocity, Discipline, and the Political Uncanny, c. 1780–1848

http://www.bucknell.edu/universitypress/

Man of Quality, Man of Letters

The Abbé Prévost Between Novel and Newspaper

Rori Bloom

Lewisburg
Bucknell University Press

Associated University Presses
2010 Eastpark Boulevard
Cranbury, NJ 08512

The paper used in this publication meets the requirements of the American National Standard for Permanence of Paper for Printed Library Materials Z39.48-1984.

Library of Congress Cataloging-in-Publication Data

Bloom, Rori, 1971–
    Man of quality, man of letters : the abbé Prévost between novel and newspaper / Rori Bloom.
        p. cm.
    Includes bibliographical references and index.
    ISBN 978-0-8387-5724-6 (alk. paper)
1. Prévost, abbé, 1697–1763 — Criticism and interpretation. I. Title.

PQ2021.Z5B56 2009
843'.509 — dc22

                                        2008022876

To my family, and especially to my mother,
I dedicate this book.

Contents

Acknowledgments

I WOULD LIKE TO ACKNOWLEDGE THOSE TEACHERS AND SCHOLARS WHO first inspired my interest in eighteenth-century French literature: Chantal Thomas, Philippe Roger, and Anne Deneys-Tunney. My thanks also go to Gregory Brown, Bill Calin, Ziad Elmarsafy, and Nancy Regalado for their help at key points in the development of this project. I must also recognize Susan Read Baker whose thoughtful reading of my manuscript made all the difference.

I wish to express my sincere appreciation to the many other teachers, colleagues, and friends at New York University and the University of Florida whose support has meant so much and to the College of Arts and Sciences and the Paris Research Center of the University of Florida for the financial support that contributed to the completion of this project. Finally, I thank the staff and readers of the Associated University Presses and Bucknell University Press for their help.

Man of Quality,
Man of Letters

Introduction

Evoking the eighteenth century's neglect of the novels of the seventeenth,[1] Prévost makes the following pronouncement: "On ne lit plus les anciens romans; ils sont trop longs, et par là ennuyeux. On parcourt encore quelques historiettes, dont une heure ou deux voient la fin" [No one reads the old novels anymore; they are too long and boring. People still skim a tale, if it takes only an hour or two to finish], but Prévost's observation on the novels of the past also proves a presentiment of his own works' reception by posterity. When he asks: "Serait-ce que les Français se lasseraient de tant de préliminaires ménagés autrefois à dessein pour conduire imperceptiblement à la fin d'une aventure? Commenceraient-ils à ne plus goûter que la conclusion du roman?" [Could it be that the French are tired of the many preliminaries used in the past to artfully lead the reader to the adventure's end? Have they begun to enjoy only the conclusion of a novel?],[2] he is predicting even more exactly the fate of his own fictions, since modern readers have dismissed almost all of Prévost's prodigious production in favor of *Manon Lescaut,* the last installment of the author's multivolume first novel, the *Mémoires et aventures d'un homme de qualité.*[3] In fact, Prévost authored a dozen novels, several of which were six times the length of the novella for which he is best known. The extent of his achievement does not end there, for like many eighteenth-century men of letters, Prévost was a polygraph whose works include translations from Latin and English (such as his highly influential adaptation of Richardson's *Clarissa*), the fifteen-volume *Histoire générale des voyages,* more than twenty volumes of journalism, and even a dictionary (*Le Manuel lexique*). If in many ways Prévost's fictions are reminiscent of those seventeenth-century novels, which the eighteenth century deemed outmoded, his nonfiction writings are ahead of their time, expressing an encyclopedic ambition that prefigures the intellectual enterprises of the Enlightenment.

His particular place in literary history may explain the relative neglect of Prévost: he comes too late to be considered a seventeenth-century author and too early to belong with those whom we study as exemplars of Enlightenment philosophy.[4] I am interested in reexamining this author precisely because of his historical situation in order to show that his career represents an important paradigm shift in the literary field. Prévost's life (1697–1763) coincides almost exactly with a period that the *Histoire de l'édition française* designates as one of profound transformation in French letters: "From 1660 to 1780, we move from Fouquet the patron of the arts to Panckoucke the captain of industry, from the gentleman amateur [*le lettré honnête homme*] to the cultural professional."[5] I will argue that Prévost translates this transition into literary terms, for while his fiction operates within structures established in the seventeenth century, his nonfiction demonstrates a new attitude toward the roles of author and public. By exploring the deep tension between Prévost's novelistic and journalistic writing, I will analyze their opposition in terms of a contrast between aristocratic and bourgeois ideals, between static and dynamic economic systems, and between premodern and modern modes of writing and reading.

While Prévost's fiction and nonfiction read as if written in two quite different periods, many of his most important novels were in fact composed during the seven-year run of his newspaper, *Le Pour et contre*, between 1733 and 1740. Although I will eventually argue that these two different genres are essentially complementary and work together to elaborate a complex discourse about what it meant to write and to read at the beginning of the eighteenth century, I will first assess their differences. Prévost himself insists on their incompatibility, affirming in *Le Pour et contre* that, despite their pretense at historicity, his novels are not factual[6] and that despite their often unbelievable aspects the stories in his newspaper are not fictions.[7] Prévost's declaration is not necessary to establish this distinction, since his writing in these two genres is as different as night and day: the dark atmosphere of the novels matches the deep solitude in which their narrators write their memoirs; in detailing the everyday happenings of busy cities, the journalist's pace is brisk and his style bright. Moreover, while the memoir-novels look back to ideas and events of the *siècle de Louis XIV*, the newspaper announces issues and attitudes of the *siècle des Lumières*. At once nostalgic and prophetic, Prévost confounds expectations and poses a problem for literary history.

The idea that Prévost's novels were already dated even when first published is present in the reactions of their earliest readers who objected to their clichéd sentiments and hackneyed plots. Of course, this accusation of archaism by readers who were also writers often served as part of a strategy to establish the modernity of their own works. For example, in the preface to his *Egarements du cœur et de l'espirit* (1736), Crébillon *fils* proposes a new kind of novel by characterizing key elements of Prévost's writing as old-fashioned: "[I]f instead of filling novels with dark and strange situations, with heroes whose character and adventures are never believable, we were to make the novel more like a comedy, an image of human life [. . . . , t]he reader would find no more extraordinary or tragic events, no more heroes who cross the seas only to be taken prisoner by Turks, no more adventures in harems, no more sultanas rescued from vigilant eunuchs . . . no more shocking deaths and infinitely fewer underground caves."[8] To cast his own work as innovative, Crébillon *fils* characterizes his most formidable predecessor as *passé*, arguing that readers are no longer interested in Prévost's Oriental episodes and underground settings. In fact, this assault on Prévost is an almost Oedipal attack, for in condemning the dark and dangerous world of Prévostian fiction, Crébillon is at the same time announcing the end of the aesthetic of the tragic plays of Crébillon *père*, his own father.

While Crébillon *fils* dismisses Prévost's work in general terms, Diderot focuses his criticism on Prévost's most ambitious novel, *Cleveland*. If *Jacques le fataliste* can be called an antinovel, *Cleveland* is the model of the novel against which it is written. Rejecting a convenient resolution to a scene by way of the facile coincidences of traditional fiction Diderot writes: "It would have stunk of *Cleveland*."[9] Diderot evokes the adventures of Prévost's hero only to deride that author's overreliance on the stock plots of the *romanesque:* "What could stop me from . . . sending Jacques off to the islands? From sending his master there? From bringing them both back to France on the same ship? How easy it is to make up stories!"[10] By concluding "but they will have to settle instead for a bad night and you for this delay," Diderot sets himself squarely against Prévost, advocating a new form of novelistic writing where writer and reader communicate and collude around the fiction, questioning its structures and mocking its clichés. However, while Diderot rejects Cleveland in favor of Jacques, the tortured introspection of Prévost's hero and the complex adventures of Cleveland's story inform Diderot's drama *Le Fils naturel*, and even Diderot's ideas on the modern novel expressed in his *Eloge de Richardson* owe a major debt to Prévost's translations of that English author.[11] In the end, Prévost's putative archaism appears to be a construction by authors like Crébillon *fils* and Diderot, eager to constitute their modernity in contrast to an important precursor.

If Prévost is relegated to the shadows of the Enlightenment, such an assignment is not due to external determination alone but also to internal structures in his novels that indicate his extreme allegiance to both the aesthetics and the ethics of the seventeenth century. Dark images of the baroque abound in the Prévostian novel where, for example, a girl is entombed with the corpse of her lover or a dying maiden marries her suitor on her deathbed.[12] Prévost sets these scenes in a typically baroque structure similar to those of Gomberville or La Calprenède: his heroes' adventures are episodic, continuing endlessly although often interrupted by embedded narratives. At the same time, Prévost's use of the memoir form is related to a renewal of interest in the memoirs (first published in the early eighteenth century) of seventeenth-century personages such as Saint-Simon or the Cardinal de Retz. Prévost's novels are mostly set during the reign of Louis XIV, and Jean Sgard has noted that the author's period of predilection for the events in his fictions is the stretch from 1680 to 1715.[13] Like his heroes', Prévost's own culture was that of the seventeenth century, since his education was complete before the Regency began, as Sgard notes: "When Louis XIV died, Prévost was eighteen years old, but his fate was already determined despite the Regency's promise of freedom."[14] Like most of the authors of his generation, Prévost was imbued with the values of classicism, as Georges May affirms in *Le Dilemme du roman au dix-huitième siècle:* "In the course of our research and our reflections, one fact has made its importance felt with particular insistence: the enormous influence of louis-quatorzian classicism on the literary values of the time. . . . Of all the legacies which weighed heavily on the novelists of the first half of the eighteenth century, the heaviest incontestably was that of classical values."[15]

Prévost inherited not only the literary values of the seventeenth century but also that era's sociocultural ideals, for his own heroes are the product of a society ruled by the privilege of birth and regulated by the ideology of *honnêteté*. However, while Prévost's fiction is founded on the principles of the past, his heroes' actions expose the fragility of these virtues when faced with the challenges of modern life. As R. A. Francis explains: "In the nascent world of the eighteenth century, they simply cannot afford to live by the old values."[16] Entitling his essay on Prévost's use of seventeenth-century settings "Fin d'un monde,"[17] Jean Sgard eloquently expresses Prévost's relationship with the past, since the structure of the memoir-novel with its hero-narrator who acts in the past but tells in the present dramatizes the difference between these two temporal moments. Moreover, the distinction between hero and narrator also suggests another distinction, the one between narrator and author, between the idealized *honnête homme* who supposedly writes his memoirs and the real, working author Prévost who writes the novels. I will argue that the fictional memoirists of Prévost's novels incarnate an ideal type of authorship (the author as *honnête homme*) typical of the seventeenth century, a type whose existence is endangered by the new realities of writing in the eighteenth.

While Prévost's novels explore the problems of their heroes' past, Prévost's newspaper is a reflection of the author's present. The rise of the genre is itself a phenomenon of the eighteenth century: Jack Censer has noted that between 1745 and 1785 the French press expanded from fifteen to eighty titles and from 15,000 to 60,000 copies in circulation. Censer estimates four to six readers per copy, bringing the audience for periodicals at that time up to about 300,000 people.[18] Prévost's *Pour et contre* anticipated this explosion and participated in the growth of the periodical genre beyond the three official titles in France at the end of the seventeenth century: *La Gazette de France, Le Journal des savants*, and *Le Mercure*. This expansion had as its impetus the emergence of a French press outside of France after the revocation of the Edict of Nantes, since with the exile of French Protestants at the end of the seventeenth century, periodicals in French prospered as a means of communication for members of the Protestant diaspora who finally wrote outside of the strict censure of the French state. Pierre Bayle's *Nouvelles de la République de Lettres* is an example of this phenomenon and is cited by Prévost as an inspiration for *Le Pour et contre*, which Prévost began during his own exile in England.

The multiplication of periodicals at this time also demonstrates the Enlightenment's interest in circulating new ideas, and at least a generation before the *encyclopédistes* began their efforts to collect and redistribute knowledge, newspapers functioned as cheap, portable encyclopedias, as Claude Labrosse and Pierre Rétat explain: "At the time when dictionaries were becoming colossal enterprises (*L'Encyclopédie*), the periodical method allowed every home to own a little encyclopedia."[19] Jean Sgard notes that Prévost's *Pour et contre* is a prime example of "an encyclopedic . . . program,"[20] as it promises in its first issue to treat an impressively wide variety of subjects including:

I. L'Etat des sciences et des arts. II. Les Ouvrages nouveaux. . . . III. Les Journaux et autres mémoires périodiques de la République des Lettres. IV. Les Mœurs et les usages du siècle. V. Les Préjugés vulgaires. VI. Le Caractère des hommes illustres. . . . VII. La Comparaison des grands hommes. VIII. Le Caractère des dames distinguées par le mérite. IX. Les nouveaux établissements, civils, militaires, littéraires. X. Les Médailles nouvelles. XII. Les Faits avérés. . . . XII. Les Inventions extraordinaires de l'art. (*PC* 1, 10–11)

[I. The State of the Sciences and the Arts. II. New Works. . . . III. Newspapers and Other Periodicals of the Republic of Letters. IV. Customs and Usages of our Time. V. Common Prejudices. VI. The Character of Illustrious Men. . . . VII. The Comparison of Great Men. VIII. The Character of Ladies Distinguished by their Merit. IX. New Civil, Military, or Literary Establishments. X. New Medals. XII. True Facts. . . . XII. The Extraordinary Inventions of Art.]

Not only does Prévost show his interest in the spread of knowledge by way of the press, he is also an important early promoter of the use of reason. After each article in *Le Pour et contre*, Prévost does not make a critical pronouncement but rather leaves the final evaluation to his readers, allowing them to take a position for or against the work reviewed or the innovation announced. Introducing reason into the public discourse through the periodical has been seen by sociologists and historians as one of the major changes in mentalities to occur in the eighteenth century. In *Les Origines culturelles de la Révolution française*, Roger Chartier associates the growth of the power of the periodical press in the eighteenth century with the loss of the power of traditional authorities and with the gain of the power of the public: "The intellectual sociability of the eighteenth century is represented as the foundation of a new public space where the use of reason and judgment is exercised without limits on critical examination and without obligatory deference to the old authorities. The various instances of literary and art criticism (salons, cafés, academies, newspapers) constituted this new, autonomous, free, and sovereign public. Understanding the emergence of the new political culture means recognizing the progressive politicization of the literary public sphere and the movement of criticism towards traditionally forbidden domains: the mysteries of the Church and the State."[21] Although to avoid problems with his censors Prévost excludes religion and politics from *Le Pour et contre*, I will argue that his newspaper's engagement of its reading public nonetheless contributes to the development of open debate in France. Despite his affinity for the past, Prévost participates in some of the most fundamental movements of his present and enables progress toward the future.

If Prévost's newspaper offers a model for modernity, this movement in time is, however, linked to a movement in space, for *Le Pour et contre* constantly evokes England as an exemplar of progress and a place of possibility. Before major figures of the French Enlightenment took England as an inspiration, Prévost saw this society as a model for new modes of being. [22] In essence, Prévost characterizes the English as a forward-thinking people and compares travel to England to a sort of time travel when he declares: "Un livre de Paris qui passe une fois la mer, se trouve tout d'un coup à l'égard des Anglais ce qu'il sera dans deux siècles à l'égard des Français mêmes" [A book from Paris that crosses the sea is immediately regarded by the English in the same manner in which the French will see it in two centuries] (*PC* 15, 349–50). If Prévost wants his *Pour et contre* to be as its title indicates a "périodique d'un goût nouveau" [periodical of a new taste], the novelty he offers is mainly news of England, for he proclaims: "Enfin, ce qui sera tout à fait particulier à cette feuille, je promets d'y insérer chaque fois quelque particularité intéressante touchant le génie des Anglais" [Finally, what will be special about this newspaper is that I promise to include in each issue some interesting peculiarity of the English character] (*PC* 1, 11). However, Prévost's study of English life is not just a means to offer novelty to his French readers but also to indicate new directions for French society.

For Prévost, one of the most important inventions of the English is the newspaper form, and his praise of England begins with an admiration of that nation's newspapers, which he will use as a model for his own. At the beginning of *Le Pour et contre* he explains: "Sachant la langue anglaise et faisant venir régulièrement de Londres toutes les feuilles périodiques qui sont comprises sous le nom de News Papers, je suis résolu pour enrichir la mienne d'en tirer tout ce que je pourrai rendre propre à l'usage de la France" [Because I know the English language and regularly receive from London all the English periodicals known by the name of News Papers, I am resolved to enrich my own by taking from the English all that I can adapt to the use of the French] (*PC* 1, 12). According to Prévost, newspapers represent what is best in English society, since the debate and discord among their countless papers demonstrate the freedom of expression that Englishmen enjoy. He is also fascinated with the companion institution of the coffeehouse where famous papers such as *The Spectator* are both written and read, and he calls this place "le siège de la liberté Anglicane" [the seat of Anglican freedom].[23] It is in the coffeehouse where he notices that the reading of newspapers leads not only to the movement of ideas but also to the fluidity of social identity, as he writes: "On m'a fait remarquer dans plusieurs maisons de café un ou deux mylords, un chevalier baronnet, un cordonnier, un tailleur, un marchand de vin et quelques gens de même trempe assis autour d'une même table, et s'occupant à fumer et à s'entretenir familièrement des nouvelles de la cour et de la ville. Les affaires du gouvernement sont l'objet du peuple comme celui des grands" [People pointed out to me in several coffeehouses one or two lords, a knight baronet, a shoemaker, a tailor, a wine merchant, and others of their kind seated around the same table smoking and speaking familiarly about the news of the court and the city] (*MHQ,* 247).

Finally, one of the most striking insights of *Le Pour et contre* is Prévost's recognition of the rise of bourgeois values in England as a result of English economic dynamism. The hybridity of discourse found in the coffeehouses accompanies a mixing of classes in a country that is not controlled by eighteenth-century French society's rigid rules of caste. As a result, the heroes of *Le Pour et contre* are not the old-fashioned gentlemen of Prévost's novels but rather modern men of means whose adventures follow the rise and fall of the new economy of speculation: the tragic ends of the banker Cantillon and the stock jobber Herby are given extended attention in Prévost's newspaper. Moreover, Prévost explains that if the French gentleman of the seventeenth and the early eighteenth century disdains commerce as an undignified activity, in England, even noblemen engage in trade, and he details the business interests of several English aristocrats. He argues that if aristocrats lower themselves to participate in commerce, men of modest origins may be more easily elevated in English society. In his study of the successful careers and social ascent of Addison, Congreve, and Swift among others, Prévost argues that in England even men of letters can, through hard work, become men of quality.

At the same time as he admires the power of the English economy, Prévost is keenly aware of the problems inherent in merging reading and writing with buying and selling. If a few English authors are rewarded with royal patronage, Prévost notes that the majority of writers in England still struggle for survival in a competitive marketplace. Prévost observes that with the multiplication of periodicals and printed matter in general, literature like all else in London has become a business, and the English newspapers that Prévost so admires are, as Erin Mackie describes them, "without financial backing from either private patrons or government" and thus exist as "purely commercial enterprises funded solely by sales and advertisements."[24] In this scheme, literature is just another commodity to be bought and sold. Although Prévost finds much to praise in the effect of the market economy on English society, he is cautious in recommending the application of market values to literature: *Le Pour et contre* is in some ways inspired by English models, but Prévost's journalistic examination of the new literary economy in England is also in many ways an indictment of it. While *Le Pour et contre* is forward-thinking in its interest in collecting and diffusing information, in its acknowledgment of the importance of the public sphere, in its vision of a more mutable society, and in its appreciation of economics as an essential influence on social change, it is nonetheless nostalgic for the past, for a system of values in which art is not commercial and in which the writer earns not financial gain but glory for his efforts. At the same time as Prévost depicts life on Grub Street, he rejects the new economy of literature he sees developing in England and portrays himself not as a hack but as a hero along the lines of the heroes of his own novels. In retreating from his position as a modern Man of Letters to reassociate himself with that of the Man of Quality, Prévost shows that even in his most modern work, he is still compelled to look back to the strong models inherited from the seventeenth century. Of course, despite his discourse of resistance to the commodification of culture, Prévost actively exploits this evolution, using techniques of marketing to sell his own writing, adopting the bourgeois ideology that hard work merits reward, and creating literary works that capitalize on capitalism.

By giving equal attention to Prévost's novelistic and journalistic writing, I am arguing for a new orientation in the scholarship that until now has considered Prévost first and foremost as an author of novels. The most in-depth examination of Prévost is still *Prévost romancier*, where Jean Sgard argues that Prévost's novels represent the most important aspect of his literary career: "[H]e was above all else a novelist and the first to understand the importance of the genre."[25] The tradition of privileging Prévost's novels over his newspaper may be traced to nineteenth-century readings that valued Prévost's first-person fiction as a form of personal expression and neglected his seemingly impersonal nonfiction writing as a result. For many nineteenth-century readers, *Manon Lescaut* was Prévost's best work because it seemed to be his most autobiographical. In an essay entitled "Manon Lescaut, did she exist?" Arsène Houssaye affirms: "Manon Lescaut is a memory." He adds: "A dreamer could never invent such a thing."[26] An anonymous prefacer to the 1847 *Suite de Manon Lescaut* writes of Prévost: "He was Des Grieux."[27] At the end of the nineteenth century, André Lebreton explains that while for other writers it is not essential to know their lives, Prévost's works are best interpreted in light of the author's biography: "It is not indispensable, before reading them [the other novelists of the time] to know how they loved. In the case of Prévost the man and the author explain each other, and the secret of his originality is in the story of his life."[28] Although the nuanced readings of *Prévost romancier* go far beyond biographical criticism, Sgard's chronological analysis insists on the strong coordination between Prévost's life and work; he sees the novels as the privileged production of this synthesis and thus as the life's work of their author: "[H]is biography may be summed up as the genesis of his novels."[29] In his recent biography of Prévost, which thoroughly examines every aspect of the author's career, Sgard stands firm in seeing the novels as the essence of the author's achievement, concluding: "That is why the life of Prévost . . . is still from beginning to end so interesting: it leads directly to his novels."[30]

What is problematic about many biographical interpretations of Prévost's novels is their reading of his writing as a confession and not a construction, an effusion of emotions unmediated by practical or even literary concerns. While Enlightenment readers may have viewed Prévost as a craven hack, Romantic readers imagined Prévost as a passionate genius. Houssaye argues that *Manon Lescaut* is a true story because he sees in it "the truth of passion." He describes its composition as the transcription of a divine dictation, proclaiming: "The most beautiful novels are made by destiny, by chance, by God himself."[31] Sainte-Beuve sets *Manon* apart from the rest of Prévost's writing, attributing it to a moment of special inspiration: "Happy are those who, like he did, have had one day, one week, one month of their life where the heart was more generous, the voice purer, vision more lucid, genius more present."[32] Jules Janin affirms that *Manon Lescaut* is the work of "a man of genius" created "in one of those moments of enthusiasm."[33] Such Romantic discourse of inspiration and enthusiasm would almost seem to exclude authorial agency and to ignore Prévost's artistic and professional ambitions.[34] Although Sgard's reading of Prévost amply demonstrates the author's artistry, his designation of *Manon Lescaut* as a "miraculous success"[35] echoes some nineteenth-century assessments of

Prévost's achievement, and he reinforces the Romantic image of Prévost as more passionate than professional by attributing to him "a poorly controlled sensibility, an ardent imagination, the gift of making his emotion visible."[36] The tendency to read Prévost's novels as the intensely personal expressions of their author's inner life is encouraged by Prévost's preference for the memoir-novel form. While refusing to read Prévost's novels as veiled autobiographies, critics such as Jean Sgard and Erik Leborgne have explained the aesthetic coherence of Prévost's fictional *œuvre* by situating its source in the author's own personal obsessions and fantasies.[37]

By privileging the narratological over the psychological, critics such as René Démoris and Jean-Paul Sermain have emphasized the skillful use of language in the novels' narration. These approaches read the narration as a manipulation and point to Prévost's able orchestration of the complex relationship between discourse and story. Démoris's study of Prévost's fiction analyzes the author's use of first-person narration as a "subtle rhetoric" responsible for explaining away the problematic actions of the hero.[38] Sermain's *Rhétorique et roman au dix-huitième siècle* studies Prévost's narrators not as tormented obsessives but as eloquent orators: "[T]he evaluation of the rhetorical character of the discourses formulated by the hero or addressed to him play an essential role in the interpretation of the novel. It decides the sense that the reader is led to give to the autobiographical act itself."[39] However, while narratological analyses of Prévost's novels reveal the author's talent as a craftsman of complex fictions, the application of these same principles to Prévost's career shows it to be a composition just as carefully controlled. Sermain distinguishes between "the internal eloquence of the work, that of the characters" and "the external eloquence of the work, that which allows the author to appeal to his public."[40] Whereas Sermain has limited himself to an examination of the internal eloquence of the novels, I propose to juxtapose the novel's communication between narrator and narratee with the newspaper's representation of the relationship between author and public. In so doing, I will expose the overarching rhetoric by which Prévost uses both his fiction and nonfiction to articulate his authorial image and to manage the public's perception of him.

By emphasizing the importance of Prévost's journalism, I am following a trend in scholarly attention to the press of the Old Regime that started with the publication of a *Dictionnaire des journalistes (1600–1789)* and a *Dictionnaire des journaux* (edited by Jean Sgard) in the 1970s. Some work has been done on Prévost's *Pour et contre,* with an introduction, tables, and index to the periodical published by Sgard in the 1960s,[41] and more recently a critical edition of the first sixty issues of the periodical published by Steve Larkin in the 1990s.[42] In 1992's *Récit et réflexion: poétique de l'hétérogène dans* Le Pour et contre *de Prévost*, Shelly Charles looks at the periodical as a unified literary work with its own poetics and definitively establishes it as an essential element of Prévost's literary achievement.[43] My treatment of *Le Pour et contre* draws on some of the ideas suggested by Charles's study but diverges from her approach by rereading the text in the context of Prévost's literary career. Where Charles's work privileges the "pacte de lecture" that unites narrator and narratee on the micro-structural level of particular articles of *Le Pour et contre*, I focus on the macrostructural level of the newspaper to examine the ways in which Prévost negotiates an author-public contract in both ethical and economic terms over the course of his journalistic enterprise.

In order to characterize Prévost as both behind the times and ahead of his time, as a case study of a paradigm shift in French letters, I am relying on a variety of approaches in literature, cultural history, and sociology that have established the eighteenth century as a moment of transition for mentalities. Specifically, I am considering the change in status of the author and of the public in the eighteenth century, since scholarship suggests that these concepts only really emerged as such in this period. In his famous essay, "Qu'est-ce qu'un auteur?" Foucault dates the origins of this question to the eighteenth century, which he secs as the beginning of an "industrial and bourgeois era of individualism and private property."[44] Because of the shifts in socioeconomic structures in this period, authorship becomes a category equivalent to ownership, according to Foucault: "[A] system of ownership of texts is established, . . . and strict rules on copyright, on author-publisher relations, on the rights of reproduction are set down."[45] In his essay "Figures de l'auteur," Roger Chartier responds to Foucault's "What is an author?" by stating that the idea of authorship was not waiting for the socioeconomic conditions of the eighteenth century in order to emerge. Nonetheless, Chartier, too, identifies an important change in the self-representation of authors in the eighteenth century, which he describes in the following terms: "In the second half of the eighteenth century, a somewhat paradoxical link is established between the professionalization of literary activity (it should result in a certain direct remuneration permitting writers to live from their writing) and the self-representation of authors in an ideology of genius, founded on the radical autonomy of the work of art and the disinterestedness of the creative gesture." He adds: "On the one hand, the work of poetry or philosophy is identified as a saleable good with a commercial value (as Diderot has written) and which consequently may be the object of contracts and monetary equivalents. On the other hand, the work of art is considered to be the product of a free and inspired activity motivated by internal drives only." Chartier sums up this moment of transition finally by describing it as "the movement from the patronage system to the marketplace which constitutes a change from a situation where compensation for writing was most often awarded before the fact or deferred in the form of positions or ranks to a situation where an immediate monetary profit is expected at the time of the sale of the manuscript to a publisher."[46] This evolution in attitudes toward writing from a pastime of the privileged to a professional activity is the same shift I see in Prévost's work.

Prévost's difficult articulation of his professional status is, of course, a function of his position as a precursor, since he was one of the first French men of letters to attempt to live directly from his income as an author. If he does not enter uncritically into a celebration of the market economy and the accompanying commercialization of the writer's work, this is because of the ideas about authorship that he inherited from the seventeenth century. Alain Viala's study *La Naissance de l'écrivain* — which its author calls a "sociology of the literary field" — argues that at the start of the seventeenth century writing can barely be considered a career. Viala notes: "For numerous authors, the production of works does not constitute an autonomous activity: their position in the literary field is an extension of their situation in the social field."[47] Aristocrats who write are considered aristocrats who write and not professional authors. Viala takes this antiprofessional attitude as a starting point for his study, which tracks the increasing professionalization of literature by nonaristocratic authors who write within an aristocratic system to earn the admiration and patronage of the nobility. He explains that such authors strive for a sort of "réussite" defined in terms of social promotion rather than the "succès" that would stem from financial gain due to popularity with the public. In the evolution toward professionalization, he notes the beginning of a divergence from this model, a development of two opposing images of the writer: "the one where a man dedicates himself to celebrating the glory of the Great Men who are his patrons and the one where a man makes money from the sale of his works to the public."[48] While Viala shows that some authors of the seventeenth century begin to operate under the second system, I will argue that

Prévost's work is a privileged place not just for the movement from an old to a new model of authorship but for the representation of the tensions inherent in this transition.

Robert Darnton's study of the literary underground of Old Regime France provides additional context to my analysis of Prévost's complicated position on professional authorship in the eighteenth century. In "The High Enlightenment and the Lowlife of Literature," Darnton depicts the problems faced by men of letters who tried to sell their wares in the newly open literary market. He explains that while more and more provincial youths flocked to Paris to embark on a literary career, few reached the heights of their idol Voltaire; Darnton states: "On the contrary, everything indicates that while the mandarins fattened themselves on pensions, most authors sank into a sort of literary proletariat."[49] He continues: "The most salient fact is that the marketplace could not support many more writers than in the days when Prévost and Lesage proved that it was possible—barely possible—to live from the pen instead of pensions."[50] He concludes: "Once he had fallen into Grub Street, the provincial youth who had dreamt of storming Parnassus never extricated himself."[51] In borrowing the term "Grub Street" from its original English context, Darnton is in a way mimicking the move made by Prévost several centuries earlier, since *Le Pour et contre* already interprets the conditions of the eighteenth-century literary field by looking to England as a model, by observing in its commercial economy an extreme case of the commodification of literature. The issues of Prévost's *Pour et contre* written in and about England give us an insider's view of Grub Street even as the Frenchman Prévost claims an outsider position: Prévost condemns the commercialization of English letters at the same time as he incorporates English techniques into his own writing. While I associate Prévost's memoir-novels with older, aristocratic attitudes, I will look at Prévost's newspaper as the source of a new approach to writing as a business. In fact, I see Prévost's paradoxical attitude toward authorship as an early attempt to address the opposition between two positions identified by Pierre Bourdieu in his study of the literary field of the nineteenth century:

> At one pole, the anti-economical economy of pure art which, founded on the obligatory recognition of the value of disinterestedness and on the denial of the economic (of the commercial) and of profit (over the short term), privileges production and its specific requirements, issued from an autonomous history; this production which can only recognize the de-

mand for what it can produce itself, but only over the long term, is ori-
ented toward the accumulation of symbolic capital. . . . At the other pole,
the economic logic of literary and artistic industries which, by making
the commerce of cultural goods into a business like any other, confers
priority on circulation, on immediate and temporary success, measured
for example by the number of printings, and is happy to adjust itself to
the preexisting demand of the clientele. [52]

While these two poles are seen by Bourdieu as moving farther apart
with the advance of industrialization, Prévost's preindustrial status encourages his effort to contain these two contradictory positions in his
own career.

As a journalist, Prévost does participate in the industrialization of
literature and contributes to the conceptualization of the reading public
as a market. This phenomenon has been studied in analyses of the English newspaper, and in her introduction to an anthology of articles
from *The Spectator* and *The Tatler*, Erin Mackie writes that "[t]he success of the project depended on making the papers attractive to the
readers and available to the largest possible audience. These criteria are
at once satisfied and complicated by the papers' status as popular, prestigious, indeed, even fashionable commodities in the market of public
opinion. *The Tatler* and *The Spectator* exist within modern conditions of
commodification and commercialization."[53] Mackie adds that "[m]ass
commercial consumption and mass culture are products of the fully in-
dustrialized nineteenth century but the blueprint for a recognizably
modern consumer society was being drawn up in the eighteenth."[54]
These ideas about the early industrialization of literature are addressed
in studies of eighteenth-century French literature such as Julia Simon's
Mass Enlightenment, where Simon cites Horkheimer, Adorno, and Habermas to talk about the effects of the rise of capitalism, the spread of the
consumer market, changes in social relations, and changes in the public
and private spheres on the production and reception of the works of
Diderot and Rousseau.[55] In order to examine not only the production of
literature and the socioeconomic status of the author but also its reception and its effect on the formation of a new kind of reading public, I
follow Mackie, Simon, and other cultural historians in adopting Habermas's model of the structural transformation of the public sphere.[56] I
reaffirm the argument that this phenomenon is initially English and undoubtedly linked to the periodical press by finding these very same
ideas omnipresent in Prévost's *Pour et contre*.

In reading *Le Pour et contre*, I will then look not only for Prévost's articulation of his position as a professional author but also at his representation of his readers. In his article on eighteenth-century periodicals in *Histoire de l'édition française*, Jean Sgard notes that it is the transformation of the readership that allows the multiplication of newspapers in France: "With a noticeable rise in the standard of living from 1760 on, it is not surprising that cultural needs grew proportionately. The educated population itself had grown; intellectual activity was booming in all the regions of France, and booksellers as well as reading clubs, schools, and learned societies profited from this phenomenon."[57] Sgard designates the periodical as a means of studying the market for literature, as a measure of the tastes and budgets of readers: "With the distribution of periodicals, booksellers learned to perform a study of the market, to respond to evolving demand, to put into place a distribution network, to use all of the resources of advertisement, to solicit a financial engagement from the reader."[58] In their introduction to a study of French periodicals in the year 1734, Rétat and Sgard write: "One may hypothesize that these networks [of periodical distribution], which periodically change, strive to grow and to refine themselves while maintaining their equilibrium, present in themselves some figure of the public." They continue: "As a mobile yet permanent device, periodicals are probably one of the first instruments for organizing, measuring, and analyzing the public in the modern sense of the term."[59] My study of Prévost will allow me to recognize similar strategies in his newspaper and his novels and to see them as sites for the construction of Prévost's authorial persona and also for the cultivation of his relationship with readers.

The first chapter of this book examines Prévost's novels and centers on the status of their narrators as the supposed authors of their own memoirs. By analyzing the aristocratic ethos of these narrators, their attachment to values more characteristic of the seventeenth than of the eighteenth century, I identify their approach to authorship as an archaic attitude of gentlemanly amateurism at odds with Prévost's professional ambitions. By studying the degradation of old images of heroism inside the novels and then exposing the erosion of old ideas about authorship in Prévost's correspondence with his novels' publishers, I push this paradox to reveal the impossible persistence of old ideals in the face of new realities.

While Prévost's novels may deny the realities of the modern literary marketplace, his newspaper provides a detailed description of the commodification of culture in the early eighteenth century. My second chapter takes as its subject *Le Pour et contre*'s presentation of Prévost's experiences in England and Holland and his observations on the importance of economic forces in these societies, especially in the book trade. This chapter examines Prévost's efforts to resist a sacrifice of quality for quantity in literary production as he strives to reclaim the title of Man of Quality for the modern man of letters. My reading of autobiographical anecdotes published in *Le Pour et contre* reveals a rhetoric in which the author likens himself to the heroes of his novels. However, I also show Prévost's systematic reference to his novels in his newspaper to be a new strategy, the marketing of an established brand that uses the Man of Quality name as its quality seal.

If *Le Pour et contre* allows Prévost to reposition himself as an author in the modern literary field, it is also the place where he represents the new reality of the modern reading public. In chapter 3, I show that Prévost's newspaper is especially interested in understanding the public sphere, first studying its operation in England (with articles on mobs at executions, crowds at freak shows, and audiences at the theater) and then adapting this English material to French readers. I argue that through his efforts to respond to readers' demand—he claims to vary his subjects to appeal to all and to change his pace to prevent boredom—Prévost ultimately equates the value of his work with its market value.

While Prévost's newspaper privileges the author's relationship with his public, his novels seem to refuse to recognize readers, since the narrators insist on their love of privacy and disdain for publication. Chapter 4 looks at the role of the reader in the novels, at first presented as unnecessary but eventually identified as the essential arbiter of the narrator's story. I show that, despite the apparent differences between his novels and his newspaper, in both genres Prévost invites the reader to be his judge. I argue that the incorporation of autobiographical anecdotes in both newspaper and novel further engages readers' judgment by playing with the public's image of Prévost—courting curiosity and cultivating scandal—in order to sell his work.

In its analysis of the prefaces of Prévost's memoir-novels, chapter 5 shows how the first pages of each novel borrow strategies from the newspaper. The prefacer draws readers into the text, yet this inward movement is accompanied by a movement outward, appealing to readers interested in the same kind of extraordinary stories found in *Le Pour et contre*. After examining the preface as a place where the techniques of the newspaper and novel meet, this chapter will focus on the transformation of the prefacer from amateur to professional. As the narrator of Prévost's first fiction becomes the prefacer of Prévost's three successive novels, these prefaces represent sites of slippage in his status from Man of Quality to Man of Letters.

Finally, chapter 6 studies a series of articles from *Le Pour et contre* known as the *Contes singuliers*, texts that situate themselves somewhere between fact and fiction, possessed of a noticeably novelistic content despite their journalistic context. After designating the *Contes* as microcosms of the Prévostian novel within *Le Pour et contre*, I will analyze the move from the novel's use of first-person narration to the newspaper's third-person narration in order to explore the unsentimental and ironic attitude that ensues. In so doing, I argue that the *Contes* are caricatures of the novels and that Prévost uses his short fictions to parody his long ones. I conclude that the *Contes* constitute a metafictional turn in Prévost's work, thus proving their author's acute self-awareness and offering to readers new and more complex ways to read his writing.

1
Authorship in Prévost's Novels:
From Man of Quality to Man of Letters

"NEVER HAS ONE MAN WRITTEN SO MUCH. HE ONLY WROTE TO MAKE money, and he never considered his reputation. He was a miserable fellow who lived in the filthiest debauchery. In the morning he would scribble a page while still in bed, a whore to his left and a writing case to his right . . . He would spend the rest of the day drinking."[1] In his description of Prévost's easy alternation between whoring and writing, Charles Collé's portrait of the author implies that Prévost prostituted his pen. For Collé, Prévost was a hack, writing a quantity of pages for profit and working outside of a system of quality. Arguing that the author "never considered his reputation," Collé claims that Prévost cared less for honor than for money. Of course, this picture of Prévost is quite different from the image that the author advances by identifying himself as "l'auteur des *Mémoires et aventures d'un homme de qualité*."[2] In this pseudonym's first occurrence, the word *auteur* is ambiguous, pointing less to a man of letters outside of the text than to the Man of Quality character as supposed author of his own memoirs. However, in subsequent publications, Prévost signs "l'auteur des *Mémoires et aventures d'un homme de qualité*" in an effort to equate the real author with his fictional hero and to share with him the noble qualities of *l'homme de qualité*; this signature, which obscures the work of Prévost as a professional, promotes an authorial persona who writes as an aristocratic amateur. By signing a series of productions with this pseudonym, Prévost extends the Man of Quality's particular authorial attitude to these publications so that the narrators of the later memoir-novels are avatars of the original character, inheriting the heroic ideals he embodies. As the narrator of Prévost's third novel explains: "Il est vrai en général que l'amour de la gloire est un aiguillon noble, qui peut agir sur l'âme d'un écrivain comme sur celle d'un héros et les exciter chacun à ne rien faire qui déshonore un si beau motif" [It is true in general that the love of glory is a noble impulse, which may act on the soul of a writer as on that of a hero and excite each of them to do nothing that dishonors such a fine motivation].[3] Characterized by his contemporaries as a literary lowlife, Prévost constructs fictional characters who write for glory instead of financial gain. Blurring the boundary between narrator and author, Prévost's memoir-novels portray writing not as the work of the hack but as the task of the hero.

THE PRÉVOSTIAN HERO
AS *HONNÊTE HOMME*

While Prévost writes under financial pressure, his heroes write from quiet retirement; their memoirs are not a product of literary labors but of aristocratic leisure. R. A. Francis has noted that "from the very title of his first novel, the *Memoirs of a Man of Quality,* Prévost makes it clear that he is working in the world of nobility."[4] However, it is the title of one of Prévost's later novels, *Mémoires d'un honnête homme,* which names *honnêteté* as the particular form of nobility to which all of his heroes aspire. Albeit an abstraction, *honnêteté* as an aristocratic ideal is grounded in the biological reality of noble birth, and so at the start of their narratives several of Prévost's heroes provide their genealogies. The Man of Quality asserts his nobility on the novel's first page, alluding to "la naissance et les grands biens" [the high birth and large fortune] that are his. He affirms: "Je sors d'une maison illustre, et qui a produit de grands hommes" [I belong to an illustrious house which has produced great men] (*MHQ,* 13). Similarly, the Doyen de Killerine writes: "Notre maison quoiqu' extrêmement déchue de son ancienne splendeur, tenait encore un des premiers rangs dans la comté *d'Antrim.* Nous faisons remonter notre origine jusqu'à ce fameux *Donewal O Neal* qui avait régné autrefois dans cette partie de l'Irlande que nous nommons *Cui Guilly* et que les Anglais appellent *Ulster*" [Our house, while fallen far from its former splendor, still held one of the first ranks in County Antrim. We trace our origin back to the famous Donewal O Neal who once reigned in the part of Ireland which we call Cui Guilly and which the English call Ulster] (*DK,* 16). Prévost's heroes also inform the reader that they belong to the *noblesse d'épée,* the oldest and most authentic form of French aristocracy. The Man of Quality tells us that his grandfather was a hero in campaigns led by Louis XIV. The hero of the *Mémoires d'un honnête homme* also alludes to his father's fighting prowess: "Mon père était homme d'honneur et de mérite. Quarante ans de service et plusieurs actions d'éclat . . . l'avaient conduit au degré de maréchal de camp" [My father was a man of honor and merit. Forty years of service and several brilliant actions . . . had led him to the rank of field marshal].[5] In *Le Monde moral,* the narrator also notes his family's tradition as fighters, proclaiming: "Ma naissance m'appelait au métier des armes" [My birth destined me for a military career].[6] In both *Histoire du Chevalier Des Grieux et de Manon Lescaut* and in *La Jeunesse du Commandeur* the hero's membership in the elite order of the Knights of Malta is indicative of his high birth.[7]

Ennobled by military exploits, these heroes pursue their adventures not only on the battlefield but also in the drawing room. In *The Aristocrat as Art,* Domna Stanton defines aristocratic culture as "the systematic refinement of a personal worldly manner . . . in such immaterial form as manners and breeding, polite usage, decorum."[8] Although the Man of Quality's grandfather was a war hero, his father never saw combat, displaying his prowess first in the military academy and then in high society:

> Il s'y distingua si glorieusement que le souvenir s'en conservait encore à l'Académie lorsque j'y fus envoyé au bout de vingt ans. Après s'être formé heureusement pour tout ce qui regarde l'esprit et le corps, il acheva de se polir dans le commerce des plus honnêtes gens de Paris et de la cour. Il passa ainsi quelques années sans autre occupation que celle de s'instruire et de se donner du plaisir. (*MHQ*, 14)

> [He distinguished himself so gloriously that he was still remembered at the Academy when I was sent there twenty years later. After having successfully perfected every skill of the mind and body, he finished his education in the company of the noblest gentlemen and ladies of Paris and the court. He spent several years with no other occupation but that of learning and enjoying himself.]

Although the *honnête homme* also undertakes military training, his adventures have the salon as their stage:

> Paris n'était pas un séjour nouveau pour moi. J'y avais passé plusieurs années mais dans un collège ou à l'Académie . . . J'étais retourné à l'âge

de dix-sept ans chez mon père, où le commerce des plus honnêtes gens
de la province m'avait assez formé l'esprit et les manières pour me rendre capable de paraître d'un air libre dans toutes les meilleures compagnies. (*MHH*, 212)

[Paris was not new to me. I had spent several years there but in a *collège*
or at the Academy . . . I had returned to my father's house at the age of
seventeen, where the company of the noblest gentlemen and ladies of
the provinces had formed by mind and manners well enough to prepare
me to appear at ease in all of the best companies.]

In showing a shift in the identity of the nobleman from valorous
warrior to drawing room darling, Prévost illustrates the evolution of
the idea of *honnêteté* which has made this term so difficult to define. In
his study of the *honnête homme*, Alain Montandon writes, "Indeed, the
first half of the seventeenth century insists on the ethical and religious
character of the *honnête homme*, but *honnêteté* is essentially founded on
membership in aristocratic society. In the second half of the century . . .
honnêteté designates, in more pragmatic fashion, a worldly manner [*la
politesse mondaine*]."[9] Domna Stanton's definition also insists on the
evolution and even the degradation of the term when she notes: "As
early as 1680, however, Richelet's dictionary had stressed the sociability of the *honnête homme*, ignored the element of virtue, and played
down the notion of honor."[10] In his *Littérature et politesse: L'Invention de
l'honnête homme 1550–1750*, Emmanuel Bury observes that the characters in Molière's *Misanthrope* represent a new and an old version of
the *honnête homme*. Bury thus opposes Philinte to Alceste: "He [Phi-
linte] is a more subtle figure who reflects the art of appropriateness
[*aptum*] which belongs to the *honnête homme*, who must adapt to a multitude of circumstances and abandon the rigorous position of the sage
or the hero."[11]

Despite the overall evolution of the *honnête homme* from a solitary
sage to a modern man of the world, Prévost's heroes are heirs to Alceste's more orthodox form of *honnêteté*.[12] In fact, Molière's play is present in Prévost's novel, *Mémoires d'un honnête homme*, in a passage that
recalls the famous *scène des portraits* of *Le Misanthrope*.[13] In Molière's
comedy, Philinte does not object to the cruel yet clever conversation of
Célimène and her circle, enacting his *honnêteté* as a sort of conformity
that brings about social cohesion, while Alceste enacts his more literal
understanding of *honnêteté* by accusing society of insincerity. In an
early scene of Prévost's *Mémoires d'un honnête homme*, the novel's hero

adopts Alceste's position when he censures one woman's slanderous portraits of her absent friends. The Prévostian *honnête homme* follows Alceste in objecting to the hyposcrisy that passes for sociable conversation: "Il me sembla que l'amitié dont elle faisait profession pour tant d'honnêtes gens, l'auraient rendue un peu plus réservée sur leurs défauts" [It seemed to me that the friendship she professed for so many gentlemen and ladies would have rendered her more reserved on the subject of their faults] (*MHH*, 214). While the preceding example relies on an instance of intertextual allusion, Prévost's election of Alceste as the true *honnête homme* is explicit when he cites *Le Misanthrope* in *Le Pour et contre:*

> Saint Evremond a prétendu que Paris, Londres ou Rome étaient le seul séjour digne d'un honnête homme. Cette idée est-elle juste? Si l'idée qu'il se forme d'un honnête homme est celle d'un homme vertueux, quelle satisfaction peut-il y avoir pour la vertu dans la présence continuelle de tous les vices qui y sont opposés? Les grandes villes sont comme leur asile. Ils y trouvent une espèce de protection dans l'exemple et d'encouragement dans l'impunité. Qu'on écoute le Misanthrope: 'Trahi de toutes parts, accablé d'injustices / Je veux sortir d'un gouffre où triomphent les vices / Et chercher sur la terre un endroit écarté / Où d'être homme d'honneur on ait la liberté' (*PC*, 213, 131).

> [Saint Evremond claimed that Paris, London, or Rome were the only cities suited to an *honnête homme*. Is he right? If he defines an *honnête homme* as a virtuous man, what satisfaction could virtue have in the continual presence of all the vices which oppose it? Big cities are the home of vice. It finds in them a kind of protection in its example and an encouragement in its impunity. Let us listen to the Misanthropist: 'Betrayed on all sides, overcome by injustice / I long to escape this abyss where vice is triumphant / And to find somewhere on earth a hidden spot / Where one might be free to be a man of honor.']

Here again, Prévost privileges a moral rather than a social conception of *honnêteté*, for his ideal *honnête homme* rejects vice by retiring from the social scene.

Modeled on Molière's Alceste, the heroes of Prévost's novels often express a desire for solitude. In her study of the *honnête homme*, Domna Stanton has traced this aspect of *honnêteté* from Alceste back through Montaigne to Seneca and the stoic philosophers of Antiquity who preserved their virtue by living outside of society. Stanton concludes that this "*otium* or *oisiveté* . . . is basic to all modes of elite existence."[14] For

Prévost, antisociability is an essential element of *honnêteté*. After all, if we look at his first novel's full title, the *"homme de qualité"* is also the *"homme . . . qui s'est retiré du monde."* Love of solitude is a key quality of the Prévostian hero, beginning with the paradigmatic Man of Quality who describes himself as "sauvage," "farouche," and "peu sociable" [savage, ferocious, antisocial] (*MHQ*, 29). He only undertakes his adventures when his father refuses to let him enter the *Trappe*. Always struggling against a fate that destines him for far-flung travels and worldwide fame, the Man of Quality hides behind the walls of the harem where he is taken prisoner, then in the underground room where he entombs himself after the death of his wife, and finally in the monastery where he retires to write his memoirs.

Prévost's other heroes embrace isolation just as eagerly. Cleveland begins his life hiding from the wrath of his father in an underground cave called Rumney Hole and spends the rest of his existence looking for a way back to this safe space, ultimately the only suitable setting for his melancholy character. He explains: "Si le silence et la solitude sont agréables dans l'affliction, c'est qu'on s'y recueille, en quelque sorte, au milieu de ses peines, et qu'on y a la douceur de gémir sans être interrompu" [If silence and solitude are agreeable in affliction, it is because one may meditate alone amidst one's pains and take comfort in groaning without interruption].[15] The Doyen de Killerine, born a hunchback, hides his handicap in an obscure Irish village, declaring his "goût de la solitude" [taste for solitude] and his "vocation marquée pour tout autre état que le monde" [marked vocation for any other state but a worldly one] (*DK*, 15). He enters the priesthood to pursue scholarly tranquility, living in "une paix profonde, partageant [son] temps entre les fonctions de [son] état et l'étude des Saintes Lettres" [a profound peace, sharing his time between his priestly duties and the study of scripture] (*DK*, 15). In Prévost's *Mémoires d'un honnête homme* the ideal of retreat is lived by one man who abandons the salon for the study, as he explains: "J'y passerais ma vie entière [dans mon cabinet] si l'on n'était redevable de quelque chose à la société. . . . J'ai tant de mépris pour le monde, si peu de goût pour ses frivoles amusements, pour ses misérables principes, pour tout ce qu'il appelle joie, fortune, et bonheur que mon cabinet est toujours l'endroit de Paris où je me trouve le mieux" [I would spend my whole life there (in my study) if one did not owe something to society . . . I have so much scorn for the world, so little taste for its frivolous amusements, its miserable principles, for all that it calls joy, fortune, happiness, that my study is always the place in Paris where I am most at ease] (*MHH*, 215). Attacked by the *intendante* for his lack of social graces, this misanthropic man is admired by the novel's hero (the *honnête homme* of the title) for his "vrai mérite" [true merit] (*MHH*, 215).

While the desire for retirement seems a personal choice in keeping with Prévost's melancholy protagonists, they portray this preference as a moral imperative. Through their retreat, Prévost's heroes establish themselves as *honnêtes gens*, affirming their virtue by rejecting the vices of the world. Writing on Montesquieu, Elena Russo cites the vices the philosopher finds in his own era as "the greed with which we desire vile rewards" and "that ambition so different from the love of glory."[16] As Montesquieu's contemporaries, Prévost's protagonists also see avarice and ambition as the primary problems in their world, and their rejection of society represents a condemnation of contemporary mores. For Prévost's heroes, self-imposed solitude represents a virtuous sacrifice, a renunciation of the vices inherent in the political power, material wealth, and sensual pleasure that could be theirs. When the Man of Quality gives up his name and claim to his family fortune in favor of his uncle, he adopts the pseudonym Renoncour (in which Erik Leborgne has read the phrase "renoncer à la cour" [to renounce the court])[17] so that his new name is synonymous with his sacrifice. Despite his status as the son of Cromwell, Cleveland, too, turns his back on family connections, explaining his choice in moral terms: "Plusieurs années se passèrent sans que rien ne fût capable de me faire sortir de ma solitude pour aller solliciter des avantages que je n'estimais point. . . . La vertu, disais-je, ne dépend point des biens de la fortune; et c'est la vertu seule qui rend un honnête homme heureux" [Several years passed during which nothing could make me leave my solitude to solicit advantages that I did not recognize as such. . . . Virtue, I always said, does not depend on wealth; it is virtue alone which makes an *honnête homme* happy] (*C*, 17). In *Le Doyen de Killerine, Mémoires d'un honnête homme*, and *Le Monde moral*, noble heroes in the mold of Renoncour display disinterestedness when their fathers remarry young brides; they are more concerned with the happiness of an elderly parent than with their own future inheritance. In the case of the *Doyen* this sacrifice is especially explicit when the hero gives his own fiancée to his widowed father, abandoning his advantages as the eldest son in order to adopt the solitary life of a country priest.

Prévost's heroes reject ambition and evoke vocation, scorning money in favor of glory. In *La Jeunesse du commandeur*, the hero abandons his fortune to a younger brother and enters the religious and military Order of Malta, describing his decision as a renunciation:[18]

> Peut-être suis-je le seul chevalier de mon ordre qui avec une fortune considérable et tous les avantages qui peuvent ouvrir dans le monde une carrière brillante, se soit déterminé par sa propre inclination à se charger des devoirs d'une vocation pénible. . . . [L]a mort de mon aîné m'ayant fait succéder à tous ses droits, on fut surpris qu'à l'âge de dix-huit ans, et lorsque tout semblait m'appeler aux fonctions du chef d'une grosse maison, je parlai de me rendre à Malte pour mes caravanes, et d'abandonner à mes cadets toutes mes prétentions. . . . Rien ne m'avait paru si noble et si grand que ma première vocation, et je ne pus me persuader que des avantages aussi frivoles que les biens de la fortune dussent balancer un sentiment qui me paraissait fondé sur l'honneur et la raison."[19]

> [I may be the only knight of my order who, with a considerable fortune and all of the advantages that can ensure a brilliant career, has decided on his own inclination to undertake the duties of a difficult vocation. . . . (T)he death of my older brother having made me the heir to my family fortune, everyone was surprised when at the age of eighteen, and when everything seemed to summon me to the head of a powerful household, I spoke of going to Malta to embark on a mission and to abandon to my younger brothers all of my claims. . . . Nothing seemed nobler or grander to me than my original vocation, and I could not persuade myself that such a frivolous advantage as wealth should change a sentiment that seemed to me based on honor and reason.]

This repeated rejection of "les biens de la fortune" [wealth], characteristic of the discourse of the Prévostian hero, affirms aristocracy by taking a strong stance against anything resembling a bourgeois attitude toward money.[20]

If sometimes Prévost's antisocial heroes must engage in the *commerce des honnêtes gens* they energetically eschew any involvement with commerce. In the first pages of the *Mémoires d'un homme de qualité*, the hero's father, disinherited and almost destitute, refuses a rich merchant's offer to adopt him. Understanding the unwillingness of an aristocrat to associate himself with a mere merchant, the businessman apologizes: "Ne croyez pas que je veuille faire de vous un marchand" [Do not believe that I wish to make a merchant of you] (*MHQ*, 17), acknowledging the nobleman's scorn for his profession. He proposes instead to manage the last of the marquis' money for him, delivering the interest payments while leaving the aristocrat ignorant of the means of production. In *Le Doyen de Killerine*, Georges objects to a merchant's proposal to marry his sister, for if his family is poor, they are noble nonetheless, and Georges is confident that he can restore the clan to its former glory without the merchant's money. Even in *Manon Lescaut* where Des Grieux is constantly pursuing new means to make money for his mistress, this young nobleman will not dirty his hands with hard work but prefers to pursue his fortunes at the gaming table.

Consequently, when Prévost's heroes eventually engage in the work of writing, they do so outside of the bourgeois logic of professional authorship which equates textual production with potential profit. Prévost's gentlemen memoirists insist that they have no interest in profiting from publication, for an *honnête homme* does not work for money, and he certainly does not write for it. Here again, the Prévostian hero is close to Molière's misanthropist, who, in response to Oronte's ridiculous sonnet, declares that the reputation of a gentleman is immeasurably more valuable than the fame of an author. Alceste explains:

De quoi s'offense-t-il? Et que veut-il me dire?
Y va-t-il de sa gloire de ne pas bien écrire?
Que lui fait mon avis, qu'il a pris de travers?
On peut être honnête homme et faire mal des vers;
Ce n'est point à l'honneur que touchent ces matières.
Je le tiens galant homme en toutes les manières,
Homme de qualité, de mérite et de cœur,
Tout ce qu'il vous plaira, mais fort méchant auteur.[21]

[Why is he offended? Whatever does he mean?
Is his reputation hurt by the fact that he writes badly?
How does my opinion affect him? He took it the wrong way in any case.
One can still be an *honnête homme* and a bad poet;
These matters do not affect one's honor.
I consider him a gallant man in all things,
A man of quality, of merit, of heart,
Anything that he pleases, just a very bad author.]

For Alceste, the figures of the *honnête homme* and *auteur* are opposites, since the gentleman refuses those very things that the author pursues: publicity and profit.

He affirms:

> Si l'on peut pardonner l'essor d'un mauvais livre,
> Ce n'est qu'aux malheureux qui composent pour vivre.
> Croyez-moi, résistez à vos tentations,
> Dérobez au public ces occupations,
> Et n'allez point quitter, de quoi que l'on vous somme,
> Le nom que dans la cour vous avez d'*honnête homme*,
> Pour prendre, de la main d'un avide imprimeur,
> Celui de ridicule et misérable *auteur*.[22]

> [One can pardon the publication of a bad book
> Only if the unfortunate writer's livelihood depends on it.
> Believe me, resist your temptations,
> Hide your writing from the public,
> And do not abandon, no matter what anyone says,
> Your reputation at court as an *honnête homme*
> To take, from the hand of a greedy printer,
> The ridiculous and miserable title of *author*.]

According to an aristocratic ideology that disdains professional authorship, Prévost's heroes all downplay their literary abilities, characterizing their efforts as amateurish. In the preface to the *Mémoires d'un homme de qualité*, the Man of Quality's prose style is described as "simple et naturel tel qu'on le doit attendre d'une personne de condition, qui s'attache plus à l'exactitude de la vérité qu'aux ornements du langage" [simple and natural as one would expect from a person of condition, who is more attached to an exact rendering of the truth than to the ornaments of style] (*MHQ*, 9). Lacking the tricks of the authorial trade, Cleveland insists that he is incapable of giving his memoirs "les grâces du roman" [the graces of a novel] (*C*, 205). Likewise, the Doyen de Killerine explains that, written by an *honnête homme*, his memoirs are a product of honesty rather than art, more truthful and thus less beautiful:

Je réponds qu'en attribuant tant de vertu à l'envie de se rendre utile, je lui suppose pour fondement toutes les qualités naturelles et acquises qui sont nécessaires d'ailleurs pour former un bon écrivain; et malheureusement ce ne sont pas celles dont je suis le mieux partagé. Il est donc vrai qu'avec des idées assez justes de ce qui serait nécessaire pour la perfection de l'ouvrage que j'entreprends, mes talents sont au-dessous de mon projet. . . . S'il [mon désir d'être utile] ne me communique point la beauté de l'imagination, qui est un présent de la nature, et les grâces du style, qui sont ordinairement des effets de l'art, il me rendra sincère dans mon récit. (*DK*, 13–14)

[I respond that in attributing so much virtue to the desire to make one-self useful, I suppose as its foundation all of the natural and learned qualities necessary to form a good writer; and unfortunately I do not possess many of those qualities myself. It is true that while I have clear ideas about what would be necessary for the perfection of the work I am undertaking, my talents are not up to my task . . . If it [my desire to be useful] does not provide me with much imagination, which is a gift of nature, or with the graces of style, which are ordinarily the effects of art, it will render me sincere in my story.]

Invested in their status as *honnêtes gens*, Prévost's heroes value privacy over publication and reject the idea of profiting from their literary endeavors. The Man of Quality writes his memoirs in retirement and is only persuaded to part with his manuscript on the condition that it be published anonymously.[23] Likewise, the heroes of *La Jeunesse du Commandeur* and the *Mémoires d'un honnête homme* insist on their anonymity before ceding their stories. In Prévost's last novel, *Le Monde moral*, the abbé Brenner perfectly represents the position of the gentleman amateur who writes for private purposes with no desire for financial reward, "avec l'indifférence pour la fortune et la haine des affaires qui sont comme inséparables du vrai goût de lettres" [with the indifference for fortune and the hatred of business which are inseparable from a true taste for letters] (*MM*, 380). In this way, Prévost's fictional memoirists emulate real authors such as "a Mlle de Montpensier, a Retz, a La Rochefoucauld [who . . .], when they wrote, only envisioned the symbolic value of their work and no market value [*nul droit d'auteur*.]"[24] In aligning themselves with these aristocratic amateurs, Prévost's heroes identify once again with the ideals of the *honnête homme* in opposition to the realities faced by their own creator, a professional participant in the new literary marketplace.

DEGRADATION OF THE HEROIC IDEAL: THE END OF THE *HONNÊTE HOMME*

Despite their attachment to the ideal of *honnêteté*, Prévost's protagonists often act in ways that cast doubt on their honor.[25] While Prévost's narrators insist on their honesty, their actions show them to be expert liars;

while their heroic rhetoric implies their valor, their stories reveal them to be cowards; and while their noble pretensions allow an aristocratic aloofness from the business of the world, their adventures reveal their ambition and align them more closely with their creator. Prévost's heroes are adventurers in every sense of the word, for while the word *aventurier* denotes the hero of glorious exploits, it can also connote a charlatan who follows a trajectory of tricks to pursue personal advancement. In *Les Aventuriers au XVIIIe siècle*, Suzanne Roth traces the evolution of the term from the seventeenth century, citing Furetière who defines it as "qui cherche la gloire par les armes et à faire fortune" [one who seeks glory in war in order to make his fortune], the *Dictionnaire de l'Académie*, where it is defined as "celui qui n'a aucune fortune et qui cherche à s'établir par des aventures. *Ce n'est qu'un aventurier*" [one who has no fortune and seeks one by pursuing adventures. *He is only an adventurer*], and finally Savary's *Dictionnaire universel de commerce*, which notes: "Aventurier signifie un homme peu ou point connu, qui n'a peut-être ni feu ni lieu, qui se mêle hardiment d'affaires, et qui communément n'est qu'un affronteur. Tous les bons négociants doivent se garder de telles personnes" [Adventurer signifies a little known or unknown man, who may have neither house nor home, who boldly becomes involved in business, and who commonly is nothing but a bluffer. All good businessmen must be wary of such persons]. [26] If Prévost's heroes define themselves as *honnêtes gens* in the oldest and strictest sense of the term, their actions define them as fortune-hunters. Their adventures chronicle the corruption of an ideal in a process that draws these characters closer to the reality of their author, who has himself been characterized by several scholars as the paradigmatic *aventurier des Lumières*.[27]

Although Molière's Alceste is the enemy of artifice, Prévost's own *honnêtes gens* are characterized by their dishonesty. Des Grieux plays the role of Manon's younger brother to dupe old G. M. out of his mistress and his money; in *Histoire d'une Grecque moderne*, Ferriol dresses like a Turk to win popularity and political power in Constantinople. Even the *Mémoires d'un honnête homme* begins with a scene in which a supposedly noble character shows himself to be an artful actor, impersonating an Englishman to gain access to a French prisoner (the *honnête homme* of the title) so that he may abscond with the man's memoirs: "Il ne restait qu'à tromper les yeux du commandant, pour éviter des explications inutiles. Je saisis le moment qu'il sortait de la chambre et je mis adroitement le manuscrit dans ma poche" [There was nothing left to do but to trick the commander in order to avoid useless explanations. I seized the moment that he left the room, and I adroitly slipped the manuscript into my pocket] (*MHH*, 210).

This talent for trickery extends into the personal lives of Prévost's heroes, who deceive even those closest to them. Ferriol portrays himself as a father figure, all the while hiding the progress of his passion for his young charge. The young commander lies to his mistress, assuring her of his honorable intentions only to lure her into an illicit existence as a kept woman. In *Campagnes philosophiques*, Montcal also displays a marked duplicity when he manages to keep two mistresses unknown to each other. While Naomi Segal sees the Prévostian story, particularly *Manon Lescaut*, as a male collusion against women,[28] the hero's dishonesty toward his mistress extends in fact to all of his relationships and even to the friendships that are central to the ideal of manly honor. If Des Grieux deceives anyone, it is the friends who stand in the way of his happiness with Manon; he constantly misleads his closest friend Tiberge and even lies in the confessional to the sympathetic priest at Saint-Lazare. In *Histoire d'une Grecque moderne*, Ferriol betrays the trust of the Bacha Chériber, his host and friend, in order to possess the Bacha's slave, Théophé. Later, he misrepresents his feelings for Théophé to the Sélictar, another friend whom he perceives as a rival. Likewise, in *Campagnes philosophiques*, Montcal deceives his friend and commanding officer, when Schomberg vies with him for the attentions of Mme de Gien and later of Mlle Fidert. By betraying the bonds of friendship, Prévost's heroes breach the code of honor upon which their identity is based.

Despite their insistence on membership in a military elite, the heroism of Prévost's narrators is also called into question by their cowardly actions. His military career barely begun, Renoncour is captured by the enemy and carried away to the Orient as a slave. In a surprise attack, Cleveland is stabbed by his enemy Gelin. Montcal, Peres, and the young commander are all three attacked and wounded by mere women. In *Le Doyen de Killerine*, after Patrice defends his beloved against bandits, it is revealed that there was never any danger; he had hired the thugs to attack the coach so that he could have the opportunity to play the part of the hero. Despite their military training, the heroes of the *Mémoires d'un honnête homme* and *Le Monde moral* share a strong aversion to dueling.[29] Finally, although Georges belongs to a regiment and the *honnête homme* owns one, neither of them ever takes up arms to serve.

When Prévost's heroes actually do engage in armed conflict, the ideals for which they fight are lost in bloody massacres. Montcal's descrip-

tion of the battle of Tilpenny reveals the degradation of valor into brutality when his troops slaughter innocent civilians, as he recounts:

> Je n'entrerai point dans un détail qui révolterait l'imagination de mes
> lecteurs. La moitié des rebelles fut étouffée par la fumée ou consumée
> par les flammes. . . . Mais lorsqu'ils [les survivants] étaient forcés de
> sortir, ils tombèrent au milieu de nos sabres, dont nous leur fendions la
> tête sans pitié, l'horreur de leur situation leur fit jeter des cris si pitoy-
> ables que dans plus d'un instant je fus tenté de faire cesser le carnage, et
> de les recevoir à composition. Cependant l'importance d'un tel exemple
> m'endurcit contre mes propres sentiments. J'ordonnai qu'on fît main
> basse jusqu'au dernier, et quoique j'eusse excepté les femmes dans ce
> cruel ordre, il fut impossible que sortant pêle-mêle avec leurs maris et
> leurs enfants, il n'y en eût pas un grand nombre qui périssent par le
> tranchant de nos sabres. Ainsi, à la réserve d'un petit nombre d'habi-
> tants qui se sauvèrent par des issues écartées, où je n'avais pu placer
> une garde, tout ce qui échappa aux flammes vint trouver une mort plus
> sanglante par nos mains. Le jour qui éclaira enfin cette affreuse bouch-
> erie nous fit voir un monceau de cendres à la place de la ville.[30]

> [I will not go into details which would revolt the imagination of my
> readers. Half of the rebels were suffocated by the smoke or consumed
> by the flames. . . . But when they (the survivors) were forced to come
> out, our sabers fell upon them, and we split open their skulls without
> pity; the horror of their situation made them cry out piteously, and at
> more than one instant I was tempted to call an end to the carnage and
> to make a truce with them. However, the importance of making an ex-
> ample hardened me against my own sentiments, and I ordered that they
> kill all of them to the very last, and although I would have excepted the
> women from this cruel order, it was impossible since they were mixed in
> among their husbands and children and so a great number of them per-
> ished by our sabers. Thus, except for a small number of inhabitants
> who escaped through hidden exits, where I had not been able to place a
> guard, any who escaped the flames found an even bloodier death at our
> hands. Finally, the dawn which illuminated that horrible butchery re-
> vealed a pile of ashes where the city had been.]

Brenner, hero of *Le Monde moral*, is also witness to the degeneration of
the martial ideal from glorious valor to brutal plunder:

> [I]l avait été difficile d'arrêter la licence du soldat . . . et nous trouvâmes,
> à notre arrivée, une véritable image des horreurs de la guerre. . . . [J]e
> fus vivement frappé de la vue d'un vieillard . . . qui se tenait sur la

poitrine un mouchoir ensanglanté. . . . La chambre du malheureux vieil-
lard à laquellle j'arrivai bientôt, m'offrit pour premier spectacle les
débris de sa porte et de plusieurs coffres qui venaient d'être forcés à
coups de hâche, un corps étendu, dont le sang coulait à grands flots,
quantité de meubles brisés. . . . Je compris facilement qu'il avait été
pillé, blessé en se défendant, et l'autre tué, sans doute, par des furieux
qui n'avaient rien respecté. (*MM*, 383).

[It was difficult to stop the soldiers from pillaging . . . and we found at
our arrival a true image of the horrors of war. . . . I was struck by the
sight of an old man . . . who was holding a bloody handkerchief to his
breast . . . . The poor man's room where I soon arrived offered me the
spectacle of the ruins of his door and of several coffers which had been
opened with axe blows, a body stretched out on the floor from which
blood was gushing, a large quantity of broken furniture. . . . I easily understood that they had been robbed, wounded in defending themselves,
and that the dead man had doubtless been killed by furious intruders
who had respected nothing.]

Despite their own objections to the horrors of battle, Prévost's protagonists often exploit the opportunities for advancement presented to
them by a military career, even if this advancement depends on abandoning initial allegiances to fight as mercenaries.[31] The philosopher-sol-
dier Montcal begins his story by pragmatically stating that men do not
go to war to win glory but rather to earn money:

Ce n'est pas toujours l'amour de la gloire qui engage un gentilhomme
dans la profession des armes, et qui lui fait prodiguer sa vie au milieu
des dangers. Le désir de s'élever à la fortune est le motif presque général qui détermine les hommes dans le choix d'une condition, et si la
gloire est un puissant aiguillon pour les âmes bien nées, elle ne les porte
ordinairement qu'à remplir avec honneur les devoirs d'un état que l'intérêt leur a fait choisir. (*CP*, 249)

[It is not always the love of glory which engages a gentleman in a military career and which makes him risk his life in the middle of dangers.
The desire to improve his fortunes is the general motive which determines men to choose a condition, and if glory is a powerful motive for
high born souls, it only causes them to fulfill with honor the duties of a
career they have chosen of their own self-interest.]

If at first he resists those who would pay him to fight against his own
country, Montcal eventually accepts their offers, which favor his own

professional promotion, explaining, "[U]n régiment de cavalerie était effectivement ce qui piquait mon ambition" [A regiment of cavalry was what flattered my ambition] (*CP*, 257).

In Prévost's rewriting of the adventure novel, the ideal of the knightly quest is corrupted until all that is left is the conquest of fortune. The chevalier Des Grieux never goes to Malta to begin his noble service but instead becomes a *chevalier d'industrie*, a gambler who cheats his fellow players out of their money. Similarly, Prévost's other *chevalier de Malte*, the hero of *La Jeunesse du Commandeur*, is a knight turned villain as his crusades for Christianity become acts of pillage. This hero of the high seas becomes a pirate in his own right, enlisting the corsairs he has just conquered in order to recapture his kidnapped mistress, as he explains: "Ils ne pouvaient me prendre dans un moment plus propre à me faire écouter leurs offres. Quoique je sentisse tout ce qu'il y avait d'humiliant pour moi à me lier avec des infâmes, leurs principes m'étaient indifférents lorsque je n'avais besoin que de leur courage et de leurs armes" [They could not have found a moment when I would have been more open to their offers. Although I understood how humiliating it would be for me to be linked with such scoundrels, their principles did not concern me at a time when I needed only their courage and their arms] (*JC*, 189).

Not only does the Prévostian hero disappoint by sacrificing noble ideals to practical necessities, he demonstrates his true departure from aristocracy by adopting the chief characteristics of the bourgeoisie: ambition and industriousness. Despite their protested love of privacy, Prévost's heroes pursue highly public careers, and even "l'homme de qualité qui s'est retiré du monde" [the man of quality who has retired from the world] seems to get out of the monastery quite often.[32] On his way into his first retreat, Renoncour makes time to meddle in two complicated love affairs (that of his uncle and a married woman and that of a retired consul and his two Oriental mistresses), and he leaves the monastery later to settle financial affairs first for his cousin the Marquise de R and then for his daughter. When he is again pressed into public life as preceptor to the son of a powerful political figure, Renoncour meets the king of Spain and an assortment of English nobles, and upon his return to France he shares the insights of his travels with the Regent and his advisers Law and Dubois. Such proximity to power seems strange for someone who claims to be totally uninterested in his own advancement.

Although Prévost's protagonists strongly insist on their rejection of worldly affairs, refusing to admit interest in their social and financial status, they still win fame and often fortune. Like Renoncour, hero of Prévost's first novel, Brenner, hero of the author's last, explains that despite his efforts to avoid public life, he is drawn into politics against his will: "Que mon sort était tranquille et mon cœur irreprochable lorsqu'on vint m'arracher de ma solitude. . . . Une vaine réputation d'esprit et de savoir m'a coûté le repos de ma vie" [How tranquil was my life and how irreprochable was my heart until they came to rip me away from my solitude. . . . A vain reputation for wit and wisdom cost me my peaceful life] (*MM*, 382). While Brenner is supposedly without ambition ("sa figure, dont l'agrément répondait à ses qualités intérieures, aurait secondé fort heureusement son ambition, s'il en eût de se distinguer" [his appealing face reflected his inner qualities and would have served his ambition to distinguish himself, had he had any] (*MM*, 380)), he is all too easily engaged in public affairs when he becomes aide to Prince Ragoczy. Once Ragoczy abandons him, Brenner renounces his stated desire for retirement in order to accompany one of the heirs to the Hungarian throne, Mlle Tekely, in her adventures across Europe. Although he ends his life alone in a prison cell, Brenner has become an infamous figure. Accused of stealing Ragoczy's fortune, the name of this onetime monk appears in newspapers throughout Europe, including Prévost's *Pour et contre*.[33]

Despite his protests to the contrary, the adventures of the Doyen reveal his interest in political, social, and economic advancement.[34] Although he has renounced his rights as eldest son by entering the priesthood, the Doyen reclaims control of the family upon his father's death and accompanies his siblings to Paris in their quest for success. Once there, the Doyen insists on attaching his family to the court of King James in order to establish their status in France. He writes: "Je l'avais pressé [Patrice] d'aller à Saint-Germain où je me reprochais de n'avoir pas encore paru moi-même. Mon dessein avait toujours été de nous faire présenter au roi Jacques par quelqu'un de nos parents, et j'avais jeté les yeux sur M. de Sercine que ce prince honorait de sa confiance" [I had urged him (Patrice) to go to Saint-Germain where I reproached myself for not having gone already. My plan had always been to have us presented to King James by one of our family members, and I had chosen M. de Sercine whom the prince honored with his confidence] (*DK*, 43). When Patrice's enthusiasm is not all that the Doyen requires, he takes matters into his own hands: "Je pris le parti d'aller moi-même à Saint Germain" [I decided to go to Saint-Germain myself] (*DK*, 43). Despite his priestly vow of poverty and his oft-stated "haine du monde" [hatred of the world], the Doyen works tirelessly for the fortune of his family, marrying two of his siblings to rich partners. "On ne se marie pas précisément pour être riche" [One does not exactly marry to be rich] (*DK*, 41), he writes, but he is ready to marry off Rose to the rich merchant Des Pesses despite the difference in social status between the two. The Doyen is less impressed with Patrice's love for Mlle L than with the security that his brother could find with the heiress Sara whose wealth would assure a return to prominence for his family. Finally, without ever admitting any professional ambition, the Doyen ends up with a career as a bishop—gained through his connections at court—and a comfortable fortune to see him into old age.

While the Doyen actively denies any desire for advancement, his brother Georges is a new breed of man, who pursues social promotion without apologies. Born into nobility, Georges at first appears the perfect aristocrat: "bon, sincère, généreux, sobre, intrépide; en un mot, pourvu de toutes les qualités qui forment l'honnête homme dans les idées communes" [good, sincere, generous, sober, interpid; in a word possessing all of the qualities commonly associated with an *honnête homme*] (*DK*, 19). However, ill-favored by fortune as a Catholic in Protestant Northern Ireland, Georges cannot assume his rightful place in the world. In his exile from the inner circles of the Irish elite, he dreams of success: "[M]algré la solitude et la tranquillité de ses occupations, il nourrissait dans le secret de son cœur un amour ardent pour le monde . . . des souhaits continuels pour quelque heureuse révolution qui mît du changement dans . . . sa fortune" [(D)espite his solitude and the tranquility of his occupations, he hid in the depths of his heart a passionate love of the world . . . and the continual hope for some happy revolution which would change his fortune] (*DK*, 19). Unable to change the social structures of his homeland, Georges follows his ambitions to France, lured by the prospect of easy advancement described by his French acquaintance Des Pesses who informs him

> que sans compter la voie du service militaire . . . il y avait mille chemins de fortune à choisir tant à la cour qu'à Paris. . . . [Le] jeu seul y mettait tous les jours dans l'opulence une quantité incroyable de Français et d'etrangers . . . [mais] qu'un homme bien fait qui étant sans goût pour le jeu seul, pouvait encore avec moins de hasard se procurer un établisse-

ment par le moyen des femmes; que les vieilles, les jeunes, les veuves et celles qui ne l'étaient pas, étaient également idolâtres de la bonne mine. (*DK*, 22)

[that without counting military service . . . there were a thousand ways to find fortune either at the court or in Paris. . . .(G)ambling alone enriched an incredible number of Frenchmen and foreigners daily . . . (but) a handsome man without a taste for gambling could still with less risk find fortune with women; old ones, young ones, widows and those who were not were equally enamored of handsome faces.]

Georges is enticed by this promise of social mobility and promptly moves the family to Paris where, less a subtle courtier than an aggressive *arriviste*, he rises to the rank of *capitaine d'infanterie*.

This shift in values from a system of quality to one of quantity is apparent in the transposition of the *scène des portraits* from the seventeenth-century version by Molière to the eighteenth-century one by Prévost. The portraitist is no longer Célimène, a noblewoman surrounded by courtiers, but rather the wife of a bureaucrat, a member not of the social but of the financial elite. Prévost's *intendante* evaluates the subjects of her slanders not in terms of their social status but rather in terms of their material wealth. She notes the incomes of each of her subjects: the *président* has "soixante mille livres de rente" [an income of sixty thousand *livres*] (*MHH*, 213); the marquise, whose husband "ne l'avait épousée que par intérêt" [married her only for money] now enjoys his "grosse fortune" [vast fortune] (*MHH*, 214); another woman was once a poor orphan but used her beauty to marry a "conseiller fort riche" [a very rich counselor] (*MHH*, 214); she says of a rich *abbé*: "[O]n dit qu'il prête sur gages" [(P)eople say he is a money lender] (*MHH*, 214); she adds that another woman ruins herself through gambling but avoids debt through the help of a gallant admirer. The paradigm shift is complete when the *intendante* ridicules a financier who would rather be well-born than wealthy, criticizing his attachment to the ideals of the old aristocracy and his distaste for the means by which he has achieved success, declaring: "[L]e financier . . . a beaucoup d'esprit, de douceur et de politesse, mais avec des entêtements ridicules de noblesse, qui le font gémir d'être réduit à la profession qu'il exerce et sans laquelle néanmoins il serait bien éloigné de la fortune dont il jouit" [(T)he financier . . . is very witty, nice, polite, but his ridiculous obsession with nobility makes him groan to be reduced to exercising his profession without which he would be far from having the fortune he possesses]

(*MHH*, 214). For the *intendante*, nostalgia for nobility is a sort of worthless sentimentalism, since in the new society of eighteenth-century Paris, wealth and power are less in the hands of the aristocracy and more and more in those of the bourgeoisie.

While in the *Mémoires d'un honnête homme*, the hero still resists these new realities, in *Voyages du capitaine Robert Lade*, a work of the same period, Prévost's protagonist embraces ambition from the outset and clearly states that his adventures are undertaken to reestablish his fortune. Instead of citing the love of glory as his motivation (that "puissant aiguillon" [powerful motive] cited in *Le Doyen de Killerine* and *Campagnes philosophiques*), Lade announces from the first line of his memoirs that the motivation for his illustrious adventures is purely pecuniary: "La pauvreté est un puissant aiguillon pour le courage, et j'ose dire pour toutes les vertus, surtout dans ceux qui sont tombés d'un état d'opulence et qui ont pour double motif la misère d'une épouse et de plusieurs enfants. Mes voyages et mes plus difficiles aventures n'ont point eu d'autres causes" [Poverty is a powerful motive for courage, and I dare say for all of the virtues, especially for those who have lost their wealth and who have the double motivation of the misery of a wife and of many children. My voyages and my most difficult adventures have nothing else as their cause].[35] Lade's first act in his attempt to recover his fortune is the "calcul de ce que je pouvais tirer de mes meubles" [calculation of what I could make from the sale of my furniture], an idea that the ruined nobles of Prévost's other novels would never entertain. Next, Lade looks to friends who have also lost fortunes in the *affaire du sud* and follows their example by embarking upon the "voie du commerce" [the means of business] where he will rely on the essentially bourgeois virtues of "probité" and "industrie" (*RL*, 17). In a pragmatic move, he approaches a merchant and asks for work, offering to lead one of the man's dangerous expeditions in exchange for a share of the profits. In the English explorer, Prévost finds a new type of hero who undertakes adventures with great valor but primarily for gain.

In *Voyages de Robert Lade*, the forces of commerce dictate the hero's adventures, but they also determine the character of his prose. Lade's writing is often less personal than practical, a chronicle of his travels and transactions valuable for planning further business ventures. His attention to documentation is praised in the preface to his memoir as an example of the enterprising spirit of the English, who write for the profit of the public, "cette disposition les portant à ne rien négliger dans leurs voyages et à publier toutes les remarques qui peuvent être utiles à leur commerce" [this disposition causing them to neglect nothing in the account of their voyages and to publish all of the remarks which could be useful to their commerce] (*RL*, 14). [36] Lade's memoir is not a heartfelt confession but rather a commercial memorandum.[37] In this move from the lyricism of Prévost's earlier heroes to the pragmatism of Lade, the memoirist's enterprise is degraded from a search for self-knowledge into the production of knowledge as a marketable commodity. If Prévost has hidden his own professional pursuits behind the aristocratic amateur figures who narrate (and supposedly author) the majority of his novels, the atypical hero Robert Lade, for whom writing is a business, typifies Prévost's own practice of producing pages for profit.

DEGRADATION OF THE AUTHORIAL IDEAL: THE AUTHOR IS NO *HONNÊTE HOMME*

While the adventures of Prévost's novelistic heroes undermine old ideas about heroism, at the same time, the status of his heroes as writers encourages a reexamination of old ideas about authorship. If Prévost's fictional characters cannot always live up to the ideal of *honnêteté,* can their creator be expected to do so? Although most of his novels are signed by "l'auteur des *Mémoires d'un homme de qualité*," the unauthorized publication of Prévost's private correspondence with his publisher shows him to be a modern *homme de lettres*.[38] In these "Extraits de plusieurs lettres de l'auteur des Mémoires d'un homme de qualité publiés par Etienne Neaulme pour se justifier de ce que la continuation du Philosophe anglais ou l'Histoire de M. Cleveland ne paraît pas encore" [Excerpts from several letters by the author of the Memoirs of a Man of Quality published by Etienne Neaulme to justify why the continuation of the English Philosopher or the Story of Mr. Cleveland has not yet appeared], Neaulme punishes Prévost's failure to produce pages by exposing him for who he really is: not an *honnête homme* but a hardworking (and sometimes less than honest) author. Prévost's letters to Neaulme provide a portrait of the author under intense pressure from his publisher, with Prévost almost pathetically begging for mercy: "Au nom de Dieu, mon cher monsieur, faites-moi un peu de quartier. . . . Je ne puis tout faire à la fois" [In God's name, my dear sir, show me some mercy. . . . I cannot do everything at once].[39] However, just as Prévost asks for God to protect him from his publisher, this defrocked priest will call upon the Lord's help to produce pages to profit Neaulme, promising: "[J]e vous ferai, Dieu aidant, un bel et bon 5e tome qui se vendra si bien que vous serez comblé de tout" [I will write for you, God willing, a very good fifth volume which will sell so well that you will be entirely satisfied] (*CDP*, 540). Neaulme only has to print Prévost's own words to reveal the author's problematic contradictions.

In providing context to Prévost's textual production, this correspondence presents writing not as aristocratic leisure but as labor. In the modern economy of authorship, Prévost supplies text in response to his publisher's demand, replying to Neaulme: "[N]ous pousserons le Cleveland aussi loin qu'il vous plaira" [(W)e will continue *Cleveland* for as long as you would like] (*CDP*, 537). Pages are not produced in an emotional or even a creative effusion but rather in response to economic imperatives, as Prévost notes by referring to his publisher's interest in the sales of his book: "J'ai fait réflexion depuis votre départ à l'empressement que vous m'avez marqué pour avoir la fin du Cleveland. Je conçois que votre intérêt le demande, et que si la première édition se vend assez bien pour vous faire penser à une seconde, il sera à propos que vous puissiez mettre l'ouvrage tout entier" [I have been thinking since your departure about the rush you are in to have the end of *Cleveland*. I understand that your interest demands it, and if the first edition sells well enough to make you consider a second, it would be best for you to be able to offer the whole work] (*CDP*, 537). Literature is presented in these letters as an industrial product calculable in terms of time spent and pages produced: "Je me suis donc proposé pour vous faire plaisir, de ménager quelque temps tous les jours pour l'achever. Je compte que le volume qui reste à faire n'aura pas moins de 22 ou 23 feuilles. Ainsi qu'en faisant une feuille tous les quatre jours, c'est une affaire à en finir en moins de trois mois" [I thus propose in order to please you to set aside a little time each day in order to finish it. I count that the remaining volume will have no fewer than twenty-two or twenty-three large format pages (*feuilles*). So if I write one *feuille* every four days, I can be done with the whole business in less than three months] (*CDP*, 537). *Cleveland* is no longer the private confession of a sensitive hero but the product of a professional author for sale in the literary marketplace, as Prévost informs his publisher: "[I]l se trouvera que vous aurez l'ouvrage tout entier pour la foire de Francfort" [You should have the whole work for the Frankfurt book fair] (*CDP*, 537). Moreover, it is not only the publisher who has an economic interest in the profits from the author's book sales. Prévost's letters to Neaulme reveal that he works not only under pressure from his publisher but from his creditors as well, for Prévost's promises to produce are contingent on a cash advance: "Mais en vous faisant ce plaisir [de continuer le roman], j'en ai de mon côté à vous demander. C'est de vouloir m'avancer une partie du prix. J'ai un besoin pressant de cent florins" [But in giving you this pleasure (of continuing the novel), I have something to ask of you. I need an advance. I have an urgent need of one hundred florins.] (*CDP*, 537). In a letter written to Neaulme over a year later, Prévost is still stalling for time and still asking for money, this time for "100 florins qui me sont absolument nécessaires pour parer une lettre de change mardi prochain 22 octobre" [100 florins are absolutely necessary so that I can pay a debt next Tuesday, October 22] (*CDP*, 541).

Although the author's relationship to his publisher appears to be a purely economic one, Prévost nonetheless couches it in a rhetoric of *honnêteté* more appropriate to his novels than to his real life circumstances. He offers his word of honor to his publisher as if the contract between two businessmen were a pact between gentlemen, trading upon the symbolic capital of his reputation as if real capital were not in question: "[J]e consens à passer pour un malhonnête homme, si je n'exécute pas fidèlement la promesse que je vous fais aujourd'hui. J'espère qu'après une expression si forte et dont je vous permets d'user à mon désavantage si je manque à ma parole vous ne ferez nulle difficulté de m'accorder cette satisfaction" [I consent to be called a dishonest man if I do not execute faithfully that which I have promised you today. I hope that my use of such a strong expression, which I allow you to use to my disadvantage if I do not keep my word, will encourage you to help me.] (541). He affirms his self-image as an *honnête homme* by insisting on the honesty of his dealings with Neaulme, informing him: "Je lui ai répondu [à Didot] que je ne pouvais honnêtement me déterminer là-dessus, sans vous l'avoir communiqué" [I told him (Didot) that I could not honestly decide on that without discussing it with you] (*CDP*, 540). However, when on this second occasion Neaulme does not send money, Prévost easily abandons his honorable ideals, exclaiming, "[J]e conclus que votre manière d'agir n'est point telle qu'elle doit être, et qu'elle me dispense de l'honnêteté que je voulais bien avoir pour vous" [I conclude that your way of behaving is not what it should be and that it dispenses me from the *honnêteté* that I wished to have in my dealings with you] (*CDP*, 542).

Like the narrators of his novels whose words contradict their actions, Prévost's pose as an *honnête homme* is countered by his dishonest conduct. When he asks Etienne Neaulme for an advance against the continuation of *Cleveland*, he also asks him to hide this request from his publisher brother for whom Prévost has other projects in progress, since the writer can only finish work for one at the expense of the other.[40] Prévost's double dealing continues when he falsely affirms to Etienne Neaulme that hereafter he will write exclusively for him: "J'ajouterai en second motif qu'en ne travaillant que pour vous, je vous donne la préférence sur plusieurs autres qui me demandent instamment quelque ouvrage de ma façon" [I will add that in working just for you, I have given you preference over several others who urgently ask to publish some of my work] (*CDP*, 541). At the same time, in order to extort the advance, Prévost admits that he has already communicated with Neaulme's rivals: "Je puis vous nommer M. Châtelain qui m'offre de me payer bien autrement que vous, et M. Didot qui me promet 25 livres de France de chaque feuille" [I can name M. Châtelain who offers to pay me much better than you and M. Didot who promises me 25 French *livres* for each *feuille*] (*CDP*, 541). When Neaulme still does not pay for pages he has not seen, Prévost is pressured into almost avowing his false representation of his own progress. He responds to Neaulme's refusal with all the indignation of a man caught in a lie:

> Vous voulez faire un homme d'esprit en concluant que d'après quelques mots de ma lettre, je n'ai point encore commencé le 5e tome, ce qui est très faux, puisque j'en ai 4 feuilles de faites depuis plus de trois mois. Mais quand il ne serait pas commencé, je me suis expliqué d'une manière à ne vous laisser aucun doute que je ne fusse disposé à finir promptement. (*CDP*, 542)

> [You wish to play the wit by concluding from certain terms of my letter that I have not yet begun the fifth volume, but that is very false, because I completed four *feuilles* of it three months ago. But even if I had not yet begun it, I have explained myself in a manner that leaves you no doubt that I am ready to finish it promptly.]

To distract from his own dishonesty, Prévost goes on the offensive and attacks Neaulme's *honnêteté*, declaring: "vos exceptions, vos excuses, vos promesses sont très malhonnêtes" [Your exceptions, your excuses, your promises are very dishonest] (*CDP*, 542). To defend himself against Prévost, Neaulme uses the closest weapon at hand — the printing press — to publish the author's letters and to reveal to his readers the man behind the mask of the Man of Quality. A year or so later in *Le Pour et contre*, Prévost argues that professional authors can be *honnêtes gens,* contrasting them with the avaricious and often dishonest publishers who exploit poor and honest artists. Prévost's correspondence with his own publisher shows that this scenario is yet another of the author's fictions.

2

Authorship in Prévost's Newspaper:
From Man of Letters to Man of Quality

WHILE THE DISCOURSE OF PRÉVOST'S NOVELS DENIES THEIR STATUS as the work of a professional author, his newspaper—*"Dans lequel on s'explique librement sur tout ce qui peut intéresser la curiosité du public, en matière de sciences, d'art, de livres, d'auteurs"* [In which we speak freely on everything that may interest the curiosity of the public in the matter of science, art, books, authors]—takes the literary field as its subject. Inaugurated in exile, *Le Pour et contre* describes the modernization and commercialization of literature within the emergent market economies of England and Holland. A dispatch direct from Grub Street, Prévost's newspaper documents the degradation of literature from an aristocratic activity to a business venture where the pursuit of honor is abandoned in the race for profit.

However, at the same time as *Le Pour et contre* seems to abandon the aristocratic universe of Prévost's novels, the newspaper's title page—signed "Par l'auteur des *Mémoires d'un homme de qualité*"—recalls it. Moreover, in an important autobiographical article published in his newspaper, Prévost's presentation of his adventures parallels plots from his novels, making the author into one of his own fictional heroes. Despite his move from the novels' ideal of quality to the newspaper's system of quantity—where the periodical publication of pages provides a constant source of income—Prévost does not relinquish his identification with the Man of Quality in *Le Pour et contre* but rather reiterates it in an effort to ennoble his literary endeavors.

Still invoking the old ideal of the author as gentleman, Prévost nevertheless uses his newspaper to stake new claims for the modern man of letters. While the narrators of his novels often insist on their desire for anonymity as a condition for the publication of their memoirs, in *Le*

56

Pour et contre Prévost affirms the identifiability of his style. Although his novelistic narrators refuse to be viewed as professionals interested in the profitability of their publications, in his newspaper Prévost affirms the author's right to be recognized and even rewarded for his work. A valiant defender of writers' rights against unscrupulous plagiarists and greedy publishers, Prévost portrays himself as an author for a new era, which sees heroism in hard work.

LE POUR ET CONTRE'S
PORTRAIT OF GRUB STREET

As presented in *Le Pour et contre,* the modern literary marketplace is not regulated by the ideal of honor so prized in Prévost's novels but rather by the baser drives that emerge when honor has been betrayed and heroism abandoned. The figures of the pirate and the mercenary, which in the novels represent the corruption of the heroic ideal, reappear in the newspaper's accounts of both rapacious publishers who pillage authors for their own profit and cynical authors who sacrifice glory for money. One article describes the Dutch literary milieu as "un pays où fourmillent tant de plumes mercenaires et où la presse fait vivre tant de misérables libertins" [a country which is swarming with mercenary writers and where the press provides a livelihood to so many miserable libertines] (*PC* 22, 168). Another notes that publishers "exercent entre eux une espèce de pyraterie . . . [et] peuvent se justifier sous le titre de corsaires" [exercise among themselves a sort of piracy . . . (and) can justify their actions by calling themselves pirates] (*PC* 47, 28–29). Prévost adds: "J'ai déjà remarqué dans plus d'une feuille qu'il n'y a point de corsaires qui ne se traitent les uns les autres avec plus de ménagement que les libraires de Londres" [I have already remarked in more than one issue that pirates treat each other with more respect than do the booksellers of London] (*PC* 291, 310).

Prévost's *Pour et contre* often portrays the literary field less as a site of energetic exchange than as the scene of a violent struggle for survival. He communicates the brutality of the book trade in one anecdote where a writer attacks his publisher and knocks out his teeth. The publisher provokes him by complaining that the author's book has not even earned enough to buy bread, and the indignant author responds by declaring that if the publisher cannot afford bread, he must not need his teeth (*PC* 89, 334–335). This sketch of English public life exposes the harsh reality of a literary economy in which bad sales can mean starvation. Although the author figure in this story does defend his honor, his actions reveal the rudeness of his character, and while his rejoinder is clever, it also demonstrates the degradation of men of letters reduced to fighting their publishers for a share of their earnings.

For Prévost, the agent of corruption in literary life is the publisher whose unprincipled pursuit of profit makes him the antithesis of the *honnête homme*. The publisher is not a man of honor, as Prévost shows in his account of a publisher who goes back on his word, refusing to give to an author the four free copies of his work that he had previously promised. By alienating the unprofitable author who subsequently ceases production, the publisher sacrifices "quatre mille ans de gloire" [four thousand years of glory] for an immediate return from the pages already printed (*PC* 17, 27). Preferring gain over glory, the publisher is no gentleman. In *Le Pour et contre*, Prévost casts the publisher as villain and the author as hero, an opposition that is explicit in the story of the publisher Burle and the explorer cum author Sir Walter Raleigh. Prévost recounts:

Ayant perdu toute espérance de pardon, il [Raleigh] fit venir un libraire nommé Burle qui avait imprimé le premier tome de l'Histoire du Monde et il lui demanda si ce livre s'était bien vendu. Le libraire, persuadé qu'il allait lui proposer d'en imprimer la continuation se crut intéressé à lui déguiser le profit qu'il avait tiré de son ouvrage dans l'espérance d'une meilleure composition. Il lui protesta que le débit des exemplaires avait été fort lent et fort difficile. Sir Rawleigh saisit aussitôt de son manuscrit, qu'il avait sur la table, et le jetant brusquement au feu: *Hé bien, mon ami,* dit-il en poussant un soupir, *si mon premier tome a fait tort à ta fortune, tu ne feras pas le même reproche au second. Ce monde ingrat n'est pas digne d'un tel ouvrage.* Il tint le pied dessus jusqu'à ce qu'il fût consumé, et tous les efforts du libraire ne purent en sauver une seule page."
· (*PC* 121, 9)

[Having lost all hope of pardon, he (Raleigh) sent for a publisher named Burle who had printed the first volume of his *History of the World* and asked him if that book had sold well. The publisher, persuaded that he would ask him to print the continuation, thought it in his own interest to hide from Raleigh the profit he had made from his work in hopes of making a better deal. He protested that the sale of the book had been very slow and very difficult. Sir Raleigh then seized his manuscript, which was laying on the table, and throwing it into the fire he said with a sigh: *Ah well, my friend, if my first volume has wronged your fortune, you will not have to make the same reproach to me in regards to the second. This ungrateful world is not worthy of such a work.* He held his foot on top of the book until it was consumed by the fire, and all of the publisher's efforts could not save even a single page.

Here again, the publisher's self-interest causes the world to lose the precious treasure that would have been the continuation of Raleigh's opus.

If, in a long ago past, the literary trades were noble vocations, according to *Le Pour et contre* printers have turned their calling into a mere career. Prévost describes the evolution of this profession as a fall from glory, a movement from an heroic past to a mercantile present in which everything is a product with a price and in which printing is no longer an art but a business:

Et comment les imprimeurs se laissent-ils ravir ainsi leur gloire? Ils ne sont même pas sensibles à cette perte. Ils ne pensent qu'à s'enrichir dans l'obscurité sans aucune estime pour la noblesse du moyen qu'ils emploient. Un Graveur, Un Peintre, un Horloger, un Fondeur, ne laissent rien sortir de leurs mains qui ne porte leur marque et leur nom; et les imprimeurs qui exercent le plus utile et le plus ingénieux de tous les Arts abandonnent l'honneur de leur travail à qui veut s'en emparer. (*PC* 7, 123)

[And how have printers allowed their glory to be stolen from them? They are not even sensitive to that loss. They only think of enriching themselves in obscurity without any esteem for the nobility of the means they employ. An Engraver, a Painter, a Clockmaker, a Smith, never let anything leave their hands without leaving their mark and their name upon it; and printers who exercise the most useful and ingenious of all the Arts abandon the honor of their work to whomever wants to take credit for it.]

Prévost takes as a prime example of the commodification and degeneration of literature the increasingly popular subscription method, writing of it: "Dès son origine, les personnes éclairées jugèrent qu'elle ne tarderait pas à se corrompre" [From its origin, enlightened people judged that it would not take long for this process to become corrupted] (*PC* 7, 148). The subscription method as described by Prévost is modernization as mechanization, where works are made on a fast-moving assemby line. Instead of a fine work of literature, a text produced in this way is a quickly pieced-together patchwork of errors,

printed to meet a deadline and to assure a regular rhythm of sales. Prévost cites "la négligence des ouvriers" [the negligence of workers] (*PC*
7, 148) as especially problematic when applied to such important books
as the Bible or Bayle.

Denouncing the subscription method as the demise of quality literature in favor of a rise in the quantity of profits, Prévost bemoans publishers' neglect of new works in favor of the sure income to be had by
producing old standards, remarking that "l'avantage que trouvent les libraires à tirer ainsi toutes les semaines un gros intérêt de leur argent,
fait qu'ils rejettent absolument toutes les autres voies dont ils ont moins
de profit à espérer. Les bons écrivains sont négligés et le Public perd
tout ce qu'il pouvait attendre de leur plume" [the advantage that publishers have in making a great profit each week makes them absolutely
reject all other means which offer less profit. Good writers are neglected, and the public loses all the good that could come of their writing] (*PC* 7, 151). Prévost also protests the effect of this method on authors who write to meet publishers' deadlines, explaining: "Ceux qui
savent qu'un livre ne se fait pas comme un ouvrage de maçonnerie, ne
peuvent douter que la composition d'un écrivain qui s'engage à donner
un certain nombre de feuilles, ne se ressente beaucoup de la précipitation avec laquelle il est obligé de travailler dans un espace si court"
[Those who know that a book is not made like a work of masonry cannot doubt that the method of a writer who promises to produce a certain number of pages is much affected by the hurry with which he is
obliged to work in such a short time] (*PC* 7, 150).

Prévost inveighs against publishers who, in their race to be first to
produce a new work, are unconcerned by the errors occasioned by
their haste. He refers to their competitive practices as "une guerre entre
les libraires" [a war among publishers] (*PC* 7, 152) and attributes to it
"des plus misérables suites" [the most miserable effects] (*PC* 7, 152).
Not only is the text corrupted but so is the honor of the literary endeavor, for each publishes with his *feuille* "une critique sanglante du
parti opposé" [a violent criticism of the opposing party] (*PC* 7, 152), a
slander of his competitor's project. The publishers' efforts to defame
one another's products eventually discredit their entire enterprise with
the public "[qui] en rit et les lit [les œuvres] plus par curiosité que par
estime" [(which) laughs upon reading (the criticism) and reads them
(the works) more out of curiosity than out of respect] (*PC* 7, 153). Literature is sacrificed to sales figures, and Prévost complains: "Mais
qu'importe aux Libraires si ce qu'ils font imprimer est estimable ou non

pourvu qu'il se vende?" [But what does it matter to the publishers if what they print is respectable or not as long as it sells?] (*PC 7*, 153)

Paradoxically, Prévost appears especially interested in condemning the commodification of literature at the very moment that he finds himself to be inextricably implicated in the new literary economy. Even more than his multivolume novels, which are treated by publisher and author alike as money-making machines, Prévost's newspaper illustrates what Pierre Bourdieu calls "la littérature industrielle": the new practice of authors supplying what readers demand at a steady rhythm with a predictable return.[1] By engaging in a journalistic enterprise, Prévost places himself in the position of practicing exactly that against which he preaches: the subscription method. Writing as if from on high, Prévost is actually knee-deep in the muck of Grub Street.

In his analysis of the Grub Street phenomenon in France, Robert Darnton sees journalism as one of the few outlets open to the hapless hacks he describes.[2] Even in the eighteenth century, the rise of journalism was seen to mark the downfall of literature, since newspapers were seen not as artistic outlets but rather as economic endeavors. According to Voltaire in the *Encyclopédie* article "Gazette," most newspapers "ont été faites uniquement pour gagner de l'argent" [were made only to make money].[3] As a figure of the "High Enlightenment," Voltaire views journalists as the "lowlife of literature":[4]

> Ces pauvres gens se partagent en deux ou trois bandes, et vont à la quête comme des moines mendiants, mais n'ayant point fait de vœux, leur société ne dure que peu de jours; ils se trahissent comme des prêtres qui courent le même bénéfice, quoiqu'ils n'aient nul bénéfice à espérer. Et cela s'appelle des *auteurs!* Le malheur de ces gens-là vient de ce que leurs pères ne leur ont pas fait apprendre une profession: c'est un grand défaut dans la police moderne. Tout homme du peuple qui peut élever son fils dans un art utile et ne le fait pas mérite punition. Le fils d'un metteur en œuvre se fait jésuite à dix-sept ans. Il est chassé de la société à vingt-quatre, parce que le désordre de ses mœurs a trop éclaté. Le voilà sans pain: il devient folliculaire: il infecte la basse littérature, et devient le mépris et l'horreur de la canaille même. Et cela s'appelle des *auteurs!*[5]

[These poor men split up into two or three groups and go looking for money like monks begging for alms, but having not taken vows, their association only lasts a few days; they betray each other like priests who are vying for the same parish, although they have little hope of earning an income from it. And they call themselves *authors*! The misfortune of such men is that their fathers did not make them learn a trade: this is a major failing of modern times. Any man of the people who can teach his son a useful trade and does not do so merits punishment. The son of an artisan becomes a Jesuit at seventeen. He is banished from the order at twenty-four because his bad behavior is too well known. There he is without bread: he becomes a journalist and infects the lowlife of literature, becoming the object of the contempt and the horror of even the lowest of the low. And these men call themselves *authors*!]

This story of the typical journalistic career could be based on the life of Prévost, a runaway priest turned newspaperman. In his efforts to counter such criticism, Prévost will use not only his novels but also his newspaper to rewrite his life story by portraying himself as the hero of *Le Pour et contre.*

Author as Hero

The authorial persona that emerges from *Le Pour et contre* is a hero in the most authentic sense of the term: a brave warrior mounted on a rearing steed, surging above the scribblers of Grub Street. Taking the reins from Desfontaines, whose periodical had been recently suppressed, Prévost describes himself as "un successeur qui ait la hardiesse de remonter sur Pégase et l'espérance de se tenir un peu plus ferme sur le dos de ce Cheval indocile" [a successor with the courage to remount Pegasus and with the hope of holding on more tightly to the reins of this indocile steed] (*PC* 1, 5). Quoting Corneille, Prévost identifies himself as a courageous man ready for a challenging endeavor: "Je suis ce téméraire ou plutôt ce vaillant" [I am this fearless or rather this valiant man] (*PC* 1, 5). This image of the author as hero arises from a long tradition of writers who describe themselves as belonging to a nobility of the mind. Viala explains: "Boileau conçoit une noblesse de lettres comme une noblesse d'épée. Aussi peut-on parler d"héroïsme littéraire': leur gloire d'écrivain leur conquiert la noblesse comme jadis les exploits au combat faisaient de l'homme un chevalier libre" [Boileau imagines a nobility of letters just as there is a nobility of the sword. In this way, one may speak of 'literary heroism': the writer's glory ennobles him just as in old times the exploits of war made men into heroes].[6] Prévost combats the image of the modern author as a mercenary by casting the writer as a noble knight in order to affirm that authorship is not the antithesis of heroism but a true expression of it.

Although others see his authorial enterprises as motivated by money, Prévost takes pains to attribute avarice to his publishers while characterizing his own actions as purely altruistic. In an article entitled "Définition d'un auteur," Prévost proclaims:

> Un imprimeur et un libraire . . . sont des marchands; mais, Madame, un auteur n'a rien de commun avec cette idée. . . . Un auteur est un homme, qui étant entré d'abord dans la carrière d'étude, pour satisfaire son propre goût et sans autre vue que son utilité particulière; et s'étant enrichi peu à peu l'esprit et le cœur de tout ce qu'il y a d'utile et d'agréable dans les sciences, tourne ensuite un œil de tendresse et de compassion sur toutes les créatures de son espèce, qu'il voit privées, par leur paresse et par d'autres obstacles, des fruits précieux qu'il a recueillis de son travail. Sa générosité s'enflamme. Il entreprend de leur communiquer ses sentiments et ses lumières: et ce zèle pour l'utilité d'autrui, lui fait prodiguer souvent dans un ouvrage de deux heures de lecture, des richesses qu'il a ramassées pendant vingt ans d'études et d'application. (*PC* 5, 102–3)

> [A printer and a publisher . . . are merchants; but, Madame, an author has nothing in common with them. . . . An author is a man who, having entered into a studious career to satisfy his own tastes and without any other aim but his own personal fulfillment and having enriched his mind and heart little by little with all things useful and agreeable in the sciences, then turns a tender and compassionate eye on his fellow creatures who are deprived, by their own laziness and by other obstacles, of the precious fruits he has gathered in his work. His generosity is enflamed. He undertakes to communicate to them his sentiments and his knowledge: and this zealous desire to be useful to others often causes him to give away in a work which only takes two hours to read the riches he has amassed over twenty years of serious study.]

For Prévost, the ideal author is not interested in filling his purse with money but rather his mind with knowledge and his heart with wisdom. He is less a mercantile than a moral being who, instead of taking his readers' money, wants to give them the wealth of his knowledge, even if he loses in this exchange.

In her essay, "Virtuous Economies: Modernity and Noble Expenditure from Montesquieu to Caillois," Elena Russo notes the importance of the gift as a demonstration of aristocratic prestige in pre-market societies.[7] Although not a noble himself, Prévost's presents the good author's writing as an aristocratic *acte gratuit,* affirming: "C'est un présent gratuit qu'il vous fait" [It is a free gift that he gives you] (*PC* 5, 104). Accordingly, the ideal author strives for glory and scorns financial rewards: "Il attend une récompense pour ses peines. Mais quelle est-elle? c'est la gloire. Et quelle gloire? celle d'avoir bien fait. C'est-à-dire la plus simple et la plus juste de toutes les récompenses. . . . Où trouvez-vous la moindre apparence d'intérêt dans une conduite si noble?" [He expects a reward for his troubles. But what is it? It is glory. And what sort of glory? The glory of a good deed. That is to say the simplest and most just of all rewards. . . . Where do you find the least appearance of interest in such noble conduct?] (*PC* 5, 103). Such an author—in his unselfish artistic endeavor—incarnates the noble ideals normally associated with the heroes of Prévost's novels.

Like the heroes of his novels, Prévost expresses an aristocratic disdain for the income associated with authorship, writing in *Le Pour et contre*, "Je n'attache point d'autre prix à ces sortes d'ouvrages [mes romans] que celui qu'ils reçoivent de l'approbation du Public" [I do not attach any other price to such works (my novels) than the approval of the public] (*PC* 47, 32). Uninterested in money, he declares himself invested in the honor his writing earns him, explaining, "[J]e n'ai pas laissé d'être extrêmement sensible au succès de mon travail et à l'honneur qu'on m'a fait d'en souhaiter la continuation" [I am still extremely sensitive to the success of my work and to the honor with which the public favors me by desiring its continuation] (*PC* 47, 32). Accordingly, Prévost portrays himself as less attentive to his revenues than to his reputation, which depends on the good opinion of gentlemen readers: "Je saisis d'autant plus volontiers cette occasion d'en marquer ma reconnaissance aux honnêtes gens, qu'étant fort jaloux de leur estime, j'ai appris avec chagrin qu'on s'efforce de me noircir dans leur esprit" [I seize this occasion even more eagerly to mark my gratitude to gentlemen and ladies, since I am so desirous of their esteem, and I am chagrined that others try to tarnish their image of me] (*PC* 47, 32).

This characterization of the author as *honnête homme* is constructed in a long autobiographical article known as Prévost's "Apologie," a supposedly factual piece in which Prévost writes his own life as if it were the plot of one of his fictions, making himself the hero of the story. Writing as if to win the sympathy of the readers of his sentimental novels, in the "Apologie" Prévost presents himself as flawed yet endearing. He portrays himself as a youth whose lively temperament makes him unsuited for monastic life: "Vif et sensible au plaisir, j'avouerai . . . que la sagesse demanda bien des précautions qui m'échappèrent" [Lively and pleasure-loving, I will admit . . . that good behavior required many precautions which were beyond me] (*PC* 47, 38). Unable to control his passionate nature, the young Prévost recalls the classic character of the knight of Malta (the chevalier Des Grieux or the Young Commander, for example) whose better intentions are undermined by his even stronger desires. To inspire compassion, the hero's passion must be tragic, and Prévost imparts an episode from his early life as if it were a scene from a baroque lovestory: "La fin d'un engagement trop tendre me conduisit enfin au Tombeau, c'est le nom que je donne à l'Ordre respectable où j'allai m'ensevelir, et où je demeurai quelque temps si bien mort que mes parents et mes amis ignorèrent ce que j'étais devenu" [(T)he unhappy end of a too tender engagement led me to the Tomb, which is the name I give to the respectable Order where I went to bury myself and where I stayed buried for such a long time that my family and friends did not know what had become of me] (*PC* 47, 39). The dark tones of this tale, in which Prévost almost literally buries himself alive, echo the adventures of his fictional heroes; when Renoncour, Des Grieux, or Patrice are disappointed in love, they too go underground, hiding their broken hearts in sepulchral solitude.

Prévost asks readers to extrapolate a portrait of the author from their familiarity with his fictional characters, explicitly inviting them to judge "quels devaient être depuis l'âge de vingt jusqu'à vingt-cinq ans le cœur et les sentiments d'un homme qui a composé le Cléveland à trente-cinq ou trente-six" [what could have been between the ages of twenty and twenty-five the sentiments of a man who wrote *Cleveland* at thirty-five or thirty-six] (*PC* 47, 38–39). In this comparison to Cleveland, Prévost underscores his serious side, and in his self-portrait as a mature man he attributes to himself the melancholy and even misanthropic qualities associated with the heroes of his novels. His "Apologie" thus offers the image of the author as

> un homme de trente-sept ou de trente-huit ans qui porte sur son visage et dans son humeur les traces des ses anciens chagrins; qui passe quelquefois des semaines entières sans sortir de son cabinet, et qui y emploie tous les jours sept ou huit heures à l'étude; qui cherche rarement les occasions de se réjouir; qui résiste même à celles qui lui sont offertes, et qui préfèrent une heure d'entretien avec un ami de bon sens, à tout ce qu'on appelle plaisirs du monde et passe-temps agréables. Civil, d'ailleurs, par l'effet d'une excellente éducation, mais peu galant; d'une humeur douce, mais mélancolique; sobre enfin, et réglé dans sa conduite. (*PC* 47, 41)

[a man of thirty-seven or thirty-eight who bears on his face and in his character the traces of his old sorrows; who sometimes spends entire weeks without leaving his library and who spends seven or eight hours a day in study; a man who rarely seeks opportunities for pleasure; who resists even those offered to him, and who prefers an hour of conversation with a wise old friend over those things that are called worldly pleasures and agreeable pastimes. Civil by the effect of an excellent education but not gallant, even-tempered but melancholy; sober and strict in his conduct.]

Portraying the scene of writing as a studious solitude and the artist as a person who shuns publicity, Prévost places himself in the position of the narrators of his novels who write their memoirs in retirement and publish them anonymously.

An Anonymous Author's Signature Style

While the narrators of the novels systematically seek anonymity to disguise their authorial enterprise, in the newspaper, authorship itself is an admirable adventure and one in which Prévost takes pride. Like a knight marching into battle carrying his coat of arms, Prévost emblazons each of his literary efforts with a highly identifiable mark, an image that appears throughout his *œuvre* and serves as a pseudosignature.[8] Prévost's *blason* is a heart smoldering under ashes, the central image of the "Apologie," where Prévost portrays his own dark yet fiery character: "[J]e reconnus que ce cœur si vif était encore brûlant sous la cendre" [I recognized that this lively heart was still smoldering beneath the ashes] (*PC* 47, 39). Prévost brands his work with the image of the smoldering heart, marking it with the fire of his mind so that even without a signature as such the identity of the author is clear. In his novels, this fusion of love and death is characteristic of the self-immolating heroes who strive to bury their burning passions.[9] When the passionate hero becomes a professional journalist, this imagery is adapted to illustrate the perils of authorship:

J'ai besoin aujourd'hui de plus de précaution que jamais, pour me renfermer dans les bornes que je me suis prescrites. *J'ai à marcher sur des cendres trompeuses,* où pour peu que la pesanteur de mes pas soit inégale, je cours le risque de sentir le feu qui est caché sous leur surface et d'être arrêté dans ma course. Je me rappelle mon titre, ma devise, les promesses que j'ai faites au public. (*PC* 18, 49)

[I need today to take more precautions than ever to contain myself within the limits I have prescribed. *I must tread on smoldering embers,* where a careless step might cause me to feel the fire hidden under the surface and stop me in my tracks. I must remember my title, my motto, the promises that I have made to the public.]

In fact, the line from Horace (*Incedo per ignes / Suppositos cineri doloso*), chosen by Prévost as the motto of *Le Pour et contre,* evokes the power of writing to inflame but also alludes to the fire that smolders beneath the calm exterior of the scholar.

Prévost points to the mark of the writer's personality even in works that would seem to leave no place for it, and he writes admiringly of Bayle's dictionary: "Qu'on retranche du dictionnaire de Bayle tout ce qui est de lui, ce ne sera plus qu'un livre ordinaire" [If one takes from Bayle's dictionary everything that is Bayle's, it would only be an ordinary book] (*PC* 15, 345). While *Le Pour et contre* may appear to be a patchwork of passages culled from already published sources, Prévost insists on the importance of authorial agency in his newspaper's composition: "L'abondance de mes matériaux, avec un peu de facilité que j'ai reçue du ciel pour les mettre en œuvre empêchera toujours que je ne tombe dans la nécessité de piller les autres" [The abundance of my materials and the little bit of facility which I have received from heaven to work with them will always save me from the necessity of stealing from others] (*PC* 90, 360). Often accused of plagiarism by his peers, Prévost protests his originality. He even contrasts his own industriousness with the laziness of plagiarists, declaring: "Le plagiat est déjà une règle sûre pour se mettre à couvert de la fatigue de penser dans toutes sortes d'ouvrages" [Plagiarism is already a surefire means to spare oneself the fatigue of thinking in all sorts of works]. (*PC* 273, 167)

In fact, Prévost uses *Le Pour et contre* to inveigh against plagiarism and to assert the inviolability of an author's right to be recognized for his writing. In issue 6 of *Le Pour et contre* Prévost accuses a playwright of stealing an episode of the *Mémoires d'un homme de qualité*—the scene of Donna Diana's horrible and unique death—to transpose it into a play about the life of Gustave Vasa (*PC* 6, 134). In a later issue, Prévost identifies and indicts an even more explicit theft of verbatim passages from his preface of *Histoire de M. de Thou* by a rival historian: "Je ne m'en plaindrais point s'il avait averti qu'elles sont de moi [les remarques . . .] mais s'approprier de suite jusqu'à sept pages de mon travail . . . sans donner un seul mot d'explication sur la source, c'est une entreprise qui blesse les lois de la République de lettres" [I would not have complained if he had noted that (those remarks . . .) were mine, but to appropriate seven pages of my work . . . without a single reference to the source breaks all of the laws of the Republic of Letters] (*PC* 61, 24). This victim vows to fight back, and Prévost even promises to publish an essay against plagiarism in order to unmask the miscreants who rob authors of their rightful glory (*PC* 19, 183).

In affirming the essential relationship between the creator and his creation, Prévost also campaigns against publishers' efforts to rob the author of control of his work by replacing him with hacks for projects already in progress. He uses his newspaper to defend himself against Etienne Neaulme, the publisher of *Cleveland*, who has hired a hack to produce the fifth tome of Prévost's unfinished novel. By publishing this unauthorized episode under Prévost's pseudonymous signature—"Par l'auteur des *Mémoires d'un homme de qualité*"—the publisher plans to exploit the success of the novel's first four volumes and their author's persistent popularity. In his argument against the publisher's replacement of the real author with a cheap imitator, Prévost emphasizes the artistic cost of this money-making move to the literary value of the novel. He protests

> que cette addition répond mal aux tomes précédents; que le caractère de Cleveland y est mal soutenu; qu'on n'y remarque point d'invention, ni d'art dans la conduite des événements et dans le ménagement des passions; que la morale y est pesante et mal distribuée; que le style n'en est point uniforme, quoiqu'on sente à tous moments les efforts que fait l'auteur pour le rendre conforme au mien. (*PC* 47, 30)

> [that this addition does not correspond to the preceding volumes; that the character of Cleveland is poorly sustained; that one notices little invention or art in the progress of the plot and in the development of the emotions; that the moral is heavy and poorly distributed; that the style is not uniform, although one notices everywhere the efforts made by the author to render his style like mine.]

Supplanted by substitutes in both his novels and his newspaper—Didot publishes issues of *Le Pour et contre* penned by Desfontaines and Lefebvre de Saint-Marc when Prévost is unavailable to produce his weekly pages—Prévost objects to this procedure. After Desfontaines has taken charge of *Le Pour et contre* from the middle of issue 19 to the end of issue 32, Prévost is adamant in announcing his return and affirming the superiority of the original over the copy:

Le public est facile à tromper, mais on ne le trompe pas longtemps. . . .
Ce n'est point l'amour propre qui me fait commencer par cette observation. Quoiqu'elle soit juste et qu'elle ait été vérifiée à mon égard par la
facilité avec laquelle j'apprends que le Public a reconnu que les
dernières feuilles du *Pour et contre* sont d'une autre main que la mienne,
je ne me flatte point que la différence qu'il a remarquée soit à l'avantage
de ma méthode et de mon style. Mais je comprends sans peine, que le
principal mérite d'un ouvrage de cette nature consistant de la variété
des sujets et dans la nouveauté des images, il est difficile qu'un écrivain
qui fait sa demeure à Paris puisse donner aussi facilement que moi cette
sorte d'agrément à son travail. (*PC* 33, 49)

[The public is easy to fool, but one can only fool it for so long. . . . It is
not vanity that makes me begin with such an observation. Although it is
true and has been verified in my case by the ease with which, as I have
learned, the public recognized that the last issues of *Le Pour et contre*
were authored by someone other than myself, I do not flatter myself
that the difference that was noticed reflects a preference for my method
and my style. But I understand easily that the principal merit of a work
of this nature consists in the variety of its subjects and in the novelty of
its images, and it is difficult for a writer who lives in Paris to provide
such things as easily as I can.]

Although Prévost attributes the merits of his work to the fact that he
lives in London, he nonetheless informs us that the public has noticed
his absence not just because of a change in the newspaper's subject
matter but because of a change in its method and its style.[10]

At the same time as Prévost battles his own publishers Neaulme and
Didot, he must combat others who produce pirated and often mutilated
editions of his work. When the Dutch publisher Vanderklotten decides
to profit by copying *Le Pour et contre,* cutting it in two, and selling it
twice a week instead of once to double his profits, Prévost is outraged
by this audacity. Without any sensitivity to Prévost's artful composition, Vanderklotten chops, stretches and ultimately deforms the text, as
Prévost sarcastically remarks: "[P]ar les mêmes raisons qui lui donnaient droit sur l'ouvrage, il avait incontestablement celui de le diviser,
de le raccourcir, de l'allonger, en un mot de le faire paraître sous telle
forme qu'il jugerait à propos" [(F)or the same reasons which gave him
the right to the work, he had an incontestable right to divide it, shorten
it, lengthen it, in a word to publish it in any form he judged appropri-
ate] (*PC* 47, 27). However, Vanderkotten is only operating under the
accepted idea that "un auteur perd tout droit sur ses ouvrages lorsqu'ils

sortent une fois de la presse" [an author loses all rights to his works once they are printed] (*PC* 47, 26). After all, it is the printer who transforms the artistic abstraction into a concrete commodity, as Prévost ironically explains: "[C]haque feuille du *Pour et contre* cessait de m'appartenir à mesure que je la publiais. . . . [E]lle devenait son bien à lui qui entreprenait de l'imprimer" [(E)ach issue of *Le Pour et contre* stopped belonging to me as soon as I published it. . . . (I)t became the property of the person who decided to print it] (*PC* 47, 26–27).

To establish both creative and financial control of his artistic output, Prévost must argue that the value of the text is not a product of the printing but rather of the writing process. Despite the divide that Prévost draws between the economic interests of publishers and the artistic ones of authors, he begins to argue that writing is one form of work that deserves both admiration and compensation. In so doing, he alternates between the characterization of writer as hero and the portrayal of author as "ouvrier" [worker] admirable for his "industrie" [industriousness] (*PC* 1, 3–4). However, unlike the careless worker associated with the printing of large quantities of low quality publications, the good writer is a careful craftsman. While he admits his fears that "les gens de lettres se trouvassent un peu avilis par cette comparaison" [men of letters might think themselves a bit insulted by such a comparison] (*PC* 1, 4), Prévost equates an author's popularity with "la préférence qu'on accorde à certains artisans" [the preference one accords to certain artisans] (*PC* 1, 3–4). Prévost persists in this parallel, even in his arguments about artistic originality. Defining the unmistakable quality inherent in the style of a good author, he writes: "Les bons auteurs ont leur coin, qui s'accrédite tout d'un coup, et qui fait reconnaître aussitôt l'ouvrier" [Good authors have their mark, which is recognized at once just as one recognizes the mark of an artisan] (*PC* 5, 107): Like the craftsman proud of his handiwork—"Un Graveur, Un Peintre, un Horloger, un Fondeur, ne laissent rien sortir de leurs mains qui ne porte leur marque et leur nom" [An Engraver, a Painter, a Clockmaker, a Smith let nothing leave their hands that does not bear their mark and their name] (*PC* 7, 123)—an author should announce his artistry.[11]

If the value of a craftsman's work is often based on the presence of his mark—the sign that identifies a chair or a plate as the product of an admired artisan—so too the value of writing is linked to its readers' ability to recognize it as the product of a particular author. If Prévost does not sign his works with his own name, he nonetheless leaves an identifiable mark on them: the sign of the smoldering heart, the mark of the Man of Quality, the imprint of a signature style. Alain Viala has insisted on the signature's central role in the organization of the modern economy of authorship, writing, "An author is above all else a name signing a work: in the eyes of his contemporaries, just as in the eyes of history, he exists primarily through this signature. The signature alone engages him, exposes him to penalties that his text might incur and gives him the right to enjoy any profit it might earn. The entire economy of publication is organized around the value of the signature: both the financial value (who profits from this publication?) and the symbolic and affective value (by signing a work one engages an image of oneself)."[12]

The signature is fundamental to a new discourse of authors' rights in early-modern France, which Viala summarizes thus: "The right to affirm 'ce texte est de moi' [this text is written by me] gives the right to affirm as well 'ce texte est à moi' [this text belongs to me]."[13] Because of this connection between symbolic and material claims, Prévost's fight against plagiarists is then a battle not only for artistic control of his writing but for financial control as well. Viala explains: "The refusal of plagiarism had begun to be deeply ingrained in the mentality of the time, and behind this denunciation one may discern a precise link established by the authors of the time between the value of the work as an original creation, which became a major criterion for literary distinction, and the market value of the work."[14] Prévost's objection to his publishers' actions in replacing him on projects he has already begun is not only an effort to protect the artistic integrity of the work but it is also a means of preventing the devaluation of a commodity (*Cleveland* or *Le Pour et contre*, for example) and of the brand that they represent: the works of "l'auteur des *Mémoires d'un homme de qualité*."

If Prévost adopts this pseudonym to associate himself with the hero-narrators of his memoir-novels who, despite their literary leanings, refuse to be identified as authors, his particular use of this pseudonym is a sign of his own professionalism. Even though he does not sign his name to his first novel, Prévost is widely known to be the author of the *Mémoires d'un homme de qualité*, and when he signs subsequent publications "par l'auteur des *Mémoires d'un homme de qualité*," the pseudonym in fact advertises the identity of the author. In the case of *Le Pour et contre*, Prévost's attribution of his newspaper to "l'auteur des *Mémoires d'un homme de qualité*," appears to assign the noble qualities of the Man of Quality to the author of this new literary endeavor, but this continuity between the novels and the newspaper is also a marketing move to ensure Prévost's continued profit. In associating his novelistic writing with his newspaper enterprise, Prévost attracts readers of the Man of Quality's past productions to this newest undertaking. The Man of Quality pseudonym is a sort of quality seal and serves as a brand name for Prévost in the business of authorship.

In choosing a pseudonym that instead of hiding his name affirms his identity, Prévost displays his desire to be recognized as an author. However, in adopting a signature that assigns his writing to a gentleman amateur, Prévost refuses to admit his need to be paid for his work. Roger Chartier has written that "the new reality of a situation [*état*] based solely on the revenue from writing emerged with difficulty from the mentality of the Old Regime."[15] To take his place in the modern literary market, Prévost must move away from the aristocratic values of Old Regime France and toward the commercial culture of Holland and England.[16]

MERCHANT AS HERO

While Prévost's novels denigrate commerce, his newspaper proclaims its nobility by establishing it as the source of England's power and greatness. Prévost's major criticism of Voltaire's *Lettres anglaises* is their superficial examination of the English economy. Prévost writes:

> Tout ce qu'on lit sur le commerce, qui fait le sujet de la dixième lettre, est dans les bornes les plus exactes de la vérité. Mais comme ce noble exercice des Anglais est le principal fondement de leur grandeur et de leur puissance, on s'attendait que l'auteur eût traité moins superficiellement ces articles. Un lecteur curieux aurait souhaité d'y apprendre à quel commerce les Anglais s'attachent particulièrement; de quels lieux ils tirent plus d'avantages; par quelle méthode ils conduisent leur négoce; quels établissements ils ont cru nécessaires pour la faciliter; quel ordre il y a dans leur banque et dans leurs compagnies; enfin c'était le lieu d'explorer tout ce qui n'est point connu hors de leur île, comme le titre de la lettre semblait l'annoncer. On n'a fait qu'effleurer une si belle matière. Les Anglais s'en plaignent. (*PC* 11, 247)

> [All that one reads about commerce, which is the subject of the tenth letter, is within the exact limits of truth. But since this noble exercise of the English is their principal claim to greatness and power, one would expect the author to treat these matters less superficially. A curious

reader would have wished to learn what kind of commerce most interests the English; which places are most advantageous to their trade; by which methods they conduct their business; what sorts of establishments they believed necessary to facilitate it; what sort of order they have in their bank and in their companies; in sum, that was the place to explore everything that is unknown outside of their isle, as the title of the letter implies. He has only skimmed the surface of such a rich matter. The English complain of this treatment.]

In *Le Pour et contre,* Prévost documents the important place of merchants in even the highest ranks of English social life. He recounts that when Elizabeth I needed to defend herself against Spain, she sent her minister to the "Corps de Marchands de Londres." The merchants' power is indeed so great that they have only to use their influence to win a war, thus proving their wealth to be more prestigious than a king's friendship:

Ils [les marchands] écrivirent à leurs commis et à leurs facteurs de Genes d'employer toute l'influence que les intérêts de commerce leur donnaient sur les Genois, pour les porter à rompre le traité qu'ils avaient avec l'Espagne. Cette manière de négocier parut nouvelle au Sénat et à la Banque de Genes: "mais après avoir mûrement pesé les choses et considéré leurs véritables intérêts, ils préférèrent l'amitié des marchands de Londres à celle d'un monarque qui se qualifiait du titre fastueux de roi des deux Indes." (*PC* 46, 5)

[They (the merchants) wrote to their clerks and correspondents in Genoa to use all of the influence that their commerce gave them on the Genovese to force them to violate the treaty that they had with Spain. This manner of negotiating seemed new to the Senate and the Bank of Genoa: "but after having carefully weighed the options and considered their true interests, they preferred the friendship of the merchants of London to that of a monarch who gave himself the pompous title of the king of the Indies."]

In England, money ennobles, and, conversely, noblemen are not ashamed to engage in business, as Prévost describes:

Il n'est pas surprenant que des services de cette importance ayant élevé la condition de marchand au degré d'honneur et de considération où elle est en Angleterre jusques là que des personnes de la plus haute naissance ne font point de difficulté de s'y engager et d'y borner toute leur ambition. (PC 46, 5–6)

[It is not surprising that, since services of this importance have raised the condition of merchant to the degree of honor and consideration where it is in England, persons of the highest birth do not hesitate to become merchants and to focus all of their ambition on commerce.]

Quoting Voltaire, he continues:

Le frère du dernier comte d'Oxford est mort facteur à Alep. Celui du Duc de Townshend est actuellement marchand à Londres; et Mylord King, Chancelier d'Angleterre, avait il y a deux ans un de ses fils en apprentissage chez un riche marchand d'Amsterdam. (*PC* 46, 6).

[The brother of the last count of Oxford died as a correspondent in Alep. The brother of the Duke of Townshend is now a merchant in London; and two years ago Lord King, Chancellor of England, placed his son as an apprentice with a rich merchant in Amsterdam.]

Unlike in France where younger sons are often doomed by the dearth of opportunities available to them—unable to inherit, they are sent to the army or the Church and often end up like Des Grieux subject to debt and disorder—young English nobles can engage in commerce to bring honor to themselves and their country. "C'est pour relever encore la dignité du commerce que les Anglais ont soin de le faire considérer à leurs enfants par tous les endroits qui peuvent l'annoblir" [It is to raise the dignity of commerce that the English are careful to present it to their children in every way that shows its nobility] (*PC* 46, 6), writes Prévost. In England, commerce is a civilizing force, and Prévost affirms: "C'est lui qui fait comme circuler dans l'univers les arts et les sciences, l'honnêteté et l'industrie" [It is (commerce) which circulates arts and sciences, *honnêteté* and industriousness throughout the universe] (*PC* 46, 7). An industrious man can thus also be an *honnête homme.*

While the heroes of Prévost's novels identify their main activity as refined social interaction or "le commerce des honnêtes gens," the heroes of Prévost's newspaper are men of commerce: Herby the merchant and Cantillon the banker for example. The stories of these men are as dramatic as any of Prévost's novelistic plots. Herby's harem is reminiscent of Oriental settings in the *Mémoires d'un homme de qualité.* Cantillon's betrayal at the hands of his servants reminds readers of Des Grieux's similar mishap. Both Herby and Cantillon are murdered for their money, but the fact that they are merchants makes them no less interesting characters. The elevation of merchant to hero is complete when Prévost observes that the most popular play on the London stage is a tragedy with a clerk as its protagonist. Prévost writes a long piece in praise of Lillo's *The London Merchant or The History of George Barnwell* and admires the play so much that he uses it as a model for *Manon Lescaut*, transposing the innocent George into Des Grieux, his good friend and fellow clerk Truman into Tiberge, and the scheming courtesan Millwood into Manon.[17]

In Prévost's move from the novel to the newspaper, from the idealization of aristocracy to a new admiration of industriousness, the merchant is ennobled and even the pirate is admired. While the figure of the pirate has traditionally been synonymous with that of the villain, the English pirates profiled in *Le Pour et contre* are portrayed as charismatic and even heroic. Although a pirate, Daniel Hillock is described as if he were a gentleman — "[i]l était d'une si belle taille qu'il paraissait né pour commander" [he was so good-loking that he seemed born to lead] — and Prévost adds that "ses manières . . . étaient fort supérieures à sa profession [his manners . . . were far superior to his profession.]" In recounting one of his exploits Prévost compares this modern-day bandit with a hero of Antiquity, likening the brave Hillock to "le troisième des Horaces" [the third of the Horatii] (*PC* 292, 238–39). In describing the physical force of another pirate, Pol Rib, Prévost portrays him as a sort of Hercules: "Ce qui imprima la terreur dans tous les lieux . . . c'est que fort souvent au lieu de se servir d'un sabre ou d'une épée, il n'employait qu'un gros bâton armé de fer, avec lequel il tuait quelquefois d'un seul coup trois ou quatre ennemis" [What inspired terror everywhere . . . was that often instead of using a saber or a sword, he used a large stick covered in iron with which he sometimes killed with one blow three or four enemies] (*PC* 292, 236). Pol Rib is a hero fit for legends but also made for modern times, for his story is one of hard work rewarded, as Prévost writes: "[I]l avait été longtemps matelot. S'ennuyant d'obéir, il forma le dessein de se rendre maître de son vaisseau" [(H)e had been a sailor for a long time. Tired of obeying, he formed the plan to become the master of his ship.] (*PC* 292, 236). As heroes of the high seas, English merchants and English pirates enjoy geographical mobility, but more importantly they represent a new kind of social mobility celebrated by Prévost in *Le Pour et contre*.

In English culture, actions can ennoble, and even the socially marginal artist may earn his or her way into acceptance. Prévost cites the story of Mlle Sallé, a French dancer living in London, whose refusal to prostitute herself to a rich lord wins the approval of the English royal family. The artist does not sell herself, and instead her superiority to mere money is rewarded with pensions, patronage, and admission into the highest echelons of society (*PC* 39, 216). Unlike in France, where actors as great as Molière are buried in unmarked mass graves, the passing of an English actor is cause for public pomp in London. Prévost portrays the funeral for the actor Barton Booth as the mourning of a great man, who despite his status as an actor was admired for his personal character: "Sérieux d'ailleurs dans la conduite ordinaire de la vie, réglé dans les mœurs, poli dans les manières, il s'était attiré l'amitié et la considération de toutes les honnêtes gens, qui n'estimaient pas moins le caractère de son cœur et de son esprit que l'excellence de ses talents" [Serious in ordinary life, sober of conduct and polite in his manners, he had earned the friendship and consideration of all gentlemen and ladies who esteemed the character of his heart and mind just as much as the excellence of his talents] (*PC* 5, 119). According to Prévost, artists' inclusion in respectable circles establishes England as an ideal society where talent reaps its rightful reward.

In allowing artists to rise to the highest ranks of society and even of government, England represents a true meritocracy, as Prévost writes in *Le Pour et contre*, paraphrasing Voltaire:

> A la vérité, le mérite trouve d'autres récompenses parmi les Anglais. On y a vu M. Adisson secrétaire d'état, M. Newton directeur de la Monnaie, M. Congreve secrétaire de la Jamaïque, et M. Prior plénipotentiaire; M. Swift qui est doyen de St. Patrice en Irlande, n'est pas moins respecté dans le pays que le Primat même. Un homme de mérite est presque sûr de faire sa fortune en Angleterre. Il est révéré pendant sa vie, il reçoit des honneurs distingués après sa mort. Les plus grands seigneurs de la cour se disputent la gloire de porter la poêle à ses funérailles. Entrez dans l'église de Westminster, vous y admirerez moins les tombeaux des rois que les monuments de l'estime et de la reconnaissance de la nation pour ces hommes illustres dont le mérite a fait la gloire. (*PC* 13, 302)[18]

> [In truth, merit finds other rewards among the English. There one has seen Mr. Addison rise to the rank of secretary of state, Mr. Newton director of the Mint, Mr. Congreve secretary of Jamaica, and Mr. Prior plenipotentiary; Mr. Swift who is the dean of Saint Patrick's is no less respected in the country than the Primate himself. A man of merit is almost sure to make his fortune in England. He is revered during his life, and he receives distinguished honors after his death. The greatest lords of the court vie for the honor of being pallbearers at his funeral. Enter Westminster Abbey and you will admire more than the tombs of kings

the monuments made to show the esteem and gratitude of the nation for the illustrious men whose merit has made England glorious.]

Prévost sees England as the perfect place to prove his proposition that a man of letters can be the equal of any man of quality. When Lenglet Dufrenoy questions Prévost's personal conduct in London,[19] Prévost replies with righteous indignation:

C'est si peu la violence qui m'obligea de quitter Londres pour passer en Hollande, que je partis chargé de présents, de faveurs et de caresses. Qu'il me soit permis de le dire, par le droit que donne une Apologie, j'eus la satisfaction d'emporter les regrets de vingt Seigneurs qui m'honoraient de leur bienveillance et de leur protection, et ceux d'une infinité d'honnêtes gens qui m'avaient accordé leur estime et leur amitié. (*PC* 47, 36)

[It is hardly violence which obliged me to leave London for Holland, and I leave loaded with presents, favors, and affection. Let me be allowed to say, by the rights given by an Apology, that I had the satisfaction of leaving with the regrets of twenty Lords who honored me with their benevolence and their protection and those of an infinite number of gentlemen and ladies who had accorded me their esteem and friendship.]

Despite his status as an author or perhaps even because of it, Prévost is accepted and appreciated in English society, befriended by aristocrats and other *honnêtes gens*. In Prévost's description of his successful English experience, his insistence that friendship can unite men of quality and men of letters is a strong argument for their equality. At the same time, in his depiction of the socioeconomic dynamism of English society, Prévost finds a justification for his own industriousness. Moreover, in casting England as a meritocracy, Prévost finds the ideal situation where an author can be an *honnête homme* but where he can also potentially earn a living from the sales of his works without having to deny his interest in their success.

3

The Public as Hero of
Le Pour et contre

WHILE PRÉVOST'S NOVELS REFLECT THE ARISTOCRATIC VALUES OF
seventeenth-century France, his newspaper responds to the social dynamism of eighteenth-century England. Nevertheless, if the author sees
in England a place where he can aspire to the status of gentleman, this
opportunity for ascension may not represent the opening of English nobility to an ambitious underclass but rather the expansion of the idea of
gentlemanliness to include a broader cross section of English society.
When, upon leaving London, Prévost remarks that he has found favor
there among "vingt seigneurs" [twenty lords] and friendship with "une
infinité d'honnêtes gens" [an infinite number of gentlemen and ladies]
(*PC* 47, 36), the appellation *honnête* seems to have lost something in its
translation to the English context, since there it seems to evoke not a
select elite but decent people in general. In any event, Prévost takes
pride in having won the esteem of the English, and in so doing he acknowledges the importance of public opinion in his career as an author.
While the narrators of Prévost's memoir-novels approach writing as a
private endeavor, shunning publication, in *Le Pour et contre* Prévost actively addresses his public, making the reader a partner in his project.

The interdependence of the press and its public has been recognized
by historians of the early modern period, most notably by Jürgen Habermas, who writes: "As instruments of institutionalized art criticism, the
journals devoted to art and cultural criticism were typical creations of
the eighteenth century. . . . . [I]t was only through the critical absorp-
tion of philosophy, literature and art that the public attained enlightenment and realized itself as the latter's living process."[1] Habermas's analyses of eighteenth-century England have been applied to France by
cultural historians such as Roger Chartier, who concurs with Haber-

78

mas on the central role of newspapers in the consolidation of the public sphere. Chartier writes: "The various instances of literary and art criticism (salons, cafés, academies, newspapers) constituted a new, autonomous, free, and sovereign public."[2] Similarly, in their study of the French press in the eighteenth century, Claude Labrosse and Pierre Rétat remark: "Because of its fundamental role in communication and propagation, the periodical is deeply connected to the development of the public."[3]

However, long before Habermas's study of the structural transformation of the public sphere in eighteenth-century England,[4] Prévost observed the energy of English public life with its mobs gathered before a street spectacle or crowds assembled for a theatrical production, and before Habermas pointed to the English moral weeklies as key to the consolidation of this new public,[5] Prévost modeled his *Pour et contre* on the periodical essays of Addison and Steele. Interpreting English tastes for his French readers, Prévost used his understanding of the operations of public opinion to ensure the sales of his own work. Moreover, because of its periodical publication, a newspaper can be constantly responsive to its public, and Prévost's manipulation of this form demonstrates his mastery of marketing. At the same time, Prévost's openness to the public's participation in the critical project of *Le Pour et contre* constructs readers as the ultimate arbiters of the value of his work. Prévost's newspaper is a place where the author comes into his own, claiming his rights to his writing, but it is also the place where he admits his dependence on readers to assure his professional success.

PRÉVOST AND THE PUBLIC SPHERE: THE ENGLISH EXAMPLE

During his English exile, Prévost's observations of public life in England and specifically of the role of the press in that country inspired him to found his own newspaper. Already, in his first novel, Prévost included a description of English society in which the Man of Quality, newly arrived in England, is impressed with the free exchange of ideas he encounters there.

> Chacun a droit d'en parler librement. On condamne, on approuve, on critique, on déchire; on s'emporte en invectives de vive voix et par écrit, sans que le pouvoir supérieur ose s'y opposer. Le roi lui-même n'est pas

à couvert de la censure. Les cafés et les autres endroits publics sont comme le siège de la liberté anglicane. On y trouve tous les libelles qui se font pour ou contre le gouvernement. On a le droit pour deux sous d'en lire une multitude, et de prendre une tasse de thé ou de café. On donne aussi à lire cinq ou six sortes de gazettes, qui contiennent les nouvelles de l'Europe et particulièrement celles de Londres. (*MHQ*, 247)

[Each man has the right to speak freely. Each condemns, approves, criticizes, rips apart; some are carried away and speak or write their invectives without fear that any power might oppose them. The king himself is open to censure. The coffeehouses and other public places are like the seat of Anglican freedom. One finds there all of the lampoons [*libelles*] written for or against the government. One has the right for two *sous* to read a multitude of them and to drink a cup of tea or coffee. One also finds there five or six kinds of gazettes which contain the news of Europe and especially of London.]

In fact, it is this open expression of opinions "pour ou contre" which eventually gives Prévost's newspaper its name.

The conclusion of the novel's description of English newspapers even provides a program for *Le Pour et contre*:

Ce dernier article [le journal anglais] renferme tout ce qui se passe dans la ville, jusqu'au moindre événement; les masques y sont toujours nommés, de quelque rang qu'ils puissent être, et l'on en rapporte indifféremment le bon et le mauvais. On y annonce les comédies, les bals, les concerts, les livres qui sortent de la presse, les remèdes des charlatans, les maisons et les terres à louer ou à vendre, les banqueroutes, l'état des compagnies de commerce, l'arrivée et le départ des vaisseaux, en un mot tout ce qui peut intéresser le public, L'avidité des Anglais est extrême pour toutes ces nouvelles. Elles se répandent de la capitale jusqu'à l'extrémité des provinces; et l'on ne trouve personne, jusqu'au moindre matelot, qui n'emploie tous les jours deux sous pour satisfaire sa curiosité (*MHQ*, 247–48).

[This last item (the English newspaper) contains all that happens in the city, even the least event; masquerades of all sorts are always mentioned, the good and bad are both reported. Plays, balls, concerts, newly published books are all announced, the remedies of charlatans, houses and land to be rented or sold, bankruptcies, the state of companies and businesses, the arrival and departure of ships, in a word, everything that can interest the public. The avidity of the English for this type of news is extreme. It is spread from the capital to the far reaches of the provinces; and there is no one, not even the lowliest sailor, who does not spend two *sous* daily to satisfy his curiosity.]

In this survey of the English press—with its comments on theater and books, charlatans and financiers, commerce and exploration, and especially with its aim to interest the public's curiosity—Prévost predicts the subject matter of his own periodical and prefigures its subtitle: *"Dans lequel on s'explique librement sur tout ce qui peut intéresser la curiosité du public"* [In which we speak freely on everything that may interest the curiosity of the public].

In his examination of English newspapers, Prévost's survey of their content is accompanied by a study of their context. In Prévost's novel, just as in the famous English periodical *The Spectator*, the coffeehouse is the scene of the production and consumption of the newspaper. When describing this setting, Prévost observes the vital interaction of the public and the press in England where a myriad of ideas inspire a multitude of periodicals, which in turn reignite debate among their readers. He also remarks that the variety of subjects included in the English newspaper appeals to every level of society so that with its reports on travel and trade, the English press is a place where an economically energized nation—from "mylords" to merchants—finds the interests of its members reflected. Consequently, in *Le Pour et contre,* London is portrayed not only as a center for the exchange of goods but also for the exchange of information; Prévost describes the city as "le quartier d'assemblée de tout ce qui arrive d'extraordinaire et de curieux dans le monde, . . . une espèce de centre où toutes les nouvelles de l'univers viennent se rendre par les lignes de la navigation" [the meeting place for everything extraordinary and curious that happens in the world . . . a sort of center where all the news of the universe arrives by way of the shipping routes] (*PC* 33, 51). Writing the initial issues of his newspaper in London, Prévost profits from the access to the exotic provided by this cosmopolitan city and the interest in novelty promoted by the English press, finding in this capital of commerce a rich source of stories.

An admirer of England as a nation of explorers, Prévost is impressed by the inquisitiveness of the English public and depicts in detail the English appetite for news. In *Le Pour et contre,* the presentation of any important event is accompanied by a description of the enthusiasm it first provoked in England, and the original English reception thus offers a model for French readers' reaction to the same circumstances recounted in Prévost's newspaper. Before beginning a long article about Egyptian mummies, Prévost incites the interest of his readers by first evoking the enthusiastic response of the English to the arrival of these rare artifacts: "L'arrivée de deux Momies d'Egypte, que le capitaine Booke apporta la semaine passée à Londres, excita la curiosité de tous les habitants de cette grande ville" [The arrival of two Egyptian mummies, which captain Booke brought to London last week, excited the curiosity of all of the inhabitants of this great city] (*PC* 16, 3). Even when a simple stranger arrives on English shores, there is always a curious onlooker to attract attention, to draw a crowd, to turn the everyday into the intriguing. When a young Italian girl arrives at the port, a servant sees her and tells his master of her beauty. In the English culture of rapid diffusion of information, this news travels fast so that "[d]e plusieurs seigneurs, qui ont cherché l'occasion de voir cette jeune personne sur le bruit de sa beauté et de sa mauvaise fortune, on assure que le plus grand nombre a conçu de la passion pour elle" [of the many lords who sought a means to see this young person because of the rumors of her beauty and her misfortunes, it is said that most of them fell passionately in love with her] (*PC* 13, 297). Prévost shows that the English are taken with the person and plight of Donna Maria, and their attachment to her encourages the readers of Prévost's newspaper to take an interest in this young woman's story as well.

While curiosity about Egyptian history or compassion for an Italian orphan may be seen as admirable forms of English inquisitiveness, Prévost's portrait of the English mob is not always so flattering. In an article on the "gladiatrices anglaises" [English lady wrestlers] Prévost describes the popularity of a strange, new sport in England: "Les Anglais sont surpris eux-mêmes d'en voir deux [femmes] depuis quelques semaines qui ont arraché le sabre des mains de leurs maris, et qui s'en servent l'une contre l'autre avec autant d'adresse que d'intrépidité. . . . [U]n spectacle si rare ne manque point d'attirer une assemblée nombreuse" [Over the last weeks, the English themselves have been surprised to see two (women) take the sabers from the hands of their husbands and use them against each other with as much skill as courage. . . . (S)uch a rare spectacle does not fail to attract a large crowd] (*PC* 13, 289–90). Prévost remarks that the crowd attending this strange spectacle is both big and bloodthirsty: "Les spectateurs ne s'en retournent point satisfaits lorsqu'ils n'ont pas vu couler le sang" [Spectators do not leave satisfied unless they have seen blood] (*PC* 13,

290). Prévost notices the same morbid curiosity when Londoners mass for public executions. In the first issue of *Le Pour et contre* he notes the popular interest in the figure of Sara Malcomb, a young Irishwoman found guilty of three murders in one night, writing: "[U]ne action si horrible a fait beaucoup de bruit à Londres" [Such a horrible action was the talk of London] (*PC* 1, 20). The case of another criminal, Molly Siblis, is closely followed by the public who crowd outside of the courthouse to hear her sentence and see her punishment: "La sentence de sa mort fut confirmée par la cour, et tout le monde en attendait l'exécution comme un spectacle extraordinaire" [Her death sentence was confirmed by the court, and everyone awaited her execution as they would some extraordinary spectacle] (*PC* 59, 315). However, when her sentence is just as soon commuted, the criminal becomes a sort of heroine whose story fascinates the people, as Prévost notes: "Un changement si peu attendu ne fit qu'augmenter la curiosité du public" [Such an unexpected change only added to the public's curiosity] (*PC* 59, 317).

In each of these cases, where the public's curiosity is morally questionable, the role of the English press in encouraging it is equally problematic. The lady gladiators' matches attract an audience only after having been advertised in newspapers: "Les jours qu'elles doivent en venir aux mains sont annoncés dans les gazettes" [The days they will fight are announced in the newspapers] (*PC* 13, 289). If a mob crowds around the gallows to watch the execution of the criminal Sarah Malcomb, their interest in her case is incited by its coverage in the press, as Prévost remarks, "[L]a peinture et la poésie ont été mises en œuvre pour publier toutes les circonstances. Pendant que la criminelle était en prison, M. Hogarth tira son portrait, et l'on en a fait une infinité de copies qui se sont vendues dans les rues" [(P)ainting and poetry have been employed to make public all of the circumstances. While the criminal was in prison, Mr. Hogarth made her portrait, and an infinite number of copies have been sold in the streets] (*PC* 1, 20). The popular fascination with Molly Siblis only intensifies with the publication and distribution of the criminal's memoirs.

In describing the English public's avidity for such horrific stories, Prévost at first attributes to his French readers a superior sensitivity: "Je sens comme mes lecteurs tout ce qu'il y a de dur et de révoltant dans le récit de Molly Siblis" [I feel, as do my readers, all that is hard and revolting in the story of Molly Siblis] (*PC* 59, 335). However, this condemnation of English curiosity is only a cover for the French appetite for such anecdotes, since according to Prévost this interest in the monstrous is shared by all, his readers included:

> La nature produit-elle un monstre? Vous y courez, cher lecteur. La curiosité vous porte à le voir de près et à l'examiner. L'horreur qu'il vous inspire rebute si peu vos yeux que c'est précisément ce qui vous conduit au spectacle, et plus l'image que vous en tracez à vos voisins est hideuse et difforme, plus elle leur donne d'empressement pour s'assurer de la vérité par eux-mêmes. En serait-il autrement des monstres de la morale? Non, car je vous vois courir avec ardeur pour assister au supplice d'un scélérat. La haine que vous avez pour ses crimes n'empêche pas que vous ne souhaitez de les apprendre et de voir celui qui les a commis (*PC* 59, 335–36).

> [Nature produces a monster? You run to see it, dear reader. Curiosity drives you to examine it more closely. The horror it inspires repulses you so little that it is this very horror which draws you to the spectacle, and the more the image that you relay to your neighbors is hideous and deformed, the more they desire to go see it for themselves. Is this any different for moral monsters? No, because I see you run to witness the execution of a criminal. The hatred you have for his crimes does not prevent you from wanting to learn about them and to see the person who has committed them.]

Although Prévost seems to condemn the sensationalistic strategies of English newspapers, he exploits the same stories they publish to ensure the success of *Le Pour et contre*. Even if he protests that "[u]n récit de cette nature n'est pas fait pour la traduction [ni pour . . .] la délicatesse de notre langue" [a story of this nature is not made for translation (. . . nor for) the delicacy of our language] (*PC* 59, 326), Prévost does translate excerpts of Molly's memoirs, entitling his article "Relation curieuse" to most effectively appeal to the curiosity of his French readers. In this case, crime does pay, at least for those who publish crime stories, for Prévost knows that the public will buy his account of Molly's outrageous adventures and that he, in turn, will profit from them. He thus concludes: "Je suis porté à croire . . . que les affreux désordres de Molly Siblis se feront lire avidement, et je parierais pour le succès de cette feuille" [I am led to believe . . . that the awful disorders of Molly Siblis will be read avidly, and I would bet on the success of this issue] (*PC* 59, 336).

While, in his accounts of everyday life in England, Prévost uses the English public's reaction as a means to predict and program the response of his French readers, he does not attempt to collapse cultural differences when it comes to aesthetic appreciation. Prévost admits that if he recounts the success of various plays with the English public, it is not to convince his French readers of their merit but rather to inform them of what the English enjoy. Thus he writes at the end of his translation of Steele's play, *The Conscious Lovers*: "Je me propose moins de plaire que de faire connaître ce qui plaît à nos voisins. C'est la curiosité plutôt que le goût de mes lecteurs que je cherche à satisfaire" [I propose less to please than to make known the taste of our neighbors. It is the curiosity rather than the taste of my readers that I seek to satisfy] (*PC* 119, 322). This is the attitude that Shelly Charles invokes when she characterizes the *Pour et contre*'s presentation of English literature as "a literature of curiosity."[6]

Each time Prévost introduces an English work to his French readers, he reminds them that he is not trying to change the French taste but rather to define the English. He always emphasizes the difference between the reception of the piece by its original English public and its potential rejection by the French public of the *Pour et contre*. He almost apologizes to his readers after publishing a long translation of a play by Dryden, writing: "[C]eux qui n'aiment point assez le théâtre pour souhaiter de le connaître dans ses différentes formes ou qui sont trop attachés au goût qui règne en France pour être fort curieux de celui de nos voisins ont pu trouver la traduction que j'ai donnée dans les feuilles précédentes un peu ennuyeuse" [Those who do not like theater enough to wish to know it in its different forms or who are too attached to the French taste to be curious about our neighbors' may have found the translation that I gave in the preceding issues a bit boring] (*PC* 101, 241). Prévost notes the persistence of prejudices which prevent the French from appreciating the most successful plays of the London stage: he acknowledges that the violence in *Caelia* would shock French sensibilities and the treatment of time and space in *All for Love* would offend French ideas of a well made play.[7] For French audiences accustomed to the rules of *bienséance* and the respect of the *trois unités*, the English theater's violations of these laws is a sort of aesthetic crime.

Prévost's discussion of the English reception of Fielding's *The Miser*, a translation and adaptation of Molière's *L'Avare*, provides particular insights into the differences in French and English taste. Again, Prévost admits that he does not expect his French readers to see these English modifications as merits, but rather he presents them as examples of the English aesthetic and allows his readers to judge their effect: "Je veux rendre compte à mes lecteurs d'une partie des changements, pour les mettre en état de juger s'ils embellissent Molière ou s'ils le défigurent" [I want to report to my readers on some of the changes, to allow them to judge if they improve or disfigure Molière] (*PC* 45, 337). Commenting on the changes that Fielding has made in his translation of Molière, Prévost notes that to produce a successful work, one must adapt it to the specific expectations of the spectator, and to do so, Fielding has transformed the simply structured French play into a complicated English comedy: "Il semble que M. Fielding, traducteur de l'Avare, ait appréhendé principalement que la simplicité du sujet ne déplût à ses compatriotes; il l'a chargé autant qu'il a pu de nouveaux incidents, pour rendre l'intrigue plus composée. Les Anglais ne s'accommodent point de ce qui est trop facile à comprendre. Il faut donner partout l'exercice à leur raison" [It seems that Mr. Fielding, translator of *The Miser*, feared that the simplicity of the subject would displease his countrymen; he added as many new incidents as he could to make the story more complex. The English do not enjoy things that are too easy to understand. They must in all things exercise their reason] (*PC* 4, 80–81). The fact that the most popular of Molière's plays in England at this time is not *Le Misanthrope* (admired by Prévost as a masterpiece) but rather *L'Avare* also supports the idea that the most successful art reflects the values of its public. While *Le Misanthrope* is an examination of the social codes of the French aristocracy, *L'Avare*'s story of financial interest and intrigue seems more apt to interest the English merchant class.

Since, according to Prévost, the salient feature of English society is its propensity for commerce, it is no surprise to him that one of the most successful English plays of the time is Lillo's *London Merchant*. In examining the popularity of Lillo's play in London, Prévost attributes much of its success to its suitability to its cultural context:

> [U]ne tragédie qui s'est attiré tant de marques d'approbation et d'estime doit faire naître à ceux qui en entendront parler, l'une ou l'autre de ces deux pensées; ou qu'elle est un des chefs-d'œuvre dont la parfaite beauté se fait sentir à tout le monde, ou qu'elle peut servir de règle certaine pour juger du goût présent de cette nation pour les spectacles. (*PC* 45, 337–38)

> [(A) tragedy which has attracted so many marks of approval and esteem must inspire in those who hear about it one or the other of these

two ideas; either that it is one of those masterpieces whose perfect beauty is felt by all, or that it may serve as a guide to judge the present state of this nation's taste in spectacles.]

Nevertheless, while the English enjoy seeing a merchant as a hero, their appreciation of this tragedy is inspired not only by their identification with its hero but by their horrified fascination with its heroine. This reaction is provoked by the character of the courtesan Millwood who, having seduced the young clerk and induced him to rob his master and murder his uncle to contribute to her upkeep, coldly betrays the hero to the police. Using a term he has already applied to the real murderess, Molly Siblis, Prévost characterizes the fictional Millwood as "monstrueuse" (*PC* 46, 18), implying that the English public's appetite for monsters in life informs the English taste in art.

While Prévost suggests that the play's success originates in its suitability to its public, his close study of its reception also suggests that the intense emotion it inspires might in fact transcend the time and place of its production:

Dans un pays où l'on peut dire qu'on est accoutumé aux spectacles tragiques et où les plus touchants ne sont pas toujours réservés pour le théâtre, on aurait peine à se figurer jusqu'à quel point le public a été frappé de cette scène [de trahison]. L'étonnement et l'horreur étaient visibles à chaque représentation sur le visage des spectateurs. C'était un silence si profond et si lugubre que pour s'en former l'idée il faudrait éprouver quelque chose du sentiment qui le causait. (*PC* 46, 23–24)

[In a country where one may say that one is accustomed to tragic spectacles and where the most touching are not always reserved for the theater, it could be hard to imagine to what point the public was struck by this scene (of betrayal). At each performance, astonishment and horror were visible on the faces of the spectators. To form an idea of their deep and lugubrious silence, it would be necessary to feel something of the sentiment which caused it.]

Whether his attention to English aesthetics is inspired by a love of beauty or a lust for profit, Prévost finds in this play, applauded by the English public, a source for his greatest success with French readers. The heroine of the typically English story is at the same time a universal archetype: the lovable yet loathsome woman. Millwood is a model for Prévost's classic French character: Manon Lescaut.[8]

THE PHENOMENON OF TASTE
AND PRÉVOST'S FRENCH PUBLIC

In his various observations on the phenomenon of taste, Prévost does not claim to understand its inner workings, and instead affirms that there is no accounting for it: "Mais il ne faut jamais entreprendre, dit l'illustre Addison, de rendre raison d'un goût général, non plus que de trouver la véritable cause d'une maladie épidémique" [But one must never endeavor, said the illustrious Addison, to explain a general taste just as one must not try to find the true cause of an epidemic] (*PC* 15, 360). If another periodical of the day proposes itself as an *Ecole du goût* [*School for taste*] (Prévost reviews this title somewhat suspiciously in *PC* 124), Prévost does not purport to teach taste but rather to learn as much as he can about it. He admits his inability to change taste and decides instead to literally go with the flow: "Il n'est donc pas au pouvoir d'un écrivain de rectifier le mauvais goût de son siècle, lorsque les racines en sont profondes et qu'elles ont gagné terrain dans un certain espace. En vain se flatterait-il de plaire en s'opposant au torrent, puisque le goût du public est ce torrent" [It is not then in the power of a writer to rectify the bad taste of his time, since its roots are deep and they have only grown deeper. It is vain to imagine pleasing the public by opposing the current, because the taste of the public is that current] (*PC* 65, 98).

According to Prévost, the success of a work of art often depends less on the fixed qualities of the work than on the contingencies of the place and time of its reception. As an example, Prévost takes the poet Ronsard whose reputation reflects the changing tastes of readers, for he is alternately considered admirable and detestable. Prévost explains: "Ce n'est pas que dans un autre sens un auteur estimé par le public ne puisse dans la suite devenir l'objet de ses mépris; mais c'est qu'alors le goût du public changera; c'est-à-dire qu'il se perfectionnera ou peut-être se corrompra" [It is not that an author esteemed by the public cannot become the object of its scorn; but that means that the public's taste will change; that is that it will become better or more corrupt] (*PC* 27, 281). This disconcerting fact that an author's fortunes depend not on the beauty of his work but rather on the public's appreciation of it is nonetheless fully accepted and assumed by Prévost who concludes: "On juge ordinairement du mérite d'un livre par l'empressement de ceux qui l'achètent et par le grand nombre qui le lisent" [A book's merit is ordinarily judged by the rush of those who buy it and the number of people who read it] (*PC* 28, 289).[9]

In fact, Prévost uses the success of a work as a reliable indicator of its value, explaining that what is popular must also be in some way good: "Ce qui plaît à tout le monde ne saurait être absolument indigne de plaire parce qu'il est comme impossible que l'ignorance et le mauvais goût soient si généralement répandus qu'ils règnent sans exception" [That which pleases everyone cannot be absolutely unworthy of pleasing because it is impossible that ignorance and bad taste are so widespread that they reign without exception] (*PC* 103, 295). He adds in a subsequent issue that the reverse is also true: "Lorsque le public s'accorde à mépriser un auteur en général, ou un ouvrage en particulier, ce jugement passe toujours pour infaillible et irréformable" [Once the public decides to scorn an author in general or a work in particular, this judgment is always accepted as infallible and irrevocable] (*PC* 21, 121). When reviewing literary works in the pages of *Le Pour et contre*, Prévost purports to put his own taste aside to defer to public opinion, determining the value of the work according to the public's appreciation of it. He begins one review by writing that "*Les Mémoires du Comte de Comminges* se sont fait lire de tout le monde avec goût, et passent tout d'une voix pour un livre bien écrit "[*The Memoirs of the Count of Comminges* have been read by all with pleasure and are acclaimed by all as a well written book.] Although he adds a disclaimer—"Quand je ne me serais pas convaincu par moi-même de la justice de cet éloge, je n'en conclurais pas moins qu'ils le méritent" [While I might not have been convinced myself that that praise was justified, I could not conclude that it was any less deserved]—and objects to certain flaws in the composition of plot and character in the novel, Prévost ends the review by reaffirming: "[M]ais il est aussi constant pour moi par le jugement unanime du public que par le mien que c'est un livre fort bien écrit" [But it is also true by the unanimous judgment of the public and by my own that is a very well written book] (*PC* 103, 292).[10]

Prévost even defines the value of his own works in terms of their popularity with the reading public when he evokes his novels in his newspaper, noting that "[l]e public a lu avec beaucoup de plaisir le dernier volume des *Mémoires d'un homme de qualité* qui contient les Aventures du Chevalier des Grieux et de Manon Lescaut" [the public has read with pleasure the last volume of the *Memoirs of a Man of Quality* which contains the Adventures of the Chevalier des Grieux and Manon

Lescaut] (*PC* 36, 137). Addressing Crébillon *fils'* criticism of his novels in the preface to *Les Egarements du cœur et de l'esprit,* Prévost evokes his own success with readers as a more important indicator of his worth than the opinion of some young and unproven author. The established author retorts: "[E]t si l'intérêt m'oblige de censurer sa réflexion sur les *souterrains,* je prierai en même temps le génie qui préside à la fortune des livres, d'accorder autant de succès à tous les siens qu'on en a vu obtenir à quelques-uns de ceux où les souterrains sont employés" [And if self-interest obliges me to respond to his reflection on underground caves,[11] I will beg the genie who presides over the fortune of books[12] to grant as much success to his as I have attained for some of mine where underground caves were used] (*PC* 105, 355).

Nevertheless, while the public determines a work's popularity, success is not entirely out of the author's control, for he is free to apply the lessons learned as an observer of readers in order to ensure the best possible reception of his writing. The author still strives for excellence, but this excellence is defined by his ability to adapt his writing to the taste of his readers, as Prévost concludes: "[L']agrément n'est autre chose que l'art de connâitre et de flatter le goût de ceux pour qui l'on écrit" [(B)eauty is nothing but the art of knowing and flattering the taste of those for whom one writes] (*PC* 61, 5). Prévost's praise for writers often cites this ability to understand their readers, as is the case of an adaptation of *L'Astrée,* which updates the old-fashioned style of the original novel to address a more modern reading public. Prévost writes:

> Si quelqu'un était capable de rappeler l'ancien goût de la nation pour les romans étendus, ce serait sans contredit celui qu'on a donné au public depuis quelque temps. . . . Il [l'adaptateur] a abrégé des dialogues qui en sont devenus plus intéressants; il a resserré la narration, qui en parâit plus coulante; il a revêtu ce beau corps d'un style fleuri, naturel, elegant. (*PC* 11, 260)

> [If someone were capable of bringing back the nation's old taste for long novels, it would be without argument the one which has been recently published. . . . He (the adapter) has abridged the dialogues to make them more interesting; he has tightened the narrative to make it flow; he has clothed this beautiful body in a natural, elegant style.]

For Prévost, the best artist of any age is the one who best knows his public, and when Prévost praises La Fontaine he admires this classic author not for his timelessness but rather for his ability to adapt to the taste of his own time. In emulating his predecessor, Prévost will not imitate his art but rather his ability to discern the taste of his era and to adhere to it: "A son exemple [celui de La Fontaine], je tâche par diverses expériences de connaître à quelle sorte de goût je dois m'attacher pour plaire, et je fonde, si je peux parler ainsi, la carrière où je marche. J'ai cru découvrir que le goût présent se porte aux faits et aux sentiments. Tout ce qui est revêtu de ces deux caractères se débite avec succès et se lit par conséquent avec plaisir" [Following his (La Fontaine's) example, I try by various means to know the kind of taste to which I must appeal in order to please, and I establish, if I may say it thus, the career I pursue. I believed that I had discovered that the present taste tends toward facts and sentiments. All that possesses these two characteristics sells with success and is read consequently with pleasure.] (*PC* 65, 100). Prévost's ultimate aim is not the achievement of some abstract ideal but rather the more palpable approval of the public, quantifiable in the sale of his books, as he explains: "Quelle autre preuve de mérite pourrait-on demander dans un livre? S'il se débite heureusement, c'est sans doute qu'il se fait goûter, et s'il est au goût du public, il a toute la perfection qui convient à son siècle" [What other proof of merit could one demand in a book? If it sells well, it has undoubtedly appealed to the taste of the public, and if it is to the public's taste, it has all the perfection required by its time] (*PC* 65, 100).

Although Prévost does take time to educate his readers about the preferences of the English public, his ultimate goal is to please the French public of *Le Pour et contre*, an aim he acknowledges once he has returned from his English exile:

[C]ar aujourd'hui que mon retour en France m'ôte l'excuse que je pouvais tirer d'un pays où l'on ne se pique pas d'une extrême régularité dans les méthodes, il me serait honteux de ne pouvoir rentrer dans le goût de ma patrie, et reprendre ces idées d'ordre et de justesse sans lesquelles il n'y a point de fortune à faire au Parnasse français. (*PC* 61, 4–5)

[(S)ince today my return to France deprives me of the excuse I could have in a country where people do not pride themselves on an extreme regularity in their methods, it would be shameful to be unable to return to the taste of my homeland and to take up anew the ideas of order and correctness without which one may not reach the summit of the French Parnassus.]

At the same time, however, Prévost observes that this French public is composed not of one but of many readers, and in order to attract the largest number Prévost addresses many different interests. The constantly changing course of *Le Pour et contre* is then not so much a reflection of its inconstant author than of his constant efforts to increase his audience, as Prévost explains:

> La variété en fait le mérite et je me flatte qu'il n'y a point de conditions où elle ne puisse trouver des lecteurs. . . . Ce que j'entame quelque fois pour plaire à un philosophe, je l'abandonne ensuite pour satisfaire une dame ou un petit maître. Pourquoi préférerais-je un lecteur à l'autre? Rendre un ouvrage public, n'est-ce pas déclarer qu'on écrit pour tout le monde? (*PC* 17, 36)

> [Its merit consists in its variety, and I flatter myself that there are no classes in which it does not find readers. . . . What I begin sometimes to please a philosopher, I abandon to satisfy a lady or a fop. Why should I prefer one reader over another? Publishing a book, doesn't that mean that one writes for everyone?]

In this same issue, which concludes with a variety of short articles, each is preceded by an appeal to the type of reader it addresses: [V]oici pour les naturalistes" [Here is something for naturalists,] "Voici pour les antiquaires" [Here is something for antiquarians,] "Voici pour les cœurs tendres" [Here is something for the tender-hearted].

The variety of subjects in *Le Pour et contre* may reveal Prévost's virtuosity, but it most certainly reflects Prévost's oft-stated desire to please his public. For Prévost, the most successful issues of his newspaper assemble diverse readers by including something for everyone:

> Ceux qui cherchent dans le *Pour et contre* les agréments de la variété, seront contents de la feuille que je commence. Ceux qui aiment les remarques savantes et les anecdotes curieuses y trouveront aussi leur compte. Ceux enfin qui respectent jusqu'aux moindres restes des Grands Hommes, et qui croient qu'on ne peut les conserver avec trop de soin sauront bon gré à mes correspondants de Londres de m'avoir communiqué ce que je vais donner au public. Que de goûts différents je compte satisfaire aujourd'hui. (*PC* 64, 73)

> [Those who look for the pleasures of variety in the *Pour et contre* will be happy with this issue. Those who like savant remarks and curious anecdotes will also enjoy it. Those who respect the last traces of Great Men

and who believe that one cannot preserve their memory carefully enough will be grateful to my correspondents in London who have communicated to me that which I am about to publish. How many different tastes will I satisfy today.]

According to Prévost, the multiplicity of readers dictates not only the diversity of subjects in *Le Pour et contre* but also the very order and length of stories, since he abridges or extends his articles according to his idea of readers' continued interest or growing impatience. Prévost explains his reason for delaying the end of a translation of an English play as a result of the distaste of some of his readers for this sort of article but promises an eventual continuation to satisfy those others who enjoy the English theater: "Je confesse même que quelques-uns m'en ont fait des plaintes, tandis que d'autres l'ont regardée au contraire comme un article si intéressant qu'ils m'ont prodigué leurs remerciements et leurs éloges. C'est cette variété de sentiments et d'inclinations dans mes lecteurs qui m'oblige de les satisfaire du moins alternativement" [I confess that some people even complained of this to me, while others regarded it as so interesting that they thanked and praised me prodigiously. It is this variety of sentiments and inclinations in my readers which obliges me to satisfy them at least in alternation] (*PC* 101, 241). Prévost insists here on his flexibility in reacting to reception and thus designates the periodical as the most supple of forms in its ability to reply to readers and to modify itself accordingly.

Prévost's desire to please often manifests itself in his stated fear of boring the reader. In issue 76, filled with scientific observations, he declares: "Brisons sur les raisonnements abstraits qui ne seraient pas du goût de nos lecteurs" [Let us end the abstract reasoning that may not be to the taste of our readers] (*PC* 76, 14). Prévost emphasizes his efforts to hold his readers' interest by expressing doubts about his ability to do just that: "Mais je crains bien, moi qui veux faire ici le plaisant, et qui parle si librement sur le compte d'autrui, que ce long article ne paraisse aussi ennuyeux que le premier" [But while I strive to be amusing here and speak freely about others, I fear that this article may seem as boring as the first] (*PC* 39, 208). Such breaks in the text are the very moments when Prévost points to his extreme attentiveness to his public, since here he allows his readers' imagined reaction to change the course of his writing. In hopes of bringing back readers he may have bored, after a long discussion of new works of mathematics, Prévost strikes a lighter note: "Quoique le passage soit bien difficile des mathématiques à la galanterie, je le hasarde d'un seul saut pour me réconcilier promptement avec ceux que je viens d'ennuyer" [Although the transition from mathematics to gallantry is very difficult, I will make the leap in order to reconcile myself promptly with those I have just bored] (*PC* 39, 200). To do so, Prévost follows complex explanations of mathematical discoveries with humorous tales of the complicated hairstyles of certain "female geometers" in an article entitled "Mathématiques des femmes" [Mathematics for women], where he writes: "Que de géométrie, par exemple, n'entre-t-il pas dans une coiffure? Que d'optique et d'architecture dans tout leur habillement?" [How much geometry, for example, goes into a hairstyle? How much optics and architecture into ladies' clothing?] (*PC* 39, 201).

Similarly, after a long article detailing the present state of intellectual affairs in Germany, Prévost worries that this subject may have tired those readers uninterested in such serious matters, but he explains: "Je me repentirais d'avoir fait un article si long, s'il n'y avait dans le sujet même une sorte de variété, qui pourra l'empêcher de paraître ennuyeux" [I would repent of such a long article if there weren't in the subject itself a sort of variety which will keep it from seeming boring] (*PC* 34, 88). However, before proceeding from a study of German intellectuals to a survey of English ones, Prévost decides to break up the issue by inserting a digression that is not another catalog but rather a narrative: "J'ose me flatter du moins que ce que j'ai à dire dans la suite sur les savants d'Angleterre ne sera ennuyeux pour personne. Mais dissipons l'ennui si je l'ai fait naître. L'histoire suivante en causera-t-elle à quelqu'un?" [I dare flatter myself that what I have to say in the next part on English scholars will bore no one. But let us end any boredom I may have caused. Will the following story cause any to anyone?] (*PC* 34, 88). The succeeding story promises to engage readers bored by the dryness of the study of German academia by telling a tale not of German intellectuals—M. Schlopflein, M. d'Uffenbach, M. Heineccius—but of Scottish lovers.

The technique of following a philosophical or scientific article with an entertaining story is characteristic of *Le Pour et contre* where Prévost tries to satisfy all tastes, both serious and light, and he declares: "Je n'ai pas honte d'interrompre un sujet lorsque sa longueur peut devenir ennuyeuse; ni de faire succéder une histoire tendre ou badine aux plus sérieuses réflexions" [I am not ashamed to interrupt a subject when its length may make it boring, nor am I ashamed to follow the most serious reflections with a tender or funny story] (*PC* 17, 36). Often, a factual article is balanced by a narrative that if perhaps not entirely fictional definitely draws on the images and techniques of the novel. In this way, Prévost encourages readers who have already appreciated his novels to become faithful subscribers to his newspaper. He emphasizes the importance of the pleasing fiction as a way to maintain the reader's interest and even reproaches Voltaire for his dryness in the *Lettres philosophiques* where long essays on Locke and Newton are rarely leavened with narrative. According to Prévost, these two letters "déplairont aux femmes et aux trois quarts des hommes. . . . [I]ls auraient souhaité [qu'il] . . . eût tempéré la sécheresse de sa matière par quelque fiction agréable, ou par quelque autre enfin de ces tours heureux qui coûtent si peu à une belle imagination. [will displease women and three quarters of men. . . . (T)hey would have wished (that he . . .) had tempered the dryness of his subject with some agreeable fiction or by another of those happy touches which cost so little to such a lively imagination] (*PC* 12, 277). In describing the mixture of fact and fiction that characterizes his own memoir-novels, Prévost explains that his goal was to "faire goûter quelques maximes de morale" [render agreeable some moral maxims] by means of a "narration agréable" [an agreeable story] (*PC* 90, 353).

This formula—"faire goûter"—is a concrete application of Prévost's exploration of aesthetic abstractions, for once the author understands his readers' taste, he may better manipulate it. According to Prévost, the ability to attract readers is just as important as the ability to write, and he even goes so far as to argue that the principal merit of an author may lie less in his talent as an artist than in his skill as an advertiser:

> Ce n'est pas un petit embarras pour un écrivain que de prévenir le public en sa faveur et de donner un tour assez insinuant à toutes ses promesses pour faire souhaiter qu'il les remplisse. Dans tous les arts il y a une industrie particulière, qui est souvent le principal mérite de l'ouvrier, et qui consiste à s'emparer, pour ainsi dire, de l'opinion des hommes. . . . De là cette préférence qu'on accorde à certains artisans. (*PC* 1, 3)

> [It is no small task for a writer to earn the favor of the public and to lend such an insinuating appeal to his promises that the public wishes him to keep them. In all of the arts, there is a particular talent, which is often the principal merit of the worker, and which consists of seizing, so to speak, upon public opinion. . . . That is how certain artisans earn the public's preference.]

In a literary marketplace where writers compete for a limited number of readers, books languish unsold not because of their lack of merit but, according to Prévost, because of a lack of marketing. Despite the fact that artists may possess "le même fonds de mérite et d'habileté" [the same amount of merit and talent,] Prévost affirms that "ceux qui n'ont pas le talent de se faire valoir languissent dans l'oubli" [those who do not have the talent to make their value known languish in oblivion] (*PC* 1, 4). In this economy, the press plays a central role in assuring literary success by advertising certain works at the expense of others: Prévost stresses the importance of publicizing new works, explaining:

> Combien ne nommerais-je pas d'ouvrages auxquels on pourrait appliquer ce qu'Horace a dit des héros? "Avec tout leur mérite et leur vertu, ils demeurent dans l'obscurité si personne ne les en tire." Je connais un livre plein de savoir et d'excellentes observations critiques qui faute d'avoir été annoncé par les affiches et les journaux, n'est presque connu jusqu'à présent que de l'imprimeur et du libraire. (*PC* 120, 337)

> [How many works could I name to which one could apply Horace's saying about heroes? "With all of their virtue and merit, they remain in obscurity if no one draws them out of it." I know a book filled with learning and excellent critical observations which, since it was not advertised in broadsheets and newspapers, is hardly known by anyone but its printer and its publisher.]

It is the task of "affiches" and "journaux," the press, to regulate and inspire the demand for books, as Jean Sgard explains in *Histoire de l'édition française*: "[F]rom 1730 on, all of the major publishers began publishing periodicals; they found this an advantageous means of announcing their own publications and of providing reviews of them immediately, of attaching their catalogue and of establishing a list of their clients. Van Duren became successful thanks to La Barre de Beaumarchais, Didot thanks to Prévost, Paupie thanks to D'Argens."[13]

The press is the place for publicity, and despite Prévost's pronounced disdain for the greed of his editors, he uses *Le Pour et contre* to advertise their publications. Not only is a catalog of the works of all of the publisher Didot's authors included at the end of Prévost's periodical, but favorable reviews of many of these works may be found in its pages. This is the case of *Les Singularités historiques* by Dom Liron, which Prévost presents in *Le Pour et contre* in a review that shows his talent for manipulating the public to serve the financial interests of a publication. Praising this work at length but deferring the revelation of its title until the article's end, Prévost encourages curiosity by creating a sense of anticipation within his review and thus around the work itself. Didot may or may not have paid Prévost for this particular service, but in looking out for his publisher's economic interests, Prévost protected his own, demonstrating his value not just as a man of letters but as a literary promoter. It is clear that Didot valued Prévost's talent of seizing on public opinion, since he commissioned him to write the preface for several publications by other authors, such as Dom Liron's *Singularités historiques* as well as Mme de Lintot's *Trois nouveaux contes de fées.*

Not only does Prévost use *Le Pour et contre* to promote the works of others, but he also sees his periodical as an important means of self-promotion. Prévost includes in his newspaper a variety of favorable references to his novels, including the *Mémoires et aventures d'un homme de qualité,* and *Le Doyen de Killerine*[14] as well as long and enthusiastic reviews of *Cleveland*[15] and *Manon Lescaut.*[16] Moreover, he also gives his public a preview of texts that he plans to publish in order to prepare the reaction of his readers in advance. He declares his intention to publish an account of his travels in the English provinces, admitting that in announcing this plan it is his "vue . . . de le faire désirer en le faisant regarder d'avance comme un ouvrage curieux et agréable" [aim . . . to make the public desire it by characterizing it in advance as a curious and agreeable work] (*PC 86,* 254). He alludes to his composition of an historical novel in order to promote interest in the topic, further intriguing his readers by having them guess at the identity of the author: "[u]n homme de lettres dont le nom est connu travaille actuellement à l'histoire de Marguerite d'Anjou" [(a) man of letters whose name is known is currently working on a life of Marguerite d'Anjou] (*PC 269,* 67). Prévost even minimizes the importance of his past successes in order to prepare the success of future projects, writing:

> Je suis bien aise . . . de pouvoir déclarer de nouveau ce que j'ai déjà répété plus d'une fois: les Mémoires d'un homme de qualité, leur suite, l'histoire de Cleveland et celle du Doyen de Killerine sont des ouvrages de pur amusement. Ma vue dans une confession si simple et si ingénue est de disposer le public à juger autrement de quelques ouvrages plus sérieux dont je fais actuellement mon occupation et surtout de *l'Histoire des Grands Hommes de la Monarchie Française* dont je me propose de publier incessamment l'essai. (*PC 135,* 342)

[I am happy . . . to be able to declare yet again that which I have already repeated more than once: the Memoirs and Adventures of a Man of Quality, their continuation, the story of Cleveland and that of the Doyen de Killerine are merely works of entertainment. My aim in such a simple and ingenuous confession is to dispose the public to judge differently the more serious works which I am currently undertaking, especially the *History of the Great Men of the French Monarchy* an excerpt of which I plan to publish soon.]

Of course, his dismissal of past achievements allows him to list them again, reminding readers of all of the titles in his catalog.

THE PUBLIC AS JUDGE

In his efforts to observe the preferences of his public and to exploit these observations for his own success, Prévost attempts to master the literary market, but at the same time he admits his readers' power over his writing. While he has assumed the reins of his journalistic endeavor with "la hardiesse de remonter sur Pégase" [the courage to remount Pegasus] (*PC* 1, 5), Prévost's newspaper writing is constantly reined in by his concern for readers' reaction. He is constrained by his need to win their approval, as he writes: "La haute opinion que j'ai du goût et de l'esprit de mes lecteurs est quelquefois un fardeau pesant pour moi. Il m'arrête lorsque je crois marcher le plus légèrement" [The high opinion I have of the taste and intelligence of my readers is sometimes a heavy burden for me. It stops me when I am treading most carefully] (*PC* 39, 208). In providing both the *pour* and the *contre*, Prévost shares the role of critic with his readers, establishing them as the ultimate arbiters in the matters before them. Deferring to their opinion, Prévost refers to his readers as his judges, writing: "Rien n'a tant d'empire sur un écrivain que l'opinion qu'il a de ses lecteurs, c'est-à-dire de ses juges" [Nothing has so much power over a writer than the opinion of his readers, that is to say his judges] (*PC* 61, 5). In *Les Origines culturelles de la Révolution française*, Roger Chartier has located the origin of the idea of the "tribunal of public opinion" in the second half of the eighteenth century in texts by Malesherbes and Condorcet as well as in the newspapers of the period immediately preceding the Revolution.[17] Even before this pre-Revolutionary politicization of the French press, *Le Pour et contre* began empowering readers, with Prévost's announcement in his first issue: "J'abandonnerai toujours la décision au lecteur" [I will always abandon judgment to the reader] (*PC* 1, 9).

To encourage the continuous exercise of his readers' judgment, Prévost often presents his public with actual court cases. The popularity of the published texts of judicial proceedings in the eighteenth century has been studied by Sarah Maza in her analysis of the era's *causes célèbres*. Maza explains that "published trial briefs were issued in quantities that outstripped those of most other kinds of printed matter at the time" and argues that "the writing and reading of sensational courtroom literature contributed to the birth of public opinion and of a new public sphere in the decades just before the French Revolution."[18] Prévost is aware of the public's interest in courtroom dramas and encourages his readers to exercise their talents as judges by presenting judicial proceedings without pronouncing judgment. He describes in detail the idiosyncrasies of English justice, but if he often presents it as arbitrary it is to offer to readers the opportunity to play the role of arbiter. Criminals are portrayed as charismatic or appealing in order to allow the public to hesitate between condemnation and admiration. Villainesses like Molly Siblis and Sarah Malcomb often appeal to readers because of their beauty. The murderer Savage is presented as a man of merit despite his illegitimate origins, which actually legitimate readers' desire to see this victim of social injustice triumph over the judicial system. Another criminal about to be executed invites appreciation of his ingenuity when he cleverly devises a method to keep the hangman's noose from breaking his neck.

Both Maza and Chartier attribute the eighteenth-century public's interest in court cases to the curiosity about private life suddenly publicized by the press coverage of legal proceedings. Chartier explains: "The old direct, discreet, exclusive relationship that linked individuals to the king as guarantor and guardian of domestic secrets yields its place to a very different model: the public exposure of private conflicts."[19] Prévost exploits this appetite for intimate details with his coverage of domestic conflicts. In recounting the scandalous affair of a woman suing her eunuch husband for divorce, Prévost panders to readers' interest in the couple's sex life or lack thereof. Playing the role of legal scholar, Prévost researches old records to look for precedents which might aid the judge in his difficult decision, and his supposedly academic interest in the case allows for the exposition of its details while encouraging at the same time the possibly perverse interest of readers. The article excites the reader's curiosity and invites his engagement, either for or against the disappointed wife or chagrined husband. Having presented arguments on both sides, Prévost does not give his own opinion. Instead, he leaves the decision to his readers, allowing them to imagine the outcome on their own: "On attend avec beaucoup de curiosité et d'impatience la décision du tribunal" [The decision of the tribunal is awaited with much curiosity and impatience.] (*PC* 40, 233).

Prévost recounts the case of the clerk who wins the hand of a young woman in a lottery in which each ticket sold contributes to the composition of her dowry. When it is revealed that the clerk bought his ticket with his master's money, his master asserts his own right to possess the girl and the money that comes with her. While Prévost's narration takes readers as far as the courtroom where the case is tried, he only hints at a number of possible outcomes and allows his public to act as the judge in this intriguing matter, affirming, "Le public qui ne consulte que les simples mouvements de la nature souhaiterait pour l'amour de la demoiselle qu'elle devînt l'épouse du marchand, et pour l'amour du commis qu'il obtînt la liberté d'épouser sa maîtresse" [(T)he public, which only consults the simple impulses of nature, might wish for the good of the girl that she marry the merchant and for the good of the clerk that he obtain the liberty to marry his mistress] (*PC* 92, 42). In a way, the difficulty in deciding leaves the reader free to maintain in his mind the two possible endings, to be sympathetic to both of the opposing parties, and thus to be charmed by the story both despite its ambivalence and because of it.

In *Le Pour et contre*, Prévost calls on the public to judge books and men, and after engaging his readers in various problems of aesthetics and ethics, he turns their attention onto himself. In issue 47, Prévost appeals to the tribunal of public opinion on his own behalf, introducing the judicial paradigm here by making his case against the Dutch publisher Vanderklotten. By asking the rhetorical question "[Q]ue sais-je si les Libraires n'ont pas leur jurisprudence à part?" [(H)ow do I know that publishers do not have their own jurisprudence?] (*PC* 47, 28) Prévost appeals to readers to decide in his favor in this business matter. When he addresses the more personal matter of defending his reputation against the libelous account of his life by Lenglet Dufrenoy, Prévost continues to call upon the public's judgment. Having established readers as the ultimate judges of his work ("[J]e n'attache point d'autres prix à ces sortes d'ouvrages que celui qu'ils reçoivent de l'approbation publique" [I attach no other price to those sorts of works than the public's approval of them] (*PC* 47, 32)), Prévost asks them to judge his life. He summarizes his accuser's account of his "crimes" (*PC* 47, 34) as if presenting them before a court of law, concluding: "Voilà le procès tout instruit" [The case has already been made] (*PC* 47, 35).

Prévost has presented himself "devant Dieu et les hommes" [before God and men] (*PC* 47, 35) and "au jugement de tout le monde" [before the judgment of all] (*PC* 47, 36), calling "le ciel et le public à témoins" [heaven and the public as witnesses] (*PC* 47, 40) and finally declaring: "Je laisse à juger au Public" [I let the public judge] (*PC* 47, 46). Prévost's self-portrait is a case presented in self-defense, and he invokes "le droit que donne une Apologie" [the right given by an Apology] (*PC* 47, 36) as if all autobiography were an appeal to the court of public opinion. While the narrators of Prévost's memoir-novels present themselves as indifferent to the opinion of others, their narrations, too, will eventually conform to the "pour et contre" paradigm established by Prévost's newspaper.

4

The Role of the Reader
in Prévost's Novels

WHILE *LE POUR ET CONTRE* ACKNOWLEDGES ITS READERS ON ALMOST every page, Prévost's memoir-novels seem to stand in diametric opposition to his newspaper by insisting on their narrator's need for privacy. The narrators of Prévost's novels write their memoirs in monastic solitude never intending to publish, and while the narrator of *Le Pour et contre* strives to "intéresser la curiosité du public" [interest the curiosity of the public], the narrator of the *Mémoires d'un homme de qualité* begins by declaring his lack of interest in potential readers: "Je n'ai aucun intérêt à prévenir le lecteur sur le récit que je vais faire des principaux événements de ma vie. On lira cette histoire si l'on trouve qu'elle mérite d'être lue. Je n'écris mes malheurs que pour ma propre satisfaction: ainsi je serai content si je retire pour fruit de mon ouvrage, un peu de tranquillité dans les moments que j'ai dessein d'y employer" [I have no interest in interesting the reader in the story that I am going to tell about the principal events of my life. This story will be read if people find that it merits reading. I write about my misfortunes for my own sake alone: thus I will be content to gain from my work the tranquility I find in writing it] (*MHQ*, 13). This writer is his own most important reader and does not especially need another, aiming only to please himself. The Man of Quality's unconcerned attitude toward reception is repeated in *Cleveland* where the memoirist characterizes his project as a private pursuit; his writing is self-expression for its own sake, a monologic moan never to be interrupted by an interlocutor. Cleveland explains: "Si le silence et la solitude sont agréables dans l'affliction, c'est qu'on s'y recueille, en quelque sorte, au milieu de ses peines, et qu'on y a la douceur de gémir sans être interrompu" [If silence and solitude are agreeable in affliction, it is because one may meditate alone amidst one's pains and take comfort in groaning without interruption] (*C*, 17). He does not envision a confidant to console him but rather designates the paper upon which he writes as the sole recipient of his story: "Mais c'est une consolation plus douce encore de pouvoir exprimer ses sentiments par écrit. Le papier n'est point un confident insensible, comme il le semble; il s'anime en recevant les expressions d'un cœur triste et passionné" [But it is an even sweeter consolation to be able to express one's feelings in writing. Paper is not an unfeeling confidant, as it might seem; it comes alive upon receiving the expressions of a sad and passionate heart] (*C*, 17). The paper functions as a mirror, reflecting back to the writer the image of his past sorrows. The writer and reader are one and the same, and no outside audience is needed.

While some of Prévost's memoirists express their disinterest in the reading public, the narrator of the *Mémoires d'un honnête homme* does not even envision the possibility of publication, for his jailers have forbidden any communication with the outside world. He acknowledges: "Je dois me regarder déjà comme séparé du monde où je n'ai plus rien à prétendre. Enfin, je suis mort, lorsque toutes les voies me sont fermées pour retourner au commerce des vivants" [I must see myself as separated from the world where I no longer have any claims. I am dead, since all routes to return to the living are closed to me] (*MHH*, 211). He writes neither to interest nor to entertain others but to distract himself: "J'ai pensé au contraire que si quelque chose était capable de remplir le vide de tant de moments et de soulager tout à la fois mon cœur et mon imagination, c'était de rappeler plus vivement que jamais toutes les circonstances de ma vie. Il dépendait même de moi de les écrire" [I thought, on the contrary, that if something were capable of filling the void of so many moments and of soothing at the same time my heart and my imagination, it was remembering more clearly than ever all of the circumstances of my life. It depended on me to write them down] (*MHH*, 212). He writes without imagining any reader but himself, sending his story into the void that surrounds him. In fact, most of Prévost's narrators represent themselves as outsiders, separate from their fellow men and thus unable to communicate with them. Renoncour describes himself as a superior being, for he has "le cœur formé d'une certaine façon" [the heart formed in a certain way.] He is not only different from but incomprehensible to others, and he adds: "Je n'expliquerai point très aisément ce que j'entends par cette façon dont on peut avoir le cœur formé" [I will not be able to easily explain what I mean by this way in which one's heart may be formed] (*MHQ*, 13). He implies that most men cannot understand the force of his feelings, concluding: "Il était donné à ma famille d'aimer comme les autres hommes adorent" [It was the destiny of men in my family to love as other men adore] (*MHQ*, 69). Likewise, Cleveland presents himself as being of a special nature, stating: "[J]e puis dire que j'ai toujours été différent des autres hommes" [I can say that I have always been different from other men] (*C*, 173). As a result, he sees himself as inevitably alone: "Pour moi je puis me placer dans une troisième classe, et je suis peut-être le seul individu de ma malheureuse espèce" [I place myself in a third class of men, and I may be the only individual of my unfortunate kind] (*C*, 173).[1]

Des Grieux goes even further than Cleveland in insisting on the specificity of his experience, stressing the unfathomable nature of his deep and abiding despair. He describes his plight in words that only emphasize his inability to describe it and thus readers' inability to relate: "Ce fut une de ces situations uniques auxquelles on n'a rien éprouvée qui soit semblable. On ne saurait les expliquer aux autres, parce qu'ils n'en ont pas l'idée; et l'on a peine à se les bien démêler à soi-même, parce qu'étant seules dans leur espèce, cela ne se lie à rien dans la mémoire et ne peut même être rapproché d'aucun sentiment connu" [It was one of those unique situations: one has never felt anything like it. It cannot be explained to others, because they have no idea of it; and one can barely understand it oneself, because it is one of a kind and is related to nothing in one's memory and cannot be compared to any known emotion] (*MHQ*, 387). To reaffirm his distinctiveness, Des Grieux constantly characterizes himself with superlatives as "le plus misérable de tous les hommes" [the most miserable of all men] (*MHQ*, 426) and describes his mistress in the same terms as "ce que la terre avait de plus parfait et de plus admirable" [one who was the most perfect and most admirable on earth] (*MHQ*, 439). Des Grieux depicts his sentiments as "une agitation que je ne saurais comparer à rien parce qu'il n'y en eut jamais d'égale" [an agitation which I could not compare to anything since it never had any equal] (*MHQ*, 436) and evokes the end of his adventures and the death of Manon as "un malheur qui n'eut jamais eu d'exemple" [a misfortune of which there has never been another example] (*MHQ*, 438). This insistence on the incomparable nature of his experience would seem to preclude any chance of its communication to readers.

EMPATHY AND THE IDEAL READER

Nevertheless, there are moments in Prévost's memoir-novels where the hero's story is understood, but these scenes still constitute a refusal of the Other, since the only narratee who truly understands him is the narrator's own double. In the *Mémoires d'un homme de qualité*, mutual confidence only occurs when the narrator finds a narratee who is a second self. In fact, it is Renoncour's double, Rosambert, who finds him, for upon observing the hero from afar, he recognizes in him a kindred spirit. The Man of Quality recounts:

> Il me dit . . . qu'ayant demandé quelque éclaircissement à un de mes domestiques sur ma naissance et sur la tristesse dont je lui avait paru possédé, il n'avait pu résisté à l'envie de me connaître; qu'étant malheureux comme moi, et peut-être encore plus solitaire, il s'était imaginé que la communication de nos chagrins pourrait avoir quelque douceur l'un pour l'autre; qu'il était rare de trouver parmi les personnes heureuses et contentes des amis qui prissent part à nos peines jusqu'à s'en affliger avec nous; au lieu que les personnes malheureuses trouvaient de la concilation à s'attendrir ensemble, et à se plaindre de la dureté de la fortune ou de l'injustice des hommes. (*MHQ*, 29–30)

> [He told me . . . that having asked that one of my servants shed light on my birth and on the sadness which seemed to possess me, he could not resist the desire to know me; as miserable as I and maybe even more solitary, he had imagined that the communication of our sorrows could provide some comfort to both of us; that it was rare to find among those who are happy and content friends to take part in our pains and to suffer with us; and that instead unhappy people could find comfort in lamenting together and in complaining about the hardness of fortune or the injustice of men.]

Communication is possible because the Other is "comme moi" [like me], someone who can understand because he has experienced the same isolation, the same affliction. The relationship between Renoncour and Rosambert then is not one of sympathy but of empathy, and in fact the two become one, as Renoncour writes: "Nous devînmes inséparables dès ce moment. Nos intérêts, nos occupations, nos chagrins, nos promenades, nos lectures, tout fut bientôt commun entre nous. Nous trouvâmes dans nos caractères et dans nos inclinations des rapports qui servirent à redoubler notre amitié. . . . Nous passions souvent des jours entiers à nous entretenir, et nous nous séparions toujours sans lassitude" [We became inseparable from that moment on. Our interests, our occupations, our sorrows, our walks, our readings, everything was soon shared by us. We found in our characters and in our inclinations similarities that served to double our friendship. . . . We often spent whole days together talking, and we were never bored when it came time to separate] (*MHQ*, 30). The repetition of the pronoun "nous" and the adjective "nos" in this passage emphasizes the community of sentiments of these two men; the reciprocal construction of the verbs establishes a system of reflections that equates speaking to another with speaking to oneself.[2]

This is constituted as the ideal narrative situation, for the narrator feels freest when he recognizes in his narratee another member of the emotional elite of *illustres malheureux*. When Renoncour and his pupil Rosemont meet the Prince of Portugal in their travels, the three men first establish their membership in a community of sorrows before beginning to confide in each other. All three have experienced similarly tragic losses in love, and thus the prince is able to tell his story not as if to strangers but to other selves who share his pain, as he explains: "Je vois bien . . . que ce n'est pas le hasard qui nous a réunis. Si vous avez été malheureux, vous en prendrez plus de part à mes peines; c'est une consolation que le ciel me procure. Il faut que vous me racontiez vos aventures et je vous promets de vous faire aussi le récit du malheureux événement qui m'oblige à m'éloigner du Portugal" [I see . . . that it is not chance which has assembled us. If you have been unhappy, you will better understand my pains; it is a consolation which heaven procures for me. You must tell me your adventures, and I promise to tell you the story of the unhappy event which obliges me to leave Portugal] (*MHQ*, 198). They are all of one mind and heart, and the consolation of this society is not very different from the comfort Cleveland takes in his solitude.

In the course of his adventures, Renoncour continues to meet other members of the exclusive club of men made superior by their suffering. Des Grieux is one of these, and his confession to Renoncour is preceded by the compulsory scene of mutual recognition, of reassurance that his secrets will not leave their circle. For his part, Renoncour sees in Des Grieux a reflection of himself, remarking: "On distingue du premier coup d'œil un homme qui a de la naissance et de l'éducation. . . . Je découvris dans sa figure et dans tous ses mouvements un air si fin et si noble que je me sentis porté naturellement à lui vouloir du bien" [One distinguishes at first glance a well-born and well-educated man. . . . I discovered in his face so many fine and noble qualities that I felt myself naturally well-disposed toward him] (*MHQ*, 366). Des Grieux in turn notes Renoncour's nobility and tells his story to him in an act of *reconnaissance*: gratitude for Renoncour's sympathy and recognition of their similarities. Des Grieux thus begins his story by remarking: "Monsieur, vous en usez si noblement avec moi que je me reprocherais comme une basse ingratitude d'avoir quelque chose de réservé pour vous" [Sir, you treat me so nobly that I would reproach myself as of a lowly ingratitude if I were to hide anything from you] (*MHQ*, 367). The chance meeting of two members of a social and emotional elite ensures compassion and encourages confession.[3] In such situations, Prévost's first and foundational narrator— the Man of Quality—is also his ideal narratee.

LES CŒURS SENSIBLES AND
THE SYMPATHETIC READER

From the initial exclusion of the narratee, to the tautological situation in which the narrator is his own narratee, to the admission of a narratee who is a double of the narrator, the memoirist strictly circumscribes his potential reading public. With his insistence on identification and empathy, he seems to imply that the only adequate reader of his story is one whose character is similar to his and whose adventures echo his own. These conditions would seem to close the text to the common reader, yet allusions to a broader reading public do appear. Despite the indifference to reception declared at the start of his own memoirs and his insistence on the public's inability to comprehend him, Renoncour envisions a broader readership from the beginning. Throughout his memoirs, he refers to his "lecteur," admitting the presence of a public inside even the most private of narratives. He even asks the reader's permission to write, begging his indulgence and solliciting his sympathy: "Qu'il me soit permis de faire quelques réflexions sur cette première époque de nos infortunes domestiques. C'est un soulagement que je ne puis refuser à ma douleur et que je prie le lecteur de m'accorder quelquefois dans cet ouvrage" [Permit me to reflect on this first series of our domestic misfortunes. This offers a relief that I cannot refuse to my pain, and I ask the reader to allow it to me from time to time in this work] (*MHQ*, 15).

However, this initial deference to the reader does not designate a total abandon of control of reception, for at the same time as he appeals to the reader, the narrator works to determine his reaction. Before recounting one of his greatest personal tragedies—the loss of his wife—Renoncour prepares the reader in these terms: "Mon lecteur s'aperçoit assez de ce qu'il doit attendre de la suite de cette histoire. Ceux qui n'aiment point que leur tranquillité soit troublée, même par la compassion, ou ceux qui craignent d'être trop attendris par un récit douloureux, doivent interrompre ici leur lecture. Je n'ai plus que des soupirs et des pleurs à leur offrir. Je sens que toutes les plaies de mon cœur vont se rouvrir, et qu'elles sont prêtes à saigner" [My reader understands well enough what he can expect of the rest of this story. Those who do not like their tranquillity troubled, even by compassion, or those who fear that they might be too affected by a painful tale must stop reading here. I have only sighs and tears left to offer them. I feel that all of the wounds of my heart are going to reopen and that they are ready to bleed] (*MHQ*, 99). In effect, he pauses dramatically, getting the reader's full attention, before asking him to steady himself and ready his emotions, to muster the compassion that is the only appropriate response to the passion of the narration. If the reader has any remaining doubts about the right response to Renoncour, other characters' reactions provide a model for reception. For instance, when Renoncour tells the story of Selima's death, his uncle declares with appropriate emotion: "Hélas! qu'ai-je appris? La fortune ne se lasse donc pas de ses injustices? Serez-vous toujours aimable et toujours malheureux?" [Alas, what have I learned? Fortune does not tire of doing injustice? Will you always be lovable and always unhappy?] (*MHQ*, 98). When Rosemont hears the same relation, he bursts into tears before exclaiming: "J'ai le cœur si pénétré d'admiration et de tendresse par votre récit, que votre père ni votre épouse n'ont jamais eu pour vous plus d'affection que moi" [My heart is so penetrated with admiration and tenderness after hearing your tale, that neither your father nor your wife have felt more affection for you than do I] (*MHQ*, 284). These demonstrations of sympathy for Renoncour by characters within the novel indicate how affecting the narration is meant to be and serve to inspire the reader's sympathy for the narrator.

Renoncour describes his ideal reader as one interested less in information than in emotion:

> Je laisse aux géographes, et à ceux qui ne voyagent que par curiosité, le soin de donner au public la description des pays qu'ils ont parcourus. L'histoire que j'écris n'est composée que d'actions et de sentiments. J'entreprends de rapporter ce que j'ai fait, et non ce que j'ai vu. Les

cœurs sensibles, les esprits raisonnables, tous ceux, en un mot, qui sans suivre une philosophie trop sévère ont du goût pour la vertu, la sagesse et la vérité, pourront trouver quelque plaisir dans la lecture de cet ouvrage. C'est pour eux seulement que j'écris. (*MHQ*, 119)

[I leave to the geographers and to those who travel for curiosity's sake the task of providing the public with a description of the countries they have traversed. The story that I write is composed solely of actions and sentiments. I strive to report that which I have done and not that which I have seen. Sensitive hearts, reasonable minds, in a word, all those who, without following too severe a philosophy still love virtue, wisdom and truth, will be able to find some pleasure in reading this work. It is for them alone that I write.]

Despite the restriction "c'est pour eux seulement que j'écris" [it is for them alone that I write], this definition of the reader broadens the range of potential narratees to include a large public of "cœurs sensibles" and "esprits raisonnables." The only real stipulation is that readers be more sentimental than severe. The ideal Prévostian narratees are these "cœurs sensibles," whom the narrator constantly incites to share his emotions. Cleveland invites readers to feel his pain, writing: "Je commence une narration que je vais accompagner de mes larmes et qui en fera couler des yeux de mes lecteurs" [I begin a narration that I will accompany with my tears and which will make tears fall from the eyes of my readers] (*C*, 85). Although Cleveland is his own first and most important narratee, he hopes that his readers' reactions to his story will mirror his own. In *La Jeunesse du Commandeur*, the narrator likewise asks for the reader to relate to him, calling upon those who have also experienced passion to have compassion for his impetuous acts: "Ceux qui ont éprouvé l'empire d'une passion violente savent avec quelle impétuosité le cœur se détermine sur les moindres apparences de justice et de raison qui semblent favoriser son penchant" [Those who have been dominated by a violent passion know with what impetuousness the heart is determined by the least appearances of right and reason which seem to favor its penchant] (*JC*, 164). In *Le Monde moral*, Brenner does not ask the reader to agree with his actions but rather to feel pity for his plight: "Je pense bien moins à les justifier qu'à vous conduire par la connaissance des evénements à la pitié que je vous demande pour leurs tristes suites" [I think much less of justifying them than of leading you, by making the events known, to the pity that I ask of you for their sad outcome] (*MM*, 389). In each case, the reader is not asked to evaluate the narrator but rather to sympathize with him.

The effectiveness of the Prévostian narrator in determining sympathetic reception extends beyond fictional narratees to the author's real readers. A contemporary of Prévost records in her correspondence this response to the first installment of the *Mémoires d'un homme de qualité:* "There is a new book here entitled *Mémoires d'un homme de qualité retiré du monde.* It is not worth much; however, its ninety pages bring the reader to tears."[4] Interestingly enough, this reader is Mlle Aïssé, the model for the heroine of Prévost's *Histoire d'une Grecque moderne.* The fictional Théophé is characterized as a reader of unique intensity, and the real Mlle Aïssé also writes of reading as an extremely emotional experience. However, while Aïssé's response to Prévost's writing would seem at first to correspond perfectly to the paradigm proposed by the narrator to his narratee, her critical reaction to her own emotions is problematic. Aïssé reproaches herself for indulging her feelings, for falling into the narrator's trap, and she seems almost ashamed of her susceptibility when she says of the work itself that "it is not worth much." However, Aïssé's ambivalent response is not just the result of an unusually alert reading, for despite their overt appeal to the emotions Prévost's novels at the same time obliquely critique the very sentimentality they encourage.

NARRATOR AS NARRATEE:
THE END OF SYMPATHY AND
THE BEGINNING OF SUSPICION

Unquestioning emotional adherence as a privileged mode of reception is challenged from within the Prévostian text itself when the narrator, who successfully garners sympathy for his own plight, shows himself to be singularly unsympathetic to the stories of others. In the role of mentor, the narrator is often called upon to judge his pupil's actions, and he often reacts to the youthful misadventures of his charge with unsentimental severity. In the *Mémoires d'un homme de qualité,* this shift from sympathy to censure is clearly marked in the movement from the first to the second half of the novel.[5] In books 1 through 5, Renoncour elicits our sympathy for his own youthful misadventures, while in books 6 through 14, the now older and cynical Renoncour calls on the reader to censure the amorous adventures of the young Rosemont. Instead of recognizing in his pupil's passions a reflection of his own, Renoncour refuses identification and maintains a critical distance from Rosemont, telling him: "Je ne vous accompagnerai plus que pour en être le spectateur et s'il est besoin pour en être le critique" [I will only accompany you further as a spectator and if necessary as a critic] (*MHQ*, 137). An impetuous lover in his youth, in old age Renoncour warns against the dangers of passion. While Rosemont is touched to tears by the story of Renoncour's romance with the Muslim Selima, Renoncour himself severely censures Rosemont for falling in love with Selima's niece Nadine, an unsuitable match for a scion of one of the noblest families of France. While Renoncour's uncle, the young Comte de C sympathizes profoundly with Renoncour's grief at losing his beloved wife, Renoncour discourages C's efforts to renew a love he thought was lost to him, condemning him for pursuing his now-married former mistress. After hearing the count confess the sad story of his doomed love, Renoncour refuses to privilege passion over reason, coldly concluding the episode by stating: "Il ne me trouva point toute l'indulgence qu'il s'était promise" [(H)e did not find in me all the indulgence he had expected] (*MHQ*, 218). While Renoncour seems to require the indulgence of all those who hear his own sad story, he has a limited ability to empathize.

Moreover, while Renoncour insists on the truth of his own tale, he problematically questions the veracity of the narratives of others, creating a double standard by which the reader must trust the main narrator's story but may distrust secondary narratives included in it. Despite the fact that he himself has once been captured and enslaved in the Orient, Renoncour replaces sympathy with suspicion when listening to the story of Sergie, a former slave rescued from a caravan of concubines by a French diplomat. Sergie tries to win Renoncour's respect by claiming that she is as noble as he is, but Renoncour questions the validity of her genealogy, which, according to him "ne portait néanmoins aucune marque qui pût empêcher de le prendre pour une fiction" [nevertheless gave no evidence that one could regard it as anything other than a fiction] (*MHQ*, 108). While Renoncour has always insisted on the truthfulness of his own story, he implies that Sergie's is an invention of her imagination, remarking on "la facilité des Géorgiennes à s'exprimer, et le tour romanesque qu'elles savent donner à leur langage" [the facility with which Georgian women express themselves and the novelistic style they know how to give to their language] (*MHQ*, 108). While her narrative may touch the sensitive heart of Renoncour's ideal reader — Sergie has been stolen from her parents, sold into slavery, and taken into the desert where she almost dies of thirst on a forced march to her new owner—Renoncour himself is immune to the girl's appeal to his emotions. In analyzing her narrative from a critical distance, Renoncour's reaction to Sergie's story marks a new model of reception for this embedded narrative that subverts the paradigm put in place by the narrative frame.

This attitude of suspicion, this hesitation that counterbalances the urge to indulge in feelings of sympathy, introduces a more complex and careful sort of reading. This new paradigm is not only described but prescribed as the right one by Renoncour in the "Avis" that precedes *Manon Lescaut.* In this text, Renoncour acknowleges that it is our first instinct to believe a story, writing: "Les âmes bien nées sentent que la douceur et l'humanité sont des vertus aimables et sont portées d'inclination à les pratiquer" [Well-born souls feel that kindness and humanity are admirable virtues and are inclined to practice them] (*MHQ*, 364). He explains that when we hear a sad story we want to sympathize, when we hear an entreaty, we want to help. However, he adds that this emotional response is often followed by a critical one in which we question the truth of the story and control our reaction accordingly, and thus at the moment when we are about to act according to our natural impulses "elles demeurent souvent suspendues" [they often remain suspended] (*MHQ*, 364). According to Renoncour, we question our first reaction by asking:

> En est-ce réellement l'occasion? Sait-on bien qu'elle en doit être la mesure? Ne se trompe-t-on point sur l'objet? Cent difficultés arrêtent. On craint de devenir dupe, en voulant être bienfaisant et libéral; de passer pour faible en paraissant trop tendre et trop sensible, en un mot, d'excéder ou de ne pas remplir assez des devoirs qui sont renfermés d'une manière trop obscure dans les notions générales d'humanité et de douceur" (*MHQ*, 364)

> [Is it really the time for it? Do we know in what measure to act? Are we mistaken about the object of our actions? One hundred difficulties stop us. We are afraid to be duped when we wish to be beneficent and generous; to seem weak if we are too tender and sensitive, in a word, to do too much or not to do enough to fulfil the duties which are vaguely contained in the general notions of humanity and kindness.]

Renoncour goes on to propose the reading of stories as a guide for evaluating situations encountered in real life, as practice for determining one's reaction to a plea that might just be a ploy. According to Renoncour then, *Manon Lescaut* is a type of conduct book, a lesson in life, an "exemple qui [peut] servir de règle à quantité de personnes dans l'exercice de la vertu" [example which (can) serve as a rule for a quantity of persons in the exercise of virtue] (*MHQ*, 364). In reading the story, we should learn when to believe and when to doubt, when to sympathize and when to censure. However, the usefulness of the story as a lesson in when to be sympathetic and when to be suspicious is limited, for when Renoncour first meets Des Grieux, he cedes immediately to his emotions and generously gives the talented storyteller the money Des Grieux needs to follow his mistress. Is Renoncour then a dupe? If so, his foolishness serves as a warning, a true *avertissement*, to readers of the novel.

This complex reaction, mixing sympathy and suspicion, reappears in *Histoire d'une Grecque moderne,* when Ferriol first responds to the heroine's story with sensitivity but later wonders whether "en voulant être bienfaisant et libéral" [in wishing to be beneficent and generous] he has been "trop tendre et trop sensible" [too tender and too sensitive]. If he first feels compassion for the slave girl and acts to save her from her fate, his initial sympathy is soon replaced by skepticism. Upon hearing Théophé's narrative of the events of her life, Ferriol's reaction evolves from admiration for its organization to suspicion at its too-perfect construction. At first he applauds her: "J'admirai même que sans autre maître que la nature, elle eût arrangé ses aventures avec tant d'ordre. . . . Je ne pouvais la soupçonner de les avoir empruntées d'autrui dans un pays où l'esprit ne se tourne pas communément à cette sorte d'exercice. Je crus donc lui découvrir un riche naturel" [I admired that with no other master except nature, she had arranged her adventures with such order. . . . I could not suspect her of having borrowed them from someone else in a country where the mind is not commonly occupied with such an exercise. I believed that I had discovered in her a natural intellect] (*HGM*, 29). Later, however, when he reconsiders the story's success in manipulating his emotions, he sees his first reaction as the effect of her dissimulated sophistication :

Je ne pus me livrer si crédulement à l'air de naïveté et d'innocence qu'elle avait su mettre dans sa contenance et dans ses regards. Plus je lui avais reconnu d'esprit, plus je lui soupçonnais d'adresse: et le soin qu'elle avait eu de me faire remarquer plusieurs fois sa simplicité, était précisément ce qui me la rendait suspecte. Aujourd'hui comme du temps des anciens la bonne foi grecque est un proverbe ironique." (*HGM*, 29)

> [I could not accept so credulously the air of naïveté and innocence
> which she had adopted in her expression and her gaze. The more I rec-
> ognized her intelligence, the more I suspected her of trickery: and the
> care she had taken on several occasions to convince me of her simplicity
> was precisely what made me suspicious of her. Today, as in ancient
> times, the good faith of a Greek is an ironic expression] (*HGM*, 29).

Her innocence would seem unbelievable, for she is after all a harem girl
educated in the arts of seduction, in playing the virgin to please her
master. Ferriol's subsequent suspicion of Théophé thus constitutes the
reception recommended by Renoncour in the "Avis" of *Manon Lescaut,*
for after his first act of generosity, Ferriol wonders whether he has
helped an innocent victim or whether he himself is the victim of her
clever scheme. He analyzes accordingly: "Elle s'est imaginée disais-je
sur l'air de bonté que je porte dans mon visage et dans mes manières,
qu'elle allait faire de moi sa première dupe; et cette jeune coquette, à
qui j'ai supposé tant de naïveté et de candeur, se promet peut-être de
me mener bien loin par ses artifices" [She imagined, I told myself, that
because of the appearance of kindness on my face and in my manners
that she was going to make me her first dupe; this young coquette,
whom I had supposed so naïve and candid, thinks perhaps that she will
lead me along quite far with her artifices] (*HGM*, 50). Despite his own
scheme to seduce her, he is afraid of being seduced, of being taken in by
a calculating con-artist.

Ferriol's fear of being deceived evolves into a permanent state of
suspicion. "Tout m'était suspect" [Everything was suspicious to me]
(*HGM*, 29), he admits. When he catches Théophé trying to leave for
Europe without him, Ferriol wants to believe her story (that she plans
to enter a convent) but cannot help but imagine another ending (that
she plans to join some secret lover). As time passes and he ages, Ferriol's anxieties increase; he sees himself turning into a doting old man
whom his younger mistress can easily fool. "Mes infirmités me ren-
daient crédule" [My infirmities made me credulous] (*HGM*, 115), he
notes, reminding himself of the need for constant vigilance against duplicity. If Ferriol listens at her closed door and searches her bed for
proof of her infidelities, even this strict surveillance does not reassure
him, for he admits that at night "le moindre bruit réveillait [ses]
soupçons" [the least noise awakened (his) suspicions] (*HGM*, 103).
He hires a governess to act as a guard, and this woman serves as a
jailer to the girl, who is imprisoned in her room even before she has

been convicted of any crime. The governess only aggravates what has become a full-fledged pathology for Ferriol, encouraging his exacerbated state of alertness, calling him in to inspect the criminal's cell for evidence of new crimes. Without proof, he can only imagine, inventing evidence to fuel his fears: "Enfin l'imagination remplie de toutes les imputations de son accusatrice, les moindres desordres que je crus remarquer dans sa chambre me parurent autant de traces de son amant, de preuves du dérèglement qu'on lui reprochait" [In the end, my imagination filled with all the imputations of her accuser, the least disorder that I thought I saw in her room appeared to me to be the traces of her lover, the proof of the misconduct of which she was accused] (*HGM*, 118).

If he is initially Théophé's mentor, Ferriol is in the end the girl's harshest censor, and he even casts himself as a *juge d'instruction*, characterizing his story as an indictment of its heroine and writing halfway through his narration: "Le procès de mon ingrate n'est instruit qu'à demi" [The case against my ingrate is only half proven] (*HGM*, 106). Moreover, while the narrator arrogates to himself the power to judge Théophé, he encourages the reader to second his opinion, for he inevitably calls upon him to judge her as well, writing at the end of his story: "C'est ici que j'abandonne absolument le jugement de mes peines au lecteur, et que je le rends maître de l'opinion qu'il doit prendre de tout ce qui lui a pu paraître obscur ou incertain dans le caractère et la conduite de Théophé" [It is here that I abandon absolutely the judgment of my pains to my reader, and that I render him the master of the opinion that he must have about all that might have seemed obscure or uncertain in the character and conduct of Théophé] (*HGM*, 117). He even states this desire to put the evidence before the public as the principal motivation behind the publication of these memoirs: "C'est immédiatement après la première nouvelle qu'on m'a donnée de la mort de Théophé que j'ai formé le dessein de recueillir par écrit tout ce que j'ai eu de commun avec cette aimable étrangère et de mettre le public en état de juger si j'avais mal placé mon estime et ma tendresse" [It is immediately after the first news I received of the death of Théophé that I formed the plan to write down all that I shared with this admirable stranger and to allow the public to judge whether I had misplaced my esteem and my tenderness] (*HGM*, 121). Conveniently, he waits until she is dead and cannot dispute his version of the facts before he asks the public to rule against her and in his own favor.[6]

APPEALING TO THE
COURT OF PUBLIC OPINION

While Prévost's hero often encourages readers to judge the heroine of his story, this suspicion cannot always be contained and can quickly turn back onto the narrator himself. If Théophé's emphasis on her simplicity makes Ferriol suspect her of scheming ("le soin qu'elle avait eu de me faire remarquer plusieurs fois sa simplicité, était précisément ce qui me la rendait suspecte" [the care she had taken on several occasions to convince me of her simplicity, was precisely what made me suspicious of her] (*HGM*, 29)), the narrator's own protestations of trustworthiness are one of the first features that allow the reader to question his disinterestedness in the reception of his story.[7] If the hero-narrator puts the heroine's tale on trial, his memoir functions as a *mémoire judiciaire*, a legal brief composed to make his own case before the public. In *Rhétorique et roman au dix-huitième siècle*, Jean-Paul Sermain sees a slippage in the Prévostian memoir-novel from an "expression of the self" to a "persuasion of the other," from the narrator's disinterestedness in the reaction of others to a dependence on their judgment as the ultimate arbiters of his identity.[8] Sermain is therefore skeptical of the hero's denial of rhetorical sophistication in the writing of his memoirs in view of this same hero's use of eloquent speech; he affirms: "[T]his distance between declared intentions and acts, and more specifically between the memoirist's writing and the set of partial images that he gives of himself in the course of his adventures, must awaken the suspicion of the reader and oblige him to question the role played by eloquence in the life and the writing of the hero-narrator."[9]

For example, while Renoncour characterizes his writing as amateurish and unskilled, his use of spoken language in the course of the story reveals his remarkable powers of persuasion. In the episode of the consul and his two mistresses, the professional diplomat concedes the inferiority of his eloquence to that of Renoncour when he asks him to speak to one of his mistresses, Sergie, and to persuade her to accept their separation so that he may marry her rival. "Personne ne serait plus capable que vous de la faire entrer dans [mon] plan" [No one could be more capable than you of making her enter into (my) plan] (*MHQ*, 107), insists the consul, entrusting Renoncour with this delicate duty. Renoncour easily wins the woman's trust by taking advantage of his vulnerable victim: "Dans les mouvements passionnés qui l'agitaient, elle prit tout d'un coup de la confiance pour moi" [In the passionate movements that agitated her, she suddenly trusted me] (*MHQ*, 107). He uses his rhetorical powers to persuade her, flattering her imagination with glowing images of the rewards that await upon her acquiescence to the consul's demands: "[J]e lui fis une peinture adroite de tous les avantages qu'une femme de son mérite pouvait se promettre en France lorsqu'elle y paraîtrait dans une situation digne d'elle" [I skillfully presented to her all of the advantages that a woman of her merit could find in France if she were to appear there in a situation worthy of her] (*MHQ*, 108). Renoncour shows himself to be not just aware of his eloquence but even proud of it, when he remarks: "[J]e commençais à m'applaudir de ma négociation" [I began to applaud myself on the success of my negotiation] (*MHQ*, 108). If his own memoirs insist on their emotional honesty and portray themsleves as unconcerned with their effects, this evidence of Renoncour's ability to affect others through language causes us to question his supposed disinterestedness in readers' reception.

If in the aforementioned case Renoncour employs his persuasive powers as a favor to a friend, his use of rhetoric is not always so disinterested. One of his most effective pleas is addressed to his grandfather on his father's behalf, but the rhetorical maneuvers meant to argue his father back into the family would also have the eventual result of making Renoncour eligible to inherit the family fortune. Renoncour uses his linguistic artistry to paint a carefully conceived word-picture: "Je commençai donc avec une peinture vive et touchante de la triste situation du marquis [mon père]" [I began with a lively and touching picture of the sad state of the marquis (my father)] (*MHQ*, 20). He pleads his father's case by providing proof of continued filial tenderness: "J'appuyais beaucoup sur le soin qu'il a eu d'envoyer plus d'une fois, tous les ans, un de ses domestiques" [I insisted on the care he had taken to send more than once each year one of his servants] (*MHQ*, 20) for news of the old man. He emphasizes his father's virtues while appealing to his grandfather's: "Pour moi, sur ce que je commence à voir aujourd'hui de vos manières généreuses et pleines de bonté, je suis persuadé, monsieur, que la douleur et le respect de M. le marquis vous toucheront à la fin, et que vous ne vous résoudrez jamais à laisser périr du regret d'avoir offensé, un fils si aimable et si vertueux" [For myself, based on what I have begun to see today of your kind and generous manners, I am persuaded, sir, that the pain and the respect of the Marquis will touch you in the end, and that you will never resolve to let such a good and virtuous son die from the regret of having offended you] (*MHQ*, 20). In this rhetorical performance words are underscored with actions, when in a seemingly spontaneous but possibly choreographed gesture Renoncour and his sister throw themselves at their grandfather's feet. However, Renoncour has been careful not to rely on instinct alone. If in the end Renoncour declares "nous sommes tous deux de votre sang" [we are all of the same blood,] (*MHQ*, 21), he does not rely on the *voix du sang* but rather on his own voice (his eloquence) to win his father's way into his grandfather's good graces.[10]

Given that in these scenes of oratorical performance Renoncour employs his eloquence first for his friend and then for his father, his memoir writing may just as well be read as another exercise in rhetoric, aimed at appealing to the reader on the memoirist's own behalf. In fact, the whole text can be read as a retrial of a case lost much earlier, as a *mémoire judiciaire* composed to appeal the decision made on the behest of his grandfather's second wife to declare Renoncour illegitimate. After her husband's death, this evil step-grandmother accuses the heir apparent of occupying the family's *château* "sans aucun droit" [without any right] (*MHQ*, 50). She takes legal measures and has Renoncour expelled by bailiffs and the property put under guard to prevent his return. Although he hires a lawyer to fight her in court, Renoncour loses not just his land but even his name: "[L]a comtesse, belle mère de mon père, me disant né d'un mariage qui s'était fait contre les lois du royaume, demandait, au nom de ses enfants, non seulement que je fusse déclaré illégitime, et exclu par conséquent de l'héritage de mes pères, mais encore qu'il me fût défendu de porter leur nom" [(T)he countess, my father's step-mother, saying that I was born of a marriage that was against the laws of the land asked, in the name of her children, not only that I be declared illegitimate and consequently exluded from any inheritance but that I be forbidden from bearing my family name] (*MHQ*, 50). While Renoncour leaves without a fight, joining the army to engage in adventures abroad and to forget his misfortunes at home, he does not altogether cede his right to reargue.

In writing his memoirs he pleads his case to the reader, proving his nobility by opening with a presentation of his genealogy. If his parents' marriage has officially been declared null by the courts, Renoncour uses his rhetorical skill to justify their union. His argument is pure casuistry, as he admits the guilt of his parents' passion but argues their lack of intent as a mitigating circumstance for their crime: "Il me semble qu'un sentiment d'amour qui naît avant la réflexion, ne saurait avoir plus d'étendue que ce qu'on appelle généralement la concupiscence. Or la concupiscence à l'égard des femmes n'est que le penchant général que nous avons pour elles. Je voudrais conclure de là que les passions extraordinaires telle que fut celle de mon père ont quelqu'autre principe" [It seems to me that a love born before any reflection may be made cannot go beyond what we generally call concupiscence. Concupiscence toward women is, however, just the general penchant that we feel toward them. Thus, I would like to conclude that extraordinary passions such as the one felt by my father have some other principle] (*MHQ*, 15). He excuses his parents by casting them as pawns of divine providence: "La Providence les permet pour des fins qui ne nous sont pas toujours connues, mais qui sont toujours dignes d'elle. Cette pensée n'a rien d'offensant pour la sainteté de Dieu: car enfin l'amour ne nous rend point criminels lorsque l'objet est légitime" [Providence permits them for other ends that are not always known but which are worthy. This idea is not at all offensive to God's holiness: for in the end love does not make us criminal when its object is legitimate] (*MHQ*, 15). His conclusion on the word "légitime" is a justification of his parents' acts but also a legitimation of his own existence. As a slave, a tutor, a monk, Renoncour's adventures do not seem those of a gentleman; it is instead his own story about himself that establishes his claim to the title Man of Quality. What Sermain writes of Des Grieux could just as easily be applied to Renoncour: "The hero occupies a marginalized social position and has recourse to eloquence to show his quality and to be accepted." [11] As an argument for his reinstitution in the aristocracy from which he has been excluded, the *Mémoires d'un homme de qualite* do not just serve to describe Renoncour's inner life but to inscribe his place in the outside world.

While Renoncour's memoirs manifest both a distaste for and dependence on publicity, the memoirs of Ferriol are those of a professional politican who accepts from the start the importance of public opinion. Even before he writes his memoirs to rhetorically recast his actions, Ferriol is aware of the need to protect his reputation. When he decides to liberate Théophé from Cheriber's harem, he does so secretly, "pour dérober la connaissance de cette aventure au public" [to hide the knowledge of this adventure from the public] (*HGM*, 16). Not only does he hide the transfer of the girl but also of the money used to buy her, worried that the public will misinterpet his generosity as mere debauchery: "Si elle était connue de nos Chrétiens, j'aurais excité la censure des gens sévères, qui m'auraient fait un crime de n'avoir pas employé pour le bien de la religion ou pour libérer quelques misérables captifs la somme qu'ils auraient crue prodiguée à mes plaisirs" [If it were known by Christians, I would have been censured by severe people who would have called me a criminal for not having used for the good of religion or to liberate some miserable captives the money that they would have imagined spent on my pleasures] (*HGM*, 19). This concern about public perception continues and even heightens when the ambassador returns to France with his beautiful young charge. He notes: "Je faisais réflexion qu'il me serait difficile à Paris d'éviter les soupçons qui naîtraient sur mon commerce avec elle" [I reflected that it would be difficult in Paris to avoid the suspicions that would be inspired by my relationship with her] (*HGM*, 111). In fact, soon after their return, Parisian society is rife with rumors about their relationship, as Ferriol recalls: "[I]l y eut . . . [beaucoup] de variété et de bizarrerie dans les jugements du public" [(T)he judgments of the public were varied and bizarre] (*HGM*, 111). Ferriol decides in the end to write his memoirs in an attempt to set the record straight. A form often characterized by Prévost's narrators as a private confession is at the same time composed out of concern for the public's perception so that the memorial narration is no longer just a mode of self-expression but also a means of persuading the reading public.

On several occasions, Ferriol refers to his memoir as "ce témoignage" [this testimony] (*HGM*, 72, 95), and in writing it he puts himself on the stand as a witness in his own defense, addressing the reader as if addressing a judge. From the very start, he pleads for the reader to consider the mitigating circumstances of his case: "On jugera si la suite de cette aventure me rend plus excusable" [One may judge whether the end of this adventure excuses me] (*HGM*, 19). One of the most important mitigating circumstances is Théophé's great beauty, which makes her irresistible and his actions towards her forgivable, as he explains: "C'est ici que je commencerais à rougir de ma faiblesse si je n'avais préparé mes lecteurs à la pardonner à une si belle cause" [It is here that I would begin to blush at my weakness if I had not prepared my readers to excuse it because of its good cause] (*HGM*, 92). He even strives to characterize himself not as the guilty seducer but as the innocent *ingénu*: "On me trouvera aussi sincère dans mes doutes et dans mes soupçons que je l'ai été dans mes éloges et qu'après avoir rapporté ingénument des faits qui m'ont jeté moi-même dans les dernières incertitudes, c'est au lecteur que j'en veux laisser le jugement" [One will find me as sincere in my doubts and in my suspicions as I was in my praise, and after having reported ingenuously the facts that have thrown me

into the greatest incertitude, it is up to the reader to make a judgment]
(*HGM*, 95).

However, in the case of Ferriol, allowing the reader's doubt becomes
a means of overcoming it: an artfully turned admission of guilt is really
an affirmation of innocence. In the opening lines of his memoirs, Ferriol
lays out this strategy: inviting the readers' doubts only to dispel them:

> Ne me rendrai-je point suspect par l'aveu qui va faire mon exorde? Je
> suis l'amant de la belle Grecque dont j'entreprends l'histoire. Qui me
> croira sincère dans le récit de mes plaisirs et de mes peines? Qui ne se
> défiera point de mes descriptions et de mes éloges? Une passion vio-
> lente ne fera-t-elle point changer de nature à tout ce qui va passer par
> mes yeux ou par mes mains? En un mot, quelle fidélité attendra-t-on
> d'une plume conduite par l'amour? Voilà les raisons qui doivent tenir un
> lecteur en garde. Mais s'il est éclairé, il jugera tout d'un coup qu'en les
> déclarant avec cette franchise, j'étais sûr d'en effacer bientôt l'impres-
> sion par un autre aveu. (*HGM*, 11)

> [Won't I be attracting suspicion to myself by the admission I am going
> to make in my exordium? I am in love with the beautiful Greek whose
> story I am going to tell. Who will believe me sincere in the story of my
> pleasures and pains? Who will not doubt my descriptions and my
> praise? Doesn't a violent passion change the nature of everything that
> passes through my eyes or my hands? In a word, what faith can one
> place in a pen guided by love? These are the reasons which must keep a
> reader on his guard. But if he is enlightened, he will judge that in
> declaring them with such openness, I was sure to soon erase their im-
> pression with another admission.]

Here the narrator invites the reader to question his honesty only to answer this question with a confession so candid that any suspicions are
to be replaced with sympathy; the shadow of distrust is illuminated by
the understanding of the enlightened reader. Just as he seems to invite
skepticism, Ferriol's use of rhetorical questions works to eliminate it,
since to each question about his character he provides an answer that
affirms his integrity.

> Si l'idée que j'ai à donner d'elle dans la suite de ces mémoires ne répond
> pas à celle qu'on en a dû prendre jusqu'ici sur des épreuves si glorieuses
> pour sa vertu, n'ai-je point à craindre que ce ne soit de mon témoignage
> qu'on se défie, et qu'on n'aime mieux me soupçonner de quelque noir
> sentiment de jalousie qui aurait été capable d'altérer mes dispositions

que de s'imaginer qu'une fille si confirmée dans la vertu ait pu perdre quelque chose de cette sagesse? (*HGM*, 95)

[If the idea that I give of her in the rest of these memoirs does not correspond to the one that I have given up to now based on her glorious proofs of virtue, should I not fear that one will mistrust my testimony and prefer to suspect me of some dark sentiment of jealousy capable of altering my dispositions rather than to imagine that a girl so virtuous could have lost some of this very virtue?]

He even admits that these questions are not meant to elicit the reader's response but to preclude it, providing the narrator with an opportunity to reply before the reader has a chance. He concludes: "Quelque opinion qu'on en puisse prendre, je ne fais cette question que pour avoir occasion de répondre. . . ." [Whatever opinion one has, I only ask this question in order to be able to answer. . . .] (*HGM*, 95).

From the start of his story where he calls his introduction an "exorde," Ferriol's memoirs are an exercise in rhetoric. If he has cast doubt on Théophé's motivations by pointing out her talent for linguistic manipulation, his own rhetorical virtuosity could cause the reader to question Ferriol's claims to innocence. His ability to argue all sides of a case is admirable, but the more we may admire his rhetorical gifts, the less we may trust his words. For example, he convinces the reader that Théophé's past errors should not prevent him from desiring her ("Car les caresses de ces amants lui avaient-ils imprimé quelque tache et devais-je me faire un sujet de dégoût de ce que je n'aurais point aperçu, si je l'avais ignoré?" [Had the caresses of those lovers stained her somehow and should I have been disgusted by something I would not have noticed had I not learned of it?] (*HGM*, 30)) and then that these same errors justify his attempts to further debauch her ("[M]ais avec tant de belles qualités et la noblesse de son origine, en aurais-je voulu faire ma maîtresse si elle n'eût rien à se reprocher du côté de l'honneur?" [(B)ut with so many good qualities and the nobility of her birth, would I have wanted to make her my mistress if she had not had something dishonorable to reproach herself?] (*HGM*, 37)). Although Ferriol does submit his case to the court of public opinion, his efforts to influence its verdict demonstrate his desire to control his public image through his mastery of language. His use of the memoir, a private and confessional form of expression, exploits the intimate communication characteristic of the genre to cultivate the sympathy of an otherwise skeptical public. Ferriol's memoir is the careful construction of a professional at persuasion, a diplomat whose last crucial negotiation is that of his own reputation in the public's imagination.

In *Le Monde moral*, the abbé Brenner is a diplomat despite himself, a solitary scholar ill at ease in the public eye. When he must accompany a Hungarian princess in her flight down the Danube, Brenner faces this strange situation with trepidation: "Je voyais toute la délicatesse du rôle que j'avais à soutenir" [I saw all of the delicacy of my role] (*MM*, 452). Although unused to the spotlight, Brenner attempts to act a "rôle," to create an appearance of propriety. He is conscious of the possible comparison of his relationship with Mlle Tekely to that of Ferriol and his *figlia anima*, whose story he evokes, and he attempts to keep up appearances by enlisting the aid of two older women to help him in his mission. Nonetheless, in the course of their travels, Brenner and Mlle Tekely attract the unwanted attention of the ship's captain who questions the unusual intimacy between the preceptor and his beautiful, young pupil: "[Q]uelques légères apparences, auxquelles nous ne renoncions pas encore, lui faisant juger que nous n'étions pas des passagers du commun, il ne put voir mon assiduité continuelle auprès de Mlle Tekely, et la familiarité de mes soins, sans former divers soupçons" [Some small gestures, which we had not yet renounced, made him judge that we were not average passengers, and he could not see my continued assiduity toward Mlle Tekely and the familiarity of my behavior without forming various suspicions] (*MM*, 454). The captain even insinuates that their final destination is a confirmation of his suspicions: "[J]e vois bien mieux pourquoi vous choisissez la Hollande, où vous serez libre de satisfaire votre tendresse et de vous marier même en dépit du caractère" [I see better now why you have chosen Holland where you will be free to satisfy your tenderness and to marry despite your status] (*MM*, 454).

After failing in his attempt to defend himself against the suspicions of a scandal-hungry public, Brenner uses his memoir to make a final appeal to readers, writing: "Vous en jugerez après m'avoir entendu" [You will judge after having heard me] (*MM*, 389). Like Ferriol, he attributes his apparent passion to the nobler motive of "la seule compassion" [compassion alone] (*MM*, 389). He characterizes his relationship with the young girl as a service to the state; after all, the object of his attentions is "l'heritière d'un sang illustre" [the heir to an illustrious bloodline] (*MM*, 412). Denying any deeper attraction, he explains their closeness as a result of his strong sense of duty: "On s'attache fortement par ses services et ses bienfaits" [Favors and good deeds form strong bonds between people] (*MM*, 452). As a priest and a diplomat, Brenner presents himself as a sober scholar and not a tender lover: "Mais il n'est pas moins certain que l'étude ayant longtemps été ma seule occupation . . . je m'étais toujours tenu fort éloigné de ces mollesses de cœur qu'on honore du nom de passions tendres, et contre lesquelles j'étais également défendu par ma qualité d'écclésiastique, par la philosophie et par le grave exercice de la politique" [But it is no less certain that study having been my sole occupation for so long . . . I had always kept myself far away from the soft-heartedness honored with the name of tender passions and which were forbidden to me by my ecclesiastic status, by my philosophy, and by the grave exercise of politics] (*MM*, 416). He insists: "[J]'étais ecclésiastique et engagé par les plus grands motifs à servir de tout mon zèle. . . . [J'étais] supérieur par conséquent aux faiblesses ordinaires de la nature. . . [et] je n'avais jamais attendu d'elle qu'une honnête et vertueuse reconnaissance" [I was a priest and engaged by the highest motives to serve with all of my zeal. . . . (I was) consequently superior to the ordinary weaknesses of nature . . . (and) I had never expected from her anything but a noble and virtuous gratitude] (*MM*, 454).

Although Brenner insists on the innocence of his actions, he does allow readers to doubt his emotional invulnerability. While he has proclaimed that his ecclesiastic occupation makes him immune to love, he admits in his memoirs his sensitive nature: "J'étais né sensible quoique l'habitude d'une vie fort appliquée m'eût rendu plus sérieux qu'on ne l'est encore à l'âge de trente-quatre ans, qui était le mien" [I was born sensitive although the habit of a studious life had made me more serious than one usually is at the age of thirty-four] (*MM*, 389). While he has presented his attentions toward Mlle Tekely as those of a generous protector, he assents that his devotion may have its source not only in his virtue but also in her charms: "La seule compassion, soutenue par le goût du mérite, animée peut-être par les charmes de la jeunesse et de la beauté, a pu me faire sortir de ses propres bornes" [Compassion alone, seconded by the love of merit, animated perhaps by the charms of youth and beauty, was able to make me cross the line] (*MM*, 389) As compassion becomes passion, Brenner pleads his inability to see what seems obvious to others, describing his attraction to Mlle Tekely as "[un] aveugle penchant" [a blind inclination] (*MM*, 412), claiming that "à mes yeux ce sentiment n'a jamais été bien éclarci" [to my eyes, this feeling has never been very clear] (*MM*, 389). While refusing to recognize his feelings, he nonetheless reveals them to the reader in a denial that is at the same time an admission: "Je ne vous préviens pas sur des sentiments dont je vous ai déjà dit que je n'ai jamais bien connu la nature. Vous me les verrez nourrir avec une constance, exercer avec un plaisir, et pousser à des excès qui m'ont toujours effrayé moi-même" [I do not wish to influence you in regards to sentiments whose nature, as I have said, I never really understood. You will see me nourish them with a constancy, exercise them with a pleasure, and push them to an excess that frightens me] (*MM*, 391). When Brenner decides to curb his attentions to Mlle Tekely and to return to the strict confines of a relationship defined by duty—renouncing the pleasure of speaking to her, looking into her eyes, kissing her hand—he suddenly realizes the depth of his desire: "J'ignorais qu'il y eut des sentiments capables de pénétrer l'âme, de troubler le sang, d'agiter tous les esprits et de mêler à ce trouble une incroyable douceur qui le redoublait jusqu'au transport" [I did not know that there were feelings capable of penetrating the soul, of troubling the blood, of agitating the mind and of combining with this an incredible sweetness capable of carrying one away] (*MM*, 455). If he has not understood his own feelings before, his struggle to repress them reveals their strength.

Brenner's characterization of his feelings as involuntary and uncontrollable constitutes an admission that is at the same time a justification. However, when he finally fights to gain control of his emotions, this recognition of his passion is also admirable since it is closely followed by a noble struggle to suppress it. Admitting the guilt of his thoughts, Brenner still wants the public to applaud his actions, presenting them perhaps as even more admirable since they represent a victory for virtue: "[L']amour est-il un crime quand il est réduit par le frein de la religion et de l'honneur aux bornes de l'honnête et simple amitié?" (Is love a crime when religion and honor keep it within the limits of a noble and simple friendship?) (*MM*, 455). Again, the rhetorical question encourages the reader to answer in the writer's favor, to find him innocent even as he admits his crime.

MEMOIR, *APOLOGIE,* AND THE RHETORIC OF PUBLIC IMAGE

The use of the memoir to justify past actions is a central strategy not only of Prévost's novels but also of his own autobiographical writing. In fact, Brenner's self-characterization as the sober yet sensitive priest echoes Prévost's own self-portrait as both serious minded and tender hearted. Moreover, Brenner's defense of his relationship with Mlle Tekely parallels a key passage in Prévost's "Apologie" where the author justifies his own questionable conduct in regards to a woman:

> Pendant mon séjour à la Haye, le hasard me fit lier connaissance avec une demoiselle de mérite et de naissance, dont la fortune avait été fort dérangée par divers accidents qui n'appartiennent point au sujet. . . . J'appris ce changement, qui devait la mettre dans le dernier embarras. J'en fus touché. Je lui offris tout ce qui était en mon pouvoir, et je la fis consentir à l'accepter. . . . [E]lle me proposa de la faire passer à Londres. . . . Elle a mérité effectivement par sa conduite et ses bonnes qualités, l'estime d'une infinité d'honnêtes gens qui s'intéressent en sa faveur; et moi qui ne lui ai jamais trouvé que de l'honnêteté et du mérite, je n'ai pas cessé de lui rendre tous les bons offices qui ont dépendu de ma situation. (*PC* 47, 42–43)

> [During my stay in the Hague, I met by chance a lady of merit and noble birth whose fortune had been damaged by various accidents which are not pertinent here. . . . I learned of her misfortunes, which had reduced her to poverty. I was touched by this news. I offered her all that was in my power and forced her to accept. . . . (S)he proposed that I help her travel to London. . . . Her good conduct and her qualities merited the esteem of an infinite number of gentlemen and ladies who have taken an interest in her plight; and I, who have found in her nothing but nobility and merit, have not ceased to do all that I can for her.]

In view of the parallels between Brenner's attentions to Mlle Tekely and Prévost's supposedly innocent attachment to Lenki, *Le Monde moral* may be read as a rewriting of an episode from the author's lifestory. In *Le Pacte autobiographique*, Philippe Lejeune has studied readers' responses to strong similarities between the life of a character and that of the author: "The reader is thus invited to read novels as fictions based on the truth of human nature but also as the fantasies which reveal the secrets of an individual. I will call this indirect form of the autobiographical pact the pact of fantasy [*le pacte fantasmatique*.]"[12] By integrating incidents from his life into his fiction, Prévost encourages readers to regard the confessions of his heroes as his own veiled avowals.[13]

Although Prévost's memoir-novels are not strictly autobiographical, their apologetic character is evident, for—as does the "Apologie" itself—Prévost's fiction responds to an imagined audience, communicating a characterization of the author in answer to existing public perceptions of him. Prévost is well aware of the scandalous stories circulated about his misadventures, and in both his fiction and his nonfiction the author invents narratives that respond to rumors about his life.[14] In both his novelistic and journalistic narratives, Prévost defends himself against slander by telling his version of the story, casting his ambiguous character in the most sympathetic light. The rhetoric of Prévost's fiction thus operates not just within the text but also at the same time outside of it in the negotiation between author and readers around Prévost's public image.[15] By encouraging the public's association of the author with his heroes, Prévost uses the novel to help clear his own name. For example, since Prévost writes the *Mémoires d'un homme de qualité* at the same time as he decides to leave the Benedictine order, the portrayal of monastic life in that novel can be seen as a source of information on Prévost's own experiences. When a young Renoncour wants to enter the *Trappe* after losing his mother and sister, his wise father prevents him from this rash decision. This novel's advice against the danger of ill-considered vows affirms a central argument in Prévost's "Apologie" where he defends his decision to leave the order by explaining that he entered it for the wrong reasons: "La malheureuse fin d'un engagement trop tendre me conduisit jusqu'au Tombeau" [The unhappy end of a too tender engagement led me to the Tomb] (*PC* 47, 39).

However, it is not the story of Renoncour but the confession of a captive Frenchman whom Renoncour saves from the slave market of Constantinople that may represent the most direct transposition of Prévost's life into literature. The young slave explains: "Dès l'âge de quinze ans, j'entrai dans l'ordre des . . . mais n'étant pas propre à l'état religieux, je me repentis bientôt de cette démarche" [From the age of fifteen, I entered the order of . . . but not being made for religious life, I soon repented this step] (*MHQ*, 76). This fundamental inadaptation of character to the religious life, the hasty entry into the monastery, followed by the inevitable regret at the decision are also found in the "Apologie," where Prévost writes: "Cependant, le sentiment me revient et je reconnus que ce cœur si vif était encore brûlant sous la cendre. La perte de ma liberté m'affligea jusqu'aux larmes. Il était trop tard" [After a time, feeling returned to me and I recognized that this lively heart was still smoldering beneath the ashes. The loss of my liberty brought me to tears. It was too late] (*PC* 47, 39). By conflating the story of a character with that of the author, Prévost uses his novel to answer questions about his conduct, making the audience for his fiction a captive audience for an apologetic account of his life. In addition, Prévost promotes the reader's sympathetic reception of the character's confessions by describing the reaction of their first hearer—Renoncour—who is in all else a model of conduct. Renoncour's reaction to the captive's state is one of "compassion" upon seeing a fellow Frenchman sold into slavery in the Orient. After hearing the man's story of rebellion against the Church, Renoncour comforts the man whom he views not as a criminal but a victim, a "malheureux" [an unfortunate] (*MHQ, 77*).

In alluding to this episode of the captive "rénégat," Jean Sgard argues that "the character with whom the author identifies is instead the Man of Quality whose adventures, loves, and misfortuntes are the only ones to be truly developed."[16] However, in view of Prévost's correspondence, the story of the renegade seems to be a means for the author to publish his own experiences with the Church. In a letter to his superior Dom Thibault, Prévost complains:

> Par quel malheur est-il donc arrivé qu'on n'a jamais cessé de me regarder avec défiance dans la Congrégation, qu'on m'a soupçonné une fois des trahisons les plus noires, et qu'on m'en a toujours crû capable, lors même que l'évidence n'a pas permis qu'on m'en accusât? (CDP 530)

> [By what misfortune am I always treated with mistrust by the Congregation so that they suspected me once of the darkest betrayals and that they still believe me capable of them even now that the evidence does not allow them to accuse me?]

He argues against the injustice of this treatment and expresses his disappointment at being continually distrusted by his superiors and deprived of responsibility:

> J'avais espéré, mon R.P., que la grâce que vous m'aviez faite de m'appeler à Paris pourrait effacer des préventions si injustes, ou qu'elles les empecherait du moins d'éclater. Cependant on m'écrit de Province qu'un visiteur se vantant à table d'avoir contribué à m'y faire venir en a donné pour raisons que j'y serais moins dangereux qu'autrepart, et qu'il fallait d'ailleurs tirer de moi tout ce qu'on peut du côté des sciences, puisqu'il serait contre la prudence de me confier des emplois. (*CDP,* 530).

> [I had hoped, my Reverend Father, that the grace that you had shown in calling me to Paris could erase the unjust prejudices against me or keep them at least from becoming public. However, I have received a letter from the provinces which reports that a visitor bragged at table about having contributed to my coming to Paris and gave as reason that I would be less dangerous here than elsewhere, and that it was necessary to put my knowledge to work since it would not be prudent to entrust me with other tasks.]

These private problems stated in Prévost's personal correspondence find a wider audience in the fictional episode of the renegade who makes similar charges against his order:

> Ma conduite, qui n'était pas des plus régulières, fit fermer les yeux à mes supérieurs sur les talents que j'avais reçus du Ciel. Ils me tinrent dans l'humiliation, en me refusant de faire prendre la prêtrise. Ce coup me fut sensible. J'avais brillé dans les études, et j'étais peu accoutumé à recevoir cette honteuse distinction qui me déshonorait. (*MHQ*, 76).

> [My conduct, which was not the most orderly, blinded my superiors to the talents that I had received from Heaven. They humiliated me by refusing to allow me to preach. I sorely felt this blow. I had been a brilliant student, and I was unaccustomed to receiving a shameful distinction which dishonored me.]

However, while in his "Apologie" Prévost insists that his conduct upon exiting the order is as blameless as if he had remained a monk—he describes his life in Holland as that of a solitary scholar whose relationship with women is limited to charitable friendship—the fictional renegade's story diverges from the author's by describing the debauchery that ensues after his transfer from a strict order to a more liberal one:

> Mon oncle eut le crédit de me faire venir à Rome. Je m'y livrai à tous les plaisirs. Mais ce qui m'acheva de me perdre fut une folle passion que je conçus pour une jeune Romaine, que je me mis dans la tête d'épouser. Mes vœux étaient un obstacle. J'employai tout le crédit de mes amis pour en obtenir la dispense. Le désespoir où me jeta l'impossibilité de réussir, me fit prendre le parti de passer en Hollande avec ma maîtresse. J'y fus reçu à bras ouverts. On y fit beacoup valoir la prétendue conversion d'un ecclésiastique qui venait de Rome. . . . Je riais intérieurement de leur crédulité, et je jugeais par mon exemple, qu'il en était de même de tous ceux à qui la débauche fait quitter l'église catholique. (*MHQ*, 76)

> [My uncle had enough influence to have me called to Rome. There, I gave myself over to a life of pleasure. But what caused my ruin was my mad passion for a young Roman woman, whom I decided to marry. My vows were an obstacle. I used the influence of all of my friends to obtain a dispensation. The impossibility of success threw me into despair, and I decided to go to Holland with my mistress. I was received with open arms. People made much of the supposed conversion of a priest who was coming from Rome. . . . I laughed secretly at their credulity,

and I judged by my own example that so did all of the others whose debauchery caused them to leave the Catholic Church.]

While Prévost energetically denies that he left the Church to live in
Holland with his mistress, the captive's story strangely resembles the
slanderous stories that circulate about the author. Nonetheless, in the
novel, the "rénégat" is punished for his crimes—he is abandoned by his
Dutch friends, forced into a deal with Jewish merchants to earn
money, and then captured by pirates and sold into slavery—and thus
Prévost would seem to condemn the character's conduct.

The question remains: why write two confessions that conflict with
each other? Why does the "Apologie" insist on innocence while the
story of the renegade serves as an admission of guilt? Prévost seems to
be playing with the reader who is never sure if he should identify the
author with one of his characters. When, within the same novel, Prévost attributes elements of his own character first to the the Man of
Quality, then to the captive, then to Des Grieux, he refuses to give the
reader a stable image of the author but instead promotes one that is
ever changing, elusive, and thus endlessly intriguing. While many readers of Prévost have implied that Prévost's novels constitute an almost
direct translation of the author's life into art, a look at the novels against
Prévost's nonfiction encourages us to see that he carefully distributes
images of himself throughout his œuvre to court the public's curiosity.
Just as he entertains readers of his newspaper with stories of famous
figures, thus contributing to the emergence of a new culture of
celebrity, Prévost's play with his own image in both his nonfiction and
his fiction creates a cult of personality around the author himself.

In *Mass Enlightenment*, Julia Simon cites Rousseau as an early example of the author as celebrity, explaining: "I will argue that the case of
Rousseau's autobiographical writing attests to the alienation and anxiety that attend the awareness of what it means to be a public figure in
the newly constituted bourgeois public sphere. These autobiographical
works suggest that it is not only culture that is commodified as a result
of enlightenment but the producers of culture as well." She continues:
"The expression of specific fears concerning the production, dissemina-
tions and reception of his writings . . . documents Rousseau's awareness
of the relationship between the reception and intepretation of his writings and the construction of his public persona."[17] In its paradoxical
paranoia, Rousseau's attitude toward the publication of his private life
resembles that of Prévost's memoirist Ferriol, who tells his story in or-

der to correct public perceptions of his actions but fears that his confession may instead be condemned. In his own *Confessions,* Rousseau mentions his admiration for *Cleveland,* and like the hero of that novel, Rousseau's self-expression is mediated by a keen consciousness of the public's perception of him.[18] In her analysis of *Les Rêveries d'un promeneur solitaire* Julia Simon explains that the solitary Rousseau is always well aware of the presence of his readers: "Despite Rousseau's claim that he writes for himself, it is evident even in the *Rêveries* that the work is aimed at a public with the specific intent of gaining its sympathy."[19] Such comments could also apply to Prévost's novels, which deny their rhetorical power only to better persuade the reader of their point.

As both author and hero of his autobiographical œuvre, "Rousseau is aware that not only his works circulate in the public sphere as commodities but that he himself does as well."[20] While the tension between an authentic private self and an artificial public image pose a problem for Rousseauistic rhetoric, the issue of authenticity is avoided by Prévost when he integrates pieces of his autobiography into his novels. Mixing fact and fiction, Prévost seems unconcerned with telling the truth about himself but interested instead in interesting his readers, providing them with more pieces of the puzzle in order to keep them playing his game. Unlike Rousseau, who argues against his adversaries to promote a positive image of himself, Prévost is not above encouraging scandal, even implying his own guilt to encourage readers to continue in their quest for evidence against him. What would seem to be a slander of himself, a story that is written at his own expense, is profitable to Prévost if his adventures continue to interest readers. In a competitive marketplace, any press is good publicity.

5

From Private to Public:
The Prefaces of Prévost's Novels

While Prévost's novels present themselves as the private efforts of amateur memoirists, his newspaper is easily identified as the work of a professional author; however, these antithetical attitudes meet in the novels' own prefaces. These paratexts affirm that the texts they introduce were never meant to be published, but at the same time they subvert the memoirist's supposed desire for privacy by promoting his writing to a broad reading public. The preface thus occupies an intermediate space between the world inside the text and the one outside, between the pure emotional expression of the memoirist's confession and the practical aspects of the text's publication in an economy where literature is a profitable commodity. The prefacer then participates in two opposing paradigms of textual production, and his precarious position demonstrates the liminality of the prefatory space and dramatizes Gérard Genette's description of the preface as a "seuil" [threshold.][1] Prévost's prefacer stands on a threshold, reaching out both to the reluctant writer and also to the cautious consumers—those "lecteur[s] incrédule[s]" [incredulous reader(s)] (*PC* 42, 247)—who make up the reading public. The prefacer is both a Man of Quality (whom the memoirist recognizes as a friend and entrusts with his manuscript) and a Man of Letters (who produces a commercially viable work and presents it to the public), and his preface provides a space in which the amateur stance of the novel meets the professional strategy of the newspaper.

TECHNIQUES OF THE NEWSPAPER

Although published as part of his novels, Prévost's prefaces often recall the discourse of his newspaper in their explicit appeal to the public.

132

Unlike the novel's narrator who insists upon his own disinterestedness toward the reception of his writing, the prefacer is very much concerned with the novel's potential readers. The narrator of the *Mémoires d'un homme de qualité* declares: "Je n'ai aucun intérêt à prévenir le lecteur sur le récit que je vais faire des principaux événements de ma vie. On lira cette histoire si l'on trouve qu'elle mérite d'être lue. Je n'écris mes malheurs que pour ma propre satisfaction" [I have no interest in interesting the reader in the story that I am going to tell about the principal events of my life. This story will be read if people find that it merits reading. I write about my misfortunes for my own satisfaction alone] (*MHQ*, 13). In opposition to the memoirist, the prefacer appears entirely invested in making the memoirs' hero attractive to readers, attributing to him "une figure très prévenante" [a very attractive face] and "le caractère le plus aimable au monde" [the most likeable personality in the world] (*MHQ*, 9). While the memoirist may be concerned only with satisfying himself, the prefacer is concerned with readers' reception and characterizes the memoirs he presents as "dignes d'être communiqués au public" [worthy of being communicated to the public] (*MHQ*, 9). In fact, the prefacer defines his role as explaining the singular and special nature of the text to the reading public, as he does in the preface to *Cleveland*: "Il faut même qu'il soit informé de ce qu'il doit y rencontrer de curieux et d'agréable" [It is necessary that he be informed of what curious and agreeable things he will find in it] (*C*, 9).

Prévost's prefaces, sometimes called "avertissements," are written like advertisements, and with their interest in readers' reception they introduce into the novel some of the commercialism of the newspaper, a genre that from its inception included advertising.[2] While Prévost's newspaper participates in the commercialization of literature by promoting the works of other authors to its readers, it is most frequently dedicated to the task of self-promotion. While *Le Pour et contre* advertises its stories in *manchettes* (marginal titles), which announce each issue's articles as "singulier," "intéressant," or "extraordinaire," the novels' prefaces use this same language to attract readers. This last adjective, "extraordinaire," appears throughout *Le Pour et contre*[3] and appears twice in the preface of *Cleveland* as well. Prévost gives one newspaper article the alluring title "Exemple merveilleux de la force de l'imagination" [Marvelous example of the strength of the imagination] (*PC* 51), and in the preface to *Manon Lescaut* he describes that story in similar terms as "un exemple terrible de la force des passions" [a terrible example of the strength of the passions] (*MHQ*, 363). Prévost promises to please readers of his newspaper with an article entitled "Relation qui n'ennuiera personne" [Relation that will bore no one] (*PC* 42), and he makes the same proposition in the preface to the *Campagnes philoso-phiques* when he announces that the novel "se fera lire sans ennui" [will be read without boredom] (*CP*, 247).

Prévost's newspaper attracts readers with the promise of the exotic by including articles on Italy, Holland, Egypt, and China, and this same exoticism is promised in the paratexts to his novels. From their very titles, *Mémoires pour servir à l'histoire de Malte (ou La Jeunesse du Commandeur)* and *Histoire d'une Grecque moderne* evoke Mediterranean settings and announce adventure on the high seas in a region where the meeting of West with East adds danger and strangeness. Most often, however, Prévost exploits his readers' interest in their English neighbors in order to sell both his fiction and nonfiction works. He attributes readers' interest in *Le Pour et contre* to the English setting of many of its articles, writing: "Londres est une espèce de centre où toutes les nouvelles de l'univers viennent se rendre par les lignes de la navigation" [London is a sort of center where all the news of the universe arrives by way of the shipping channels] (*PC* 30, 51). In the same way, Prévost capitalizes on French interest in England by announcing the Anglo-Saxon ascendancy of several of his novels with such titles as *Cleveland ou Le Philosophe anglais*, *Le Doyen de Killerine*, and *Voyages du capitaine Robert Lade*, and he emphasizes their English allure by adding to each the subtitle *"Ouvrage traduit de l'anglais"* [Work translated from the English].

The appeal of the exotic is used to greatest effect in the preface to *Voyages du capitaine Robert Lade en différentes parties de l'Afrique, de l'Asie et de l'Amérique: contenant l'histoire de sa fortune et ses observations sur les colonies et le commerce des Espagnols, des Anglais, des Hollandais, etc.* [Voyages of Captain Robert Lade in Different Parts of Africa, Asia, and America: containing the story of his fortune and his observations on the colonies and commerce of the Spanish, English, and Dutch, etc.] While these adventures are exotic in the extreme, it is also the fact that the adventurer is English which, according to the preface, guarantees their interest. The prefacer exclaims: "De qui attendrait-on des relations de voyages plus utiles et plus intéressantes que des Anglais? La moitié de leur nation est sans cesse en mouvement vers les parties du monde les plus éloignées. . . . Aussi voit-on paraître à Londres plus de journaux de mer et de recueils d'observations que dans tout autre lieu" [From whom could we expect more useful and more interesting accounts of travel than from the English? Half of their nation is always in movement to the most distant parts of the world. . . . Thus one sees in London more travel logs and more collected observations than in any other place] (*RL*, 13).[4] Like the narrator of the newspaper who admires the intelligence of the English, calling them "le peuple le plus singulier de l'univers" [the most singular people of the universe] and noting their "heureuse inclination . . . à se perfectionner autant qu'ils ont pu dans la voie qui leur est propre" [happy inclination . . . to perfect themselves as much as possible in the career that is theirs] (*PC* 33, 53), the prefacer of the novel also praises the unique talents of this nation: "Les Anglais joignent à la facilité de s'instruire par les voies de la navigation, le désir d'apprendre, qui vient du goût des sciences et de la culture des beaux arts" [The English combine their facility in learning by means of travel with the desire to learn which comes from a taste for the sciences and the arts] (*RL*, 13). Like *Le Pour et contre* which sees its English setting as an endless source of episodes, the preface to *Robert Lade* praises this story of an English explorer for the "variété" of its objects and the "multitude" of its scenes (*RL*, 15).

THE SPACE OF THE PREFACE: FROM THE OUTSIDE IN

While many of Prévost's prefaces offer readers a journey into the exotic unknown, others describe reading itself as an adventure. The preface to *Cleveland* compares the book to "un pays nouvellement découvert" [a newly discovered land] and reading to "une espèce de voyage que le lecteur entreprend" [a sort of voyage that the reader undertakes] (*C*, 9). The preface to *Le Monde moral* evokes Cyrano's *Voyage dans la lune* only to explain that Prévost's exploration of the human heart will be even more exciting "moins imaginaire, plus riche, plus variée, plus intéressante et sans comparaison plus utile" [less imaginary, richer, more varied, more interesting, and without a doubt more useful] (*MM*, 289). Prévost proposes a journey to the ends of the earth but also into the far reaches of the psyche, and his prefacer stands looking into the abyss, dramatizing the Prévostian desire to explore hidden depths. Leading us into the closely guarded inner world of the hero, the prefacer is both a gatekeeper and a guide, occupying a threshold and inviting readers to cross it.

By presenting the space of the text as almost impenetrable, the prefacer designates the story as a secret and heightens the reader's curiosity about the dark solitude from which the text emerges. In *Le Pour et contre* Prévost compares an unread book to a "sépulture" [sepulcher] (*PC* 276, 199), which the journalist's attention brings to light and to life; in Prévost's novels, the prefacer is also a gravedigger, plumbing darkest depths to discover stories that would otherwise be unknown. For the prefacer, this action is made literal when he discovers the memoirist buried in a sepulchral retreat, prepared to die without publishing his life's work. By following the paths of the prefacer into the hero's solitude, we gain access to what would otherwise be inaccessible. In the preface to the *Mémoires d'un homme de qualité*, the prefacer finds the hero hidden behind the walls of an abbey. In the preface to the *Mémoires d'un honnête homme*, the prefacer finds the hero imprisoned in a fortress walled in by mountains; unable to communicate with his German-speaking captors, the *honnête homme*'s only link to the outside world is the visitor who will publish and preface his story.

In presenting his interest in the memoirist's story, the prefacer offers his own desire to meet the man and read his manuscript as a model for the reader to imitate. Like Prévost's *Pour et contre*, which counts on readers' curiosity, the novels' prefaces appeal to the public's by starting with the prefacer's own. The prefacer of the *Mémoires d'un homme de qualité* opens his preface by explaining: "Cet ouvrage me tomba l'automne passé entre les mains dans un voyage que je fis à l'abbaye de . . . où l'auteur s'est retiré. La curiosité m'y avait conduit" [This work fell into my hands last autumn during a voyage I made to the Abbey of . . . where the author has retired. Curiosity had led me there] (*MHQ*, 9). This admission instantly designates the hero of the novel as an enigmatic figure worthy of the reader's attention. Although in the preface of the *Mémoires d'un honnête homme* the prefacer meets the memoirist by accident, he is immediately intrigued by the man's strange situation and eager to read his secret writings. He notes: "Nous entrâmes dans un jardin formé en terrasses sur les boulevards, où nous aperçumes un homme de très bonne mine qui se promenait seul et sans épée, suivi d'un soldat. Le commandant prévint notre curiosité" [We entered a terraced garden where we saw a very good-looking man walking alone and unarmed, followed by a soldier. The commandant responded to our curiosity.] In explaining that the unknown man is a French prisoner, the commandant can supply neither his name nor his story, leaving a mystery that draws the prefacer further in. He follows the prisoner to his cell where "[à] la vue de plusieurs papiers qui paraissaient écrits de sa main, [il eut] la curiosité de lui demander quel était le sujet" [having seen several papers that appeared to have been written by him (he had) the curiosity to ask him about their subject] (*MHH*, 210). Again, the prefacer's curiosity compels the reader's own.

Often, the very difficulty of procuring the hero's secret story makes it all the more precious, and the prefacer often obtains it only after agreeing to hide the hero's identity. Paradoxically, the hero's desire for privacy only enhances his prestige, and the prefacer then adds to this mystique by hinting that the hero's pseudonym hides a famous name. In the *Mémoires d'un homme de qualité*, the prefacer refers to the Man of Quality by the pseudonym Renoncour so as not to reveal his identity, to hide the hero's recognizable real name: "Tous ceux qui ont quelque commerce avec les Pères . . . ne sauraient ignorer le nom de cet illustre aventurier: je serai néanmoins fidèle à la promesse que je lui ai faite, de ne le pas placer à la tête de son histoire" [All those who have any business with the Fathers of . . . cannot help but know the name of this illustrious adventurer: I will nevertheless be faithful to the promise I made him not to put his name at the start of his story] (*MHQ*, 9). In the preface to the *Mémoires d'un honnête homme* the promise of anonymity is again the pact upon which publication depends, as the novel's prefacer explains in his "Avant-Propos": "Il [le héros-mémorialiste] ne mit que trois conditions à la grâce qu'il m'accordait: ce fut de ne jamais permettre que son manuscrit fût imprimé sans la participation d'une dame qui y joue le premier rôle, de retrancher de bonne foi ce qu'elle ne voudrait pas publier, et de supprimer les noms de quelques personnes connues" [He (the hero-memoirist) placed three conditions on the grace he accorded me: they were to never permit the printing of the manuscript without the participation of a lady who plays the leading role in it, to cut without question that which she would not wish to be published, and to suppress the names of several known persons] (*MHH*, 210). The fact that the narrator's story involves well-known people whose identity cannot be revealed both frustrates and piques the curiosity of readers who might recognize their famous names. In fact, the prefacer does immediately recognize the name of the protagonist as soon as it is spoken: "[S]entant le prix de l'occasion, il me découvrît son nom. . . . Son nom ne m'était point inconnu" [(R)ealizing the importance of the occasion, he revealed his name to me. . . . His name was not unknown to me] (*MHH*, 210). By keeping his hero anonymous but implying that he is in fact famous, the prefacer ensures the memoirist's privacy while encouraging a curious public's interest in his memoirs.

In refusing to name potentially recognizable names, the prefacer designates his protagonists as real people. This technique of hinting that his characters are well-known figures is borrowed from the popular press, which often invites the public into the private affairs of the famous. In the "Avertissement" to *Histoire d'une Grecque moderne,* the prefacer implies the protagonists' celebrity by denying it, warning: "Mais qu'on se garde bien aussi de confondre l'héroïne avec une aimable Circassienne qui a été connue et respectée d'une infinité d'honnêtes gens et dont l'histoire n'a point eu de ressemblance avec celle-ci" [But one must refrain from confusing the heroine with an admirable Circassian who was known and respected by an infinite number of gentlemen and ladies and whose story did not resemble this one] (*HGM*, 9).[5] This admonition is tantamount to an admission that the novel's Greek heroine is the real Circassian Mlle Aïssé and the hero is her admirer Ferriol, ex-ambassador to Constantinople; this "Avertissement" functions as an advertisement by promoting the novel as the true story of their scandalous affair.[6]

In Prévost's novels, the preface is a doorway where the prefacer stands dangling the keys, encouraging the reader's inquisitiveness by offering clues that can only be confirmed by reading the text. Even when witholding information, the prefacer intrigues the public all the more, as he does in the paratext to *Histoire d'une Grecque moderne,* stating of this preface: "Celle-ci ne servira qu'à déclarer au lecteur qu'on ne lui promet pour l'ouvrage qu'on lui présente ni clé des noms, ni éclaircissements sur les faits, ni le moindre avis qui puisse lui faire comprendre ou deviner ce qu'il n'entendra point de ces propres lumières" [This one only serves to declare to the reader that it offers no key to the names or clarification of the facts nor the least opinion that might allow him to understand or guess that which he does not understand himself] (*HGM*, 9). Refusing to enlighten the reader, the prefacer nevertheless engages him in a guessing game, pointing him to the first of a series of the story's locked doors. The reader, ready to enter the text, is like the novel's hero who stands outside a locked door intent on penetrating the secret space of the heroine: "Je m'approchai même plusieurs fois de la porte. J'y prêtai curieusement l'oreille. Le moindre bruit réveillait mes soupçons" [I even approached the door several times. I listened there curiously. The least noise awakened my suspicions] (*HGM*, 103). The novel is structured around a series of closed spaces—the closed society of Turkey, the Bacha's walled harem, the Greek girl's bedroom—and the hero's desire to penetrate is a model for the reader's own.

MAN OF LETTERS OR MAN OF QUALITY: THE PREFACER AS *HONNÊTE HOMME*

While refusing to name names, Prévost's prefacers all imply that their heroes are real people and thus that their stories are not fiction but fact. To firmly establish his own honesty, Prévost's prefacer insists on his strict refusal of all that is not real, even when the temptation for invention is strong. In piecing together the story of Robert Lade from the explorer's various travel logs, the prefacer explains: "Avec moins de respect pour la vérité, il aurait été facile de remplir le vide par des suppositions imaginaires" [(W)ith less respect for truth, it would have been easy to fill the gaps with imaginary suppositions] (*RL*, 15). The prefacer of the *Campagnes philosophiques* confesses "le penchant qui l'aurait porté à tirer parti de plusieurs situations fort heureuses pour en augmenter l'intérêt par quelques ornements de son imagination" [the penchant which would have led him to exploit several situations in order to increase the interest of the story with some ornaments from his imagination], but he protests that instead of trying to attract readers with imagined ornaments, he will win them with his strict adherence to truth, determined as he is "à ne pas faire d'autres changements dans le manuscrit de M. de Montcal que ceux qui regardent l'expression" [to make no other changes to the manuscript of M. de Montcal than those regarding style] (*CP*, 247). Where the prefacer of *Cleveland* could have surreptitiously filled in the gaps in the memoirist's story with episodes of his own invention, he refuses to make the story more verisimilar in order to present it as completely veracious. Evoking an awkward transition between episodes, he writes: "J'ai mieux aimé qu'elle subsistât [ma faute dans le manque de raccord entre deux épisodes] que de mettre une interruption désagréable dans mon ouvrage, ou de la remplir par quelque aventure de mon imagination" [I preferred that it remain (my error in the lack of transition between episodes) than to add a disagreeable interruption to my work or to fill in the gap with some adventure from my imagination] (*C*, 11).

In this presentation of fiction as fact, Prévost's prefacers engage in a practice common to eighteenth-century French novels;[7] however, at the same time as Prévost's prefacers emphasize their honesty, they argue even more persuasively for their *honnêteté*. The Prévostian preface is not only the site of a pact between prefacer and reader but also of a promise between the prefacer and the putative author (the narrator of the novel). The preface presents the fundamental scene of the story's first transmission, and when the memoirist surrenders his manuscript to the prefacer, their accord is established not by a legal contract but rather by an agreement based on the honor of both participants. In the preface of the *Mémoires d'un homme de qualité*, the memoirist's anonymity is the first condition for publication, and the prefacer promises on his honor to abide by this term: "Je serai fidèle à la promesse que je lui ai faite, de ne le pas placer [son nom] à la tête de son Histoire. Je ne l'ai obtenue qu'à cette condition; et l'honneur ne me permet pas d'y manquer" [I will be faithful to the promise that I made to him not to place (his name) at the start of his story. I only obtained it on this condition; and honor does not allow me to violate it] (*MHQ*, 9). The prefacer of the *Mémoires d'un honnête homme* also gives his word as a man of honor to protect the memoirist's privacy, swearing "un serment redoutable" [a formidable oath] and engaging his own "foi et . . . honneur" [faith and . . . honor] (*MHH*, 210). In *Cleveland* and *Le Doyen de Killerine* when the hero's heirs entrust the manuscript to the prefacer, they acknowledge his worthiness to receive their precious inheritance. In all of these scenes, the preface proposes an ethics of communication based on trust.

Despite the prefacer's status as a Man of Letters, the preface allows him to affirm his identity as a Man of Quality, establishing his *honnêteté* through his dealings with the memoirist, their close contact making the prefacer an aristocrat by association. This is certainly the case of the prefacer of the *Mémoires d'un honnête homme*, whose identity as an honorable man depends on his relationship with "un seigneur anglais qu' [il avait] l'honneur d'accompagner dans ses voyages" [an English nobleman whom (he had) the honor of accompanying on his travels] (*MHH*, 209). Although the prefacer himself cannot claim an aristocratic name, he convinces the memoirist of his honor by reminding him of the important post with which he has been entrusted: "Quoique je ne fusse pas d'un nom qu'il pût connaître, je lui représentai que le poste que j'occupais auprès d'un jeune homme de la plus haute naissance devait lui faire prendre une idée avantageuse de mon caractère" [Although I did not bear a name he could have known, I persuaded him that the position I occupied in the service of a young man of the highest birth ought to give him an advantageous idea of my character] (*MHH*, 210).[8] If he is not a man of high birth himself, the prefacer wants to be recognized for his noble nature and invokes well born friends as references: "Enfin je lui parlai de mes amis qui étaient capables de lui rendre service, et d'une sorte de considération que diverses circonstances m'avaient fait obtenir entre les honnêtes gens" [Finally, I spoke to him of my friends who could offer him their services and of a kind of consideration among gentlemen which various circumstances had allowed me to obtain] (*MHH*, 210). Eventually, the memoirist decides to entrust his manuscript to the prefacer who vows to respect the various conditions that come with it, with one notable exception. The prefacer remarks: "L'unique droit que je me réserve regarde le titre . . . [et] je n'ai rien trouvé qui corresponde mieux à l'impression qui me reste de sa personne et de ses principes que la qualité d'*Honnête homme*" [The sole right I reserve is in regards to the title . . . (and) I have found nothing which corresponds better to the impression I have of his person and his principles than the name of *Honnête homme*.] At the same time, he informs us that he is only returning the compliment already made to him by the memoirist who, he recalls, had already awarded him the same title: "Mon air et mon discours, dit-il, lui annonçaient un honnête homme" [My air and my speech, he said, were those of an *honnête homme*] (*MHH*, 210). Identity is constructed mutually as each man proclaims the *honnêteté* of the other.

This sort of personal reaffirmation is all the more important when the prefacer occupies a precarious social position. Despite Renoncour's claims to past fame, when he writes the preface to *Manon Lescaut* he has the same low social status as the prefacer of the *Mémoires d'un honnête homme*: he is the traveling tutor of a young aristocrat (Rosemont). Disinherited and *déclassé*, Renoncour uses his role as prefacer to reestablish his heroism by identifying with the hero of the story he presents. Although both Renoncour and Des Grieux are financially and socially ruined, their mutual admiration serves to reaffirm the worth of both men. In the first pages of *Manon Lescaut*, Renoncour endows Des Grieux with all the attributes of a hero, identifying in him an inherent aristocracy despite his apparent degradation. "Il était mis fort simplement; mais on distingue, au premier coup d'œil, un homme qui a de la naissance et de l'éducation" [He was dressed very simply, but one distinguishes at first glance, a well born and well educated man] (*MHQ*, 366). Des Grieux returns the favor by remarking on Renoncour's own nobility, proclaiming: "Monsieur . . . vous en usez si noblement avec moi que je me reprocherais comme une basse ingratitude d'avoir quelque chose de réservé pour vous" [Monsieur . . . you treat me so nobly that I would reproach myself of a lowly ingratitude if I were to hide anything from you] (*MHQ*, 367). Instead of ingratitude Des Grieux enacts its opposite, expressing to Renoncour his "reconnaissance" [recognition] (*MHQ*, 367), recognizing him as a man worthy of hearing his story.

In this and other examples, Prévost's prefaces work not just as windows onto the texts but as mirrors in which the prefacer as Man of Letters comes face to face with the memoirist as Man of Quality in a moment where each can recognize in the other some of himself. This mirror paradigm is nowhere stated more clearly than in the preface to *Cleveland*, where Renoncour as prefacer sees himself in the memoirs of the hero, Cleveland: "Je trouvai en effet tant de rapport entre les inclinations de M. Cleveland et les miennes, tant de ressemblance dans notre manière de penser et dans nos sentiments, que je confessai au fils que je m'étais reconnu dans les traits de son père, et que nos cœurs, si l'on me permet l'expression, étaient de la même trempe et sortaient du même moule" [I indeed found so many resemblances between the inclinations of Mr. Cleveland and my own, so many likenesses in our manner of thinking and in our sentiments, that I confessed to his son that I recognized myself in the features of his father, and that our two hearts, if I may permit myself the expression, were made of the same stuff and in the same mold] (*C*, 9). The hero's glory is reflected on the writer, allowing the reader to associate the qualities of the illustrious protagonist with the obscure scribbler who edits his adventures.

RENONCOUR, PREFACER

This blurring of inside and outside, of text and paratext, is most evident when a character emerges from his own memoir to serve as a prefacer for someone else's. This is the case of Prévost's first hero, Renoncour, who becomes the prefacer of the author's next three novels: *Manon Lescaut, Cleveland*, and *Le Doyen de Killerine*. Although the paratext to Renoncour's own memoirs presents him as resistant to the prefacer's efforts to publish his manuscript, he later becomes a prefacer himself and thus publisher of the private lives of others. When the hero becomes a prefacer he also moves from the position of Man of Quality to that of Man of Letters since the preface is the professional literary act par excellence, a sophisticated marketing strategy in a competitive literary economy as described by Prévost in *Le Pour et contre*: "[T]out ce qu'on appelle aujourd'hui projets d'ouvrages, préfaces, avertissements, introductions sont autant de stratagèmes que les auteurs emploient pour se supplanter les uns les autres et pour surprendre l'estime du public" [(A)ll that we now call plans for works, prefaces, forewords, introductions are all strategies that authors use in order to rival each other and to seize the esteem of the public] (*PC* 1, 4). In the case of the preface to *Manon Lescaut*, the "Avis de l'auteur des *Mémoires et aventures d'un homme de qualité*," Carole Dornier has noted that the very title of this paratext closes the gap between Renoncour as character and Renoncour as author. She explains: "It is the word *Auteur* as we have shown before which is used by Prévost to designate in the title of the preface the source of the utterance [*l'instance d'énonciation*]. He is addressing the *reader* and the *public* and is clarifying his intentions in regards to his addressees [*destinataires*]. The relation suggested here is not that of a memoirist writing for himself or for a few chosen readers but rather of a 'writer' attentive to his public role."[9] The hero has become a prefacer and the prefacer an author: through the course of the three prefaces he composes, Renoncour becomes Prévost.

Despite his increasing professionalization as a writer of prefaces, Renoncour continues to insist on his amateurism when he presents his introduction to *Cleveland* not as a complicated game but rather as a helpful explanation to readers. Unlike certain hypocritical authors who pretend that they never wanted to write a preface in the first place, Renoncour approaches the task with the straightforwardness of an *honnête homme*:

Je n'imiterai point l'affectation de quantité d'auteurs modernes qui semblent craindre offenser le public ou du moins l'importuner par une préface, et qui font paraître autant de répugnance et d'embarras lorsqu'ils en ont une à composer que s'ils avaient à redouter effectivement le chagrin et le dégoût de leurs lecteurs. J'ai peine à concevoir ce qui peut causer leurs alarmes et leurs difficultés. Car si leurs ouvrages ne demandent point les éclaircissements préliminaires d'une préface, qui les oblige de prendre le soin inutile d'en composer? Et s'ils croient au contraire que leurs lecteurs aient besoin de quelque explication pour l'intelligence de ce qui leur est présenté, pourquoi craindre de leur déplaire en leur offrant un secours qu'ils ne sauraient manquer de trouver agréable dès qu'ils auront reconnu qu'il est nécessaire? (*C*, 9)

[I will not imitate the affectation of a quantity of modern authors who seem to fear offending the public or at least bothering it with a preface and who display as much repugnance and hesitation when they have to compose one than if they had really to fear the sorrow and disgust of their readers. I have trouble understanding what can cause their alarm and their difficulties. For if their works do not need the preliminary clarifications of a preface, who forces them to take on the useless task of writing one? And if they believe on the contrary that their readers need some explanation to understand that which is presented to them, why fear displeasing them by offering them a help that they can only find agreeable once they have recognized its necessity?]

In composing a preface, Renoncour does not employ affectation or artifice but rather simplicity and good sense, insisting that "on sent, par exemple, qu'il manquerait quelque chose à un livre tel que celui que je donne au public s'il n'était pas précédé par une introduction" [one feels, for example, that something would be lacking in a book such as this one if it were not preceded by an introduction] (*C*, 9).

Nevertheless, his attention to the reader's needs shows the prefacer's awareness of his public and attests to a heightened interest in a positive reception of the work he presents. According to the introduction to *Cleveland*, the paratext itself is both useful and agreeable, but at the same time the paratext applies these qualities to the text itself, emphasizing especially the work's potential to please its public. In his preface to *Cleveland*, Renoncour qualifies these memoirs as an "ouvrage qui plairait vraisemblablement au public" [a work which would likely please the public] (*C*, 9), promoting the work through the preface by guaranteeing the public's satisfaction. Although in the preface to *Le Doyen de Killerine* Renoncour stresses his refusal to pander, distinguishing himself from "l'écrivain qui plaît" [the writer who pleases], and condemning this kind of author as a "ministre des honteux plaisirs" [minister of shameful pleasures] (*DK*, 9), he nonetheless displays a desire to satisfy his readers. In this preface, Renoncour worries about the work's reception ("Croira-t-on qu'un but si sérieux puisse rendre mon sujet susceptible de l'agrément que j'ai fait espérer?" [Will the public believe that such a serious goal could make my subject as agreeable as I have promised?] (*DK*, 10)) but responds to his own rhetorical question by assuring his public that despite the seriousness of his subject he has high hopes for its popular success. He reassures readers thus: "Cependant le fonds de la matière me paraît si riche que je ne crains d'exhorter mes lecteurs à l'espérance" [However, the material seems to me so rich that I do not fear urging my readers to hope] (*DK*, 10). Although at the start of his own memoirs Renoncour insists that he writes only for himself, the prefaces he writes thereafter reveal a growing interest in the reaction of his readers.

Renoncour's desire to please his public even causes him to present one important episode from his past as separate from his own story, a decision he explains in the preface to *Manon Lescaut*:

> Quoique j'eusse pu faire entrer dans mes Mémoires les aventures du chevalier des Grieux, il m'a semblé que n'ayant point un rapport nécessaire, le lecteur trouverait plus de satisfaction à les voir séparément. Un récit de cette longueur aurait interrompu le fil de ma propre histoire. Tout éloigné que je suis de prétendre à la qualité d'écrivain exact, je n'ignore point qu'une narration doit être déchargée des circonstances qui la rendraient pesante et embarrassée. C'est le précepte d'Horace: *Ut jam nunc dicat jam nunc debentia dici/Plerarque differat, ac praesens un tempus omittat.* Il n'est même pas besoin d'une si grande autorité pour prouver une vérité si simple; car le bon sens est la première source de cette règle. (*MHQ*, 363)

> [Although I could have included in my Memoirs the adventures of the chevalier Des Grieux, it seemed to me that having no necessary relationship to my story, the reader would find more satisfaction in reading them separately. A story of such length would have interrupted the course of my own story. Although I am far from imagining myself a professional author, I do know that a narration should not be burdened with circumstances that would make it heavy and unwieldy. That is Horace's precept: *Ut jam nunc dicat jam nunc debentia dici/Plerarque differat, ac praesens un tempus omittat.* I do not even need such a great authority to prove a very simple truth; for common sense is the first source of this rule.]

This denial of professionalism through an affirmation of the amateur's reliance on common sense is accompanied by a problematic show of aesthetic consciousness and an impressive knowledge of aesthetic ideas such as those found in Horace's poetics. Renoncour's radical decision to displace a central episode, one that even functions as a sort of *mise en abyme* for the main narrative, is a move motivated not by nature but by art. His writing is not a simple reflection of reality but rather a sophisticated representation of it, reconfigured to better suit the taste of readers. This "homme de qualité" who rejects "la qualité d'écrivain exact" shows in his inexact rendering of events the skill of a professional writer. Finally, the aesthetic maneuver of issuing *Manon Lescaut* in its own volume has an important economic effect as well since this "petit ouvrage" [little work] (*MHQ*, 364) benefits from its relationship with the bestselling *Memoires d'un homme de qualité* but can also be sold separately from the whole, increasing overall profits.

Renoncour's multiple insistences on amateurism notwithstanding, his prefaces appear as the productions of a literary professional. In the preface to *Le Doyen de Killerine,* Renoncour demonstrates knowledge of the literary scene that seems less compatible with his status as a cloistered monk and more in keeping with Prévost's position as a cosmopolitan journalist. His familiarity with the period's most successful works seems strange for someone whose monastic retirement should prevent him from keeping up with the latest fashions in reading, yet he reels off the titles of recent bestsellers in the fields of science, history, and theater (*le Traité des Aurores boréales, l'Histoire des anciennes monarchies,* and *le Préjugé à la mode*). Despite his retreat into private life, Renoncour is an observer of the public. He understands the popularity of the scandalous and the satirical: "On nommerait aussi aisément quantité de mauvaises productions qui se sont fait applaudir. . . . [et qui ne] plaisent que par le misérable agrément de la médisance et de la satire . . . [et] par la licence avec laquelle on y fait la guerre aux mœurs ou à la religion" [One could easily name a quantity of bad productions which have been applauded . . . (and which only) please through the miserable ornament of libel and satire . . . (and) by the license with which they treat morals and religion] (*DK,* 9). He nonetheless holds out hope that his "histoire morale" will meet with approval, explaining: "Malgré les déclamations qu'on entend tous les jours contre le goût du siècle, je ne vois pas que les bons écrivains manquent de succès" [Despite the declarations one hears everyday against the taste of the time, I do not see good writers lacking success] (*DK,* 9). In his attention to reception and study of taste, Renoncour reveals the same concerns as any literary professional preoccupied with the success of his works, and he quite closely resembles Prévost, whose interest in taste permeates *Le Pour et contre.*

This resemblance continues as the retired Renoncour approaches his role as a prefacer less as leisure and more as work, bringing to the task the techniques of journalist and historian upon which Prévost has built his career. In the preface to *Manon Lescaut,* Renoncour acts as a reporter: looking, listening, and writing. At the ready with the tools of the writer's trade, he notes the stories of the people he meets on his travels. After hearing Des Grieux's tale, he records it almost on the spot, explaining: "J'écrivis cette histoire presque aussitôt après l'avoir entendue" [I wrote down this story almost as soon as I had heard it] (*MHQ,* 367). Prévost uses the same approach in *Le Pour et contre* with stories such as "Histoire intéressante d'Amsterdam," whose mysterious heroes he meets at an inn during his travels (*PC* 291, 193–210). In the preface to *Cleveland*, Renoncour affirms that he has traveled to interview people who knew the story's characters and has explored the English countryside in order to see the settings firsthand, displaying in these activities the instincts of a good reporter. In his description of the historical research he has done to verify the events of Cleveland's life, Renoncour's preface to this novel closely resembles Prévost's prefaces to the various volumes of his *Histoire générale des voyages* where he insists on his tireless efforts to verify sources.

An essential skill possessed by Renoncour is his ability to translate from English to French, an aptitude that also ensured some of Prévost's greatest professional successes.[10] In the prefaces to *Cleveland* and *Le Doyen de Killerine*, Renoncour assigns himself the role of translator, attributing authorship to another in order to deny his own role in the text's inception. In the preface to *Cleveland (ouvrage traduit de l'anglais)*, Renoncour tries to deny any authorial agency in the text, reminding us of the "extrême différence entre une traduction simple et un ouvrage qu'on a tiré de son propre fonds" [extreme difference between a simple translation and a work that one invents from one's own imagination] (*C*, 13). Despite this attempt to limit his role in the text's invention, Renoncour nonetheless admits to a certain amount of intervention in it. Renoncour has not just translated the manuscript but in some places transformed it, for this prefacer and translator also takes on the task of editor when the heirs to Cleveland and the Doyen call on him to use his literary talents to "retoucher avantageusement" [advantageously alter] (*DK*, 9) the amateurish original. In the case of *Cleveland* he goes on to explain: "La seule [raison] qui l'empêchait [le fils de Cleveland] de le publier était la difficulté de mettre le manuscrit en ordre et de donner un air d'histoire et de narration suivie à des événements dont le fil était interrompu en quantité d'endroits" [(T)he only (reason) which prevented (the son of Cleveland) from publishing it was the difficulty in putting the manuscript in order and giving the feel of a story and a continuous narrative to a series of events whose connecting thread was broken in many places] (*C*, 9). Renoncour must reweave the worn tapestry into a text, making its separate pieces into a "narration suivie," creating from history a story. While such references to the existence of a manuscript that Renoncour only touches up and pieces together serve the fiction that the memoirs are nonfiction, these attempts to minimize the Man of Quality's role in the story's creation paradoxically emphasize his activity as a Man of Letters. In the eighteenth century when novels so often called themselves translations in order to attribute to their work an authentic albeit exotic origin, Renoncour's adoption of the task of translator is almost an avowal of his work as novelist.[11]

Despite the Man of Quality's care to avoid being unmasked as a Man of Letters, Renoncour does sometimes slip and admits his invention of episodes and even of characters in works for which his only responsibility is supposedly that of prefacer. In a note to the preface of the second edition of *Manon Lescaut*, Renoncour alludes to "quelques additions qui ont paru nécessaires pour la plénitude des principaux caractères" [some additions which seemed necessary for the fullness of the principal characters] (*MHQ*, 364), but if the original text were a faithful transcription of Des Grieux's story, these additions can only represent inventions imagined by another to further an aesthetic goal. This note probably refers to the addition of the episode of the Italian prince, which offers a more positive depiction of Manon, since it shows her preferring the penniless Des Grieux to a wealthy aristocrat.[12] With this scene and its more positive perspective on Manon's character, the understanding of her motivations becomes more difficult and the meaning of the text as a whole more enigmatic. The pretense to authenticity in Renoncour's representation of Des Grieux's spoken story cedes to the realization of an artistic vision.

If situations are invented to flesh out characters, the prefacer also implies that characters may be invented to instigate evolution in the plot. In *Le Doyen de Killerine*, the prefacer almost admits that his characters are not members of a real family but a series of opposing types: "Georges est un honnête homme, mais sans autres principes que ceux de la morale naturelle. Le doyen est un chrétien du premier ordre. . . . Patrice et Rose me paraissent deux caractères ambigus; bons mais faibles . . . faits comme exprès pour donner occasion aux deux autres d'exercer continuellement leurs principes" [Georges is an *honnête homme*, but without any other principles than those of natural morality. The Doyen is a Christian of the first order. . . . Patrice and Rose seem to me two ambiguous characters; good yet weak . . . made as if on purpose to give to the two others the opportunity to continuously exercise their principles] (*DK*, 10). Patrice and Rose thus seem to have been created to illustrate the conflict between a man of the world and a man of God, but what is ambiguous here is not so much the characters as the identity of their creator. Is it the priest who uses his own siblings to make a point or is their whole family part of someone else's plan? In fact, the preface to *Le Doyen de Killerine* is a site of slippage where the paradigm of hero as author gives way to that of prefacer as author of the text he presents. Initially, Renoncour attributes authorial intent to the Doyen, writing: "En lisant l'ouvrage tout entier, j'ai conçu que le doyen de Killerine s'était proposé de réunir dans l'histoire de sa famille toutes les règles de la religion qui peuvent s'accorder avec les usages et les maximes du monde, pour faire savoir jusqu'à quel point un chrétien peut se livrer au monde, et à quelles bornes il doit s'arrêter" [In reading the whole work, I understood that the Doyen de Killerine had proposed to unite in the story of his family all of the rules of religion that can be adapted to worldly existence in order to make known to what point a Christian can live in the world and what limits he must respect] (*DK*, 10). However, in a subsequent section, Renoncour refers to the goals of the text as his to meet or miss and identifies the vision behind its composition as his own. He is no longer just a publisher who receives manuscripts written by other men but rather an author who has penned them: "Les ouvrages que j'ai publiés dans le même genre auraient peut-être beaucoup moins promis, si j'eusse commencé par annoncer leur but. Soit que je l'aie manqué, néanmoins, ou que je l'aie rempli, il est certain qu'il n'en est pas sorti un de ma plume qui n'ait été composé dans des vues aussi sérieuses que ce genre d'écrire peut les admettre" [The works that I have published in the same genre would perhaps have promised less, if I had begun by announcing their goal. Either I would have missed it or I would have met it, but it is nevertheless certain that each one that I have penned has been composed with views as serious as this genre of writing permits] (*DK*, 10). In evoking *Cleveland*, Renoncour alludes to the limits of its "genre," admitting that despite that work's religious themes, it can only serve the cause of morality up to a point "autant du moins qu'un ouvrage d'imagination peut y servir" [as much as a work of fiction may serve it] (*DK*, 10). These so-called memoirs are, in fact, novels, and the prefacer is their author.

If, according to the Foucauldian paradigm, the author is the individual held responsible by the legal system and by the public for the text,[13] Renoncour reveals himself to be a writer when he publicly accepts criticism of *Cleveland* in his preface to *Le Doyen de Killerine*. At first, the prefacer attributes Cleveland's apparent impiety to the character, explaining that "M. Cleveland l'apprend lui-même à ses lecteurs, et . . . parle avec douleur de ses faiblesses; ce qui suppose qu'en les écrivant il est dans un état de lumière qui les lui fait condamner" [Mr. Cleveland himself informs his readers of this, and . . . speaks with sadness about his weaknesses, which implies that while writing about them he was in an enlightened state that made him condemn them] (*DK*, 11). However, later in the same preface Renoncour accepts responsibility for any appearance of immorality in the novel, arguing that his intention in writing it was to use examples of impious behavior in order to argue for the importance of religion: "Le *Cleveland*, par exemple, dans lequel on m'a reproché fort injustement d'avoir donné quelque atteinte à la religion, était fait au contraire pour en montrer la nécessité" [The *Cleveland*, for example, in which I have been very unjustly reproached for having attacked religion in some way was written on the contrary in order to show the necessity of religion] (*DK*, 10). He continues his defense of his work by proceeding to enumerate the good intentions behind it in order to show "dans quel esprit il a été composé" [in what spirit it was composed](*DK*, 10). At the end of this list, it is evident that the mind behind the composition is not the character's but the author's.

In the course of this preface, Renoncour's arguments continue to illustrate the Foucauldian model for the evolution of the author by moving from a defensive to an offensive mode in demanding recognition as the creator of his works. The end of the preface of *Le Doyen de Killerine* is an attack on imitators, specifically on the hack hired by Neaulme to produce a fifth tome of *Cleveland* when the novel's original author failed to furnish one on time. In disclaiming the apocryphal fifth tome of *Cleveland*, Renoncour distinguishes the other man's work from "les volumes qui sont de moi" [the volumes which are mine]. He adds "car après le désaveu éclatant que j'ai fait du supplément imprimé en Hollande, sous le titre de cinquième tome, il est bien étrange qu'il se trouve encore quelqu'un qui me l'attribue" [for after the dramatic disavowal that I made of the supplement printed in Holland, under the title of fifth volume, it is very strange that anyone else still attributes it to me] (*DK*, 11). This disavowal of the fifth tome is an avowal of authorship of the others, for he continues: "Je proteste de nouveau que ce qui est de moi finit à Saint Cloud . . . [et] que je n'ai pas eu la moindre part au volume suivant" [I protest again that what is by me finishes at Saint Cloud . . . (and) that I did not have the least part in the succeeding volume.] He ends: "Il verra par ma propre conclusion, qui paraîtra en deux tomes avant la fin de cette année, qu'il est fort mal entré dans mes vues" [(H)e will see by my own conclusion which will appear in two volumes before the end of the year that he has poorly understood my vision] (*DK*, 11). Unlike in *Le Pour et contre,* where Prévost criticizes a substitute for imagining an ending to the story of Donna Maria instead of waiting for factual information to arrive, in this instance Prévost does not argue that his imitator does not know the real story but that he cannot know the story that the original author had in mind. Renoncour's response in the preface to *Le Doyen de Killerine* is not an objection that this impostor does not tell the truth but rather that he does not "entrer dans mes vues," that he does not follow the plot as imagined by its creator.

Instead of insisting on the fiction of a preexisting manuscript written by the Doyen, Renoncour refers to both *Cleveland* and *Le Doyen de Killerine* as works in progress, estimating the time that it will take him to finish them: "Pour le *Doyen de Killerine*, mon dessein est de donner la seconde partie dans six semaines, et de continuer ensuite d'en faire paraître une tous les mois. J'ai assez d'avance pour être exact à suivre cet arrangement. Tout l'ouvrage consistera en douze parties, qui composeront à la fin de l'année six volumes" [For *Le Doyen de Killerine*, my plan is to give the second part in six weeks and to continue thereafter to publish one part every month. I have enough prepared in advance to follow this plan exactly. The whole work will be composed of twelve parts which will make six volumes by the end of the year] (*DK*, 11). Again, these supposed memoirs are not a text written by someone else and altered a bit by the editor-prefacer but rather altogether authored by him. They are not already written but to be written in six weeks, they are not historical but virtual. This description of the regular rhythm of textual production also demonstrates that Renoncour approaches writing not as the leisure of a Man of Quality but as the labor of a Man of Letters who calculates pages to be produced and is conscious of deadlines. Where he has previously rejected the title of "écrivain exact," here he claims this exactitude as if drafting a contract between a professional author and his publisher.

In the description that the prefacer provides of the conditions in which he writes, his circumstances are less those of a retired aristocrat than of an exiled author struggling to make ends meet. In the preface to *Le Doyen de Killerine*, Renoncour's self-portrait could well be that of Prévost:

> L'état de ma fortune ne me permettant pas de choisir pour sujet de mon travail tout ce qui demande du temps et de la tranquillité, je me réduis à ce qui se présente à ma plume de plus simple, de plus honnête et de plus agréable. Ces trois caractères s'accommodent fort bien à ma situation; le premier parce qu'il abrège mes peines, le second parce qu'il convient à ma profession et à mes principes, et le dernier parce que facilitant le débit de l'ouvrage, il répond à la principale vue qui me le fait entreprendre." (*DK*, 9)

[The state of my fortune not permitting me to choose as a subject for my work anything that demands time and tranquility, I am reduced to writing that which seems simple, *honnête*, and agreeable. These three qualities are well adapted to my situation; the first because it eases my pains, the second because it agrees with my profession and principles, and the last because in facilitating the production of the work it responds to the principal aim which made me undertake it.]

The prefacer refers here to his fortune and to his work, ideas that would not normally trouble a Man of Quality retired from the cares of the world. The allusion to his profession reminds the reader that the prefacer (Renoncour? Prévost?) is a priest but at the same time points to the fact that he is a professional author. In the end, the life portrayed in this preface is less that of a tranquil monk than of a harried hack who lacks time for reflection and must write quickly enough to pay the creditors who never leave him in peace.

6

Prévost's *Contes singuliers:*
Between Novel and Newspaper

"Le *Pour et contre* n'est point un ouvrage d'imagination" [The
Pour et contre is not a work of fiction] (*PC*, 59, 314) Prévost writes in an
effort to oppose the facts in his newspaper to the fictions in his novels.
Using his newspaper to reject the novels as unimportant and to cast
them as inferior to his nonfiction writing, he affirms:

> Je suis bien aise . . . de pouvoir déclarer de nouveau ce que j'ai déjà
> répété plus d'une fois: les *Mémoires et aventures d'un homme de qualité*, leur
> suite, l'Histoire de Cleveland et celle du Doyen de Killerine sont des
> ouvrages de pur amusement. Ma vue dans une confession si simple et si
> ingénue est de disposer le public à juger autrement de quelques ouvrages
> plus sérieux dont je fais actuellement mon occupation. (*PC* 135, 342)

> [I am happy . . . to be able to declare yet again that which I have al-
> ready repeated more than once: the *Memoirs and Adventures of a Man of
> Quality*, their continuation, the story of Cleveland and that of the Doyen
> de Killerine are merely works of entertainment. My aim in such a sim-
> ple and ingenuous confession is to dispose the public to judge differ-
> ently the more serious works which I am currently undertaking.]

However, despite the author's attempt to draw a distinction between
the two forms, Prévost's novels and newspapers do borrow from each
other. While the techniques of the newspaper are present in the prefaces to Prévost's novels, Prévost's newspaper is punctuated throughout
its twenty volumes by narratives which read like novels in miniature.

Despite their initial publication in *Le Pour et contre*, some of the newspaper's articles were recognized even by their earliest readers as de-
tachable from their original context, and shortly after their author's

153

death, these texts were excerpted and reassembled in a volume entitled *Contes, avantures et faits singuliers.* In this volume's preface, Prévost's *Pour et contre* is described as "an ingenious mixture of little stories and graver essays" from which the volume's editor has culled certain texts for his readers' enjoyment, separating lively fiction from dull fact.[1] The editor of a 1767 collection also confirms that these stories are of a different nature from the rest of the newspaper; they are the periodical's most pleasurable part: "We believed that those texts which spiced up *Le Pour et contre* would make for amusing and agreeable reading on their own."[2] Finally, a nineteenth-century edition makes explicit the connection between Prévost's *contes* and his novels by proclaiming on the volume's cover: "Today we present, certain of their success, these *Contes* which are so many small masterpieces, so many pretty little love stories, the worthy brothers of the immortal *Histoire de Manon Lescaut.*"[3] Readers of Prévost's novels may indeed recognize Manon in the heroine of the newspaper's "Relation curieuse" [Curious relation], just as they may see the Oriental exploits of Renoncour in "Aventures d'une belle musulmane" [Adventures of a Beautiful Muslim] or the love life of Montcal in "Effet héroïque de vertu morale" [Heroic Example of Moral Virtue] to cite only a few examples.

In *Récit et réflexion: poétique de l'hétérogène dans* Le Pour et contre *de Prévost,* Shelly Charles notes "the omnipresent reminders of Prévost's novelistic œuvre"[4] found in Prévost's newspaper, and she highlights these novelistic narratives in her argument about the hybrid nature of *Le Pour et contre.* However, while their presence contributes to the newspaper's hybridity, the *contes* are also essential to the creation of a greater aesthetic unity in which Prévost's novels and newspaper form a whole. Tzvetan Todorov has written that "the meaning (or the function) of an element of the work is in its possibility to enter into a correlation with other elements of the work and with the entire œuvre to which it belongs,"[5] and Prévost's *Contes singuliers* are most meaningful when taken not as fragments but as an integral part of the Prévostian project. While in some ways the incursion of the novelistic on the journalistic weakens the newspaper's claim on the reader's credulity, the presence of Prévost's novels in his newspaper reconfirms this author's complex relationship with his public. These texts enter into a dynamic interaction with their reader by requiring a reaction to their difference from their context, and when these texts make the reader see them not just as fictional in nature but Prévostian in character, they force a recognition of the author's presence in them.

The resurgence of the novels in the newspaper may be explained as a form of repetition compulsion, the reverberation of what Jean Sgard presents as Prévost's personal obsessions. Sgard suggests in several places that Prévost's writing is a projection of his personality, and Sgard's use of Charles Mauron's psychocritical perspective implies that connections between Prévost's works are the result of an unconscious process.[6] In Prévost's own time, the author's redundancies were seen as rather more conscious, clear evidence of his desire for an easy profit. By reusing already successful elements in successive works, Prévost does show his awareness of the literary market. In the case of the novelistic narratives published in *Le Pour et contre,* he delivers to readers of his newspaper that which they have come to expect from his novels, making good on the promise implied when he signs *Le Pour et contre* with the name *l'Auteur des Mémoires d'un homme de qualité.* The novelistic elements of the newspaper function then as a signature, a conscious gesture through which Prévost asserts his authorship by asking his readers to recognize his signature style. Paradoxically, while the novel strives to efface the author in order to reinforce the reader's faith in the narrator, the newspaper's evocations of the novel are a constant reminder of the author's presence in the work. By profiting from this identification, Prévost transforms the aristocratic ideal of loyalty into the consumer's loyalty to his brand.

SIGNATURE STORIES

While the news stories of *Le Pour et contre* recount the business of everyday life in London, Amsterdam, and Paris, the novelistic narratives of the newspaper transport the reader into the dark world of Prévost's fiction. "Relation d'un événement extraordinaire envoyée de Flandres" [Relation of an Extraordinary Event from Flanders] — where a young man watches his pregnant mistress die in childbirth — and "Exemple merveilleux de la force de l'imagination" [Marvelous Example of the Power of Imagination] — where a bereaved widower returns each night to his wife's grave — exemplify the juxtaposition of love and death characteristic of the Prévostian novel. The former story recalls the obsessive adoration of the beloved on her deathbed in the episode of Rosemont's marriage to the dying Donna Diana in the *Mémoires d'un homme de qualité*; the latter echoes the extravagant mourning rituals of Renoncour after the death of his wife, Selima, in the same novel. While Prévost's continued insistence on this theme may be attributed to the importance of a lost love in the author's own past, his conversion of this episode into a sort of trademark suggests an exploitation of his personal life for profit. The passionate heart buried in the ashes of a burned-out love is the easily identifiable brand burned into all of Prévost's works, and in his newspaper such novelistic narratives become privileged sites for authorial self-identification.

In "Aventure intéressante" [Interesting Adventure] (also known as "Histoire d'un désespéré" [Story of a Despairing Man]) the nocturnal wanderings of the story's hero have the same obsessive quality as the adventures of Prévost's novelistic protagonists. The appearance of this structure in the *conte* appears to argue for Prévost's compulsive repetition of the scenario where the jealous hero imagines his virginal beloved to be a cynical whore. Like Des Grieux, the "désespéré" recounts the story of his doomed love for a girl who is not the innocent ingenue he first imagined but a scheming hussy instead. Like Manon, the heroine of the *conte* is both appealing and dangerous, and the hero describes her in the same sentence as "charmant[e]" [charming] and "monstre" [a monster,] in the next breath as "vertue[use]" [virtuous] and "rusée" [cunning] (*CS*, 244). Although the couple is married, the hero has promised to wait to consummate their union until the heroine comes of age, and on the appointed night, he searches for her desperately, trailing her carriage through the streets of Paris. The "désespéré" tracks his beloved as if in a trance, but this dream state ends as he awakens to his worst nightmare when he reaches the Quai des Orfèvres and pursues her into an unknown house. Each moment leads him closer to the terrible secret of her crime, and a dark foreboding fills the obscure spaces of nocturnal Paris and makes them a maze in which the anxious lover turns. He follows her "dans une allée obscure qui me conduisit au pied d'un escalier" [into a dark alley which led to the foot of a staircase], which he ascends "avec quelque frayeur" [with some trepidation], arriving at the top only to be "alarmé du silence qui régnait" [alarmed by the silence there] and is horrified to discover his young bride in a "funeste lieu" [fateful place] with "le plus vil des hommes" [the vilest of men] to whom she offers her virginity and with whom she laughs at her husband's shame (*CS*, 246–47). In its particular characterization of the hero and heroine, its setting in the Parisian underworld, and especially in the sequence of the desperate youth's nocturnal pursuit of his perfidious beloved, this story resembles Prévost's most famous novel; the reader of *Le Pour et contre* derives a special pleasure from this identification and the exercise of comparison and contrast that ensues. Whether the recurrence of certain motifs has its source in compulsion or calculation, Prévost's success as a novelist contributes to his success as a journalist. He signs *Le Pour et contre* "Par l'auteur des *Mémoires d'un homme de qualité*," but this particular story bears the mark of the author of *Manon Lescaut* and consolidates his claim to fame as such.

While Prévost reminds readers of his newspaper of his work as a novelist through references to scenes from his novels, he also indicates his artistic presence in *Le Pour et contre* through the incorporation of a structure usually associated with his more elaborate fictions: the labyrinth. The subtitle of Jean Sgard's 1986 collection of essays on Prévost, *Labyrinthes de la mémoire*, evokes the mazelike quality of Prévost's fictional world; Sgard explains: "Prévost is doubtless the first to have affirmed the complete independence of his novelistic universe, to have conceived of his work as a labyrinth walled off from the rest of the world."[7] However, this signature structure is present not only in the author's fiction but in his nonfiction as well. In the first pages of *Le Pour et contre*, Prévost compares his navigation of censors' sensibilities to the adventures of Theseus following Ariadne's thread: "[J]e n'ai pas eu de peine à découvrir ce qui a causé en France la disgrâce de certains écrivains, ni à reconnaître qu'elle est juste, ni à comprendre que pour éviter les mêmes écueils, en marchant dans la même voie, je devais me conduire avec des précautions dont ils ont manqué. La difficulté consistait à trouver un fil assez sûr pour me servir de guide dans ce labyrinthe" [I have had no trouble discovering what has caused the disgrace of certain writers in France nor in recognizing that this disgrace is justified nor in understanding that in order to avoid the same pitfalls while following the same path, I would have to take precautions that they did not. The difficulty consists in finding a strong enough thread to guide me through this labyrinth] (*PC* 1, 5).

While the labyrinth structure may be seen as an externalization of the author's dark imagination, it should be remembered that Prévost is not only the hero turning in the maze but also the architect of this carefully designed disorientation. In "Relation qui n'ennuiera personne" [Relation which will bore no one], Prévost's narrative design draws the reader into the story's mysterious center: the English estate of the Turkish merchant Herby, a private retreat from the public spaces of the port and the stock market of London. Herby's home is his haven: "peu de personnes connaissaient l'intérieur de cette belle solitude" [few people had seen the inside of his beautiful retreat] (*CS*, 130). Even his servants are excluded from their master's inner sanctum around which he has established "des bornes qu'il était défendu de passer" [boundaries which it was forbidden to cross] (*CS*, 130). Into this retreat, Herby lures local girls "en les faisant conduire par des chemins détournés . . . [et] par les détours qu'on leur fit faire sur la route" [by having them take circuitous routes . . . (and) by the detours that he had them make] (*CS*, 132). Just like the girls who abandon their everyday English existence to live out the hero's Oriental fantasy, so the reader leaves behind the newspaper's reports on reality to follow this detour into fiction. In this story, Prévost constructs a narrative architecture to involve his readers, leading them inward by encouraging their desire to penetrate the story's secret. The representation of everyday English life is inflected with Prévost's particular interest in the exotic, the erotic, the enigmatic.

In "Triomphe d'une femme sur un adversaire de son sexe" [Triumph of a lady over an enemy to her gender,] the reader follows the hero into another labyrinth, losing himself again in the English countryside:

> Il connaissait peu les environs, mais ne se défiant point qu'il pût s'égarer dans un lieu qui n'est qu'à quelques milles de Londres, il se livra insensiblement au plaisir de parcourir un des plus beaux cantons de Middlesex. . . . ne se lassant point de pénétrer de tous les côtés où il remarquait des ouvertures, [il] s'écarta beaucoup dans l'espace d'une heure, et s'aperçut enfin qu'il ne lui serait pas aisé de retourner sur la même route. (*CS*, 189)

> [He did not know the surroundings well, but not imagining that he could get lost in a place that was only a few miles from London, he thoughtlessly gave himself over to the pleasure of exploring the most beautiful parts of Middlesex . . . . never tiring of entering anywhere he noticed an opening, (he) traveled far in the space of an hour and noticed in the end that it would not be easy to find his way home.]

At the center of this maze is a hidden house inhabited by a woman whose beauty and mystery attract the hero and the reader. Just as Prévost's novels call into question the virtue of heroines such as Sergie and Théophé, the Prévostian *conte* often crystallizes around a compelling yet morally questionable heroine, and in "Triomphe d'une femme," *Mistriss* Anna is an enigma, for she refuses to explain the reason for her retreat from society. Although her resistance to the hero's attempts at seduction argues in favor of her virtue, her reluctance to explain her strange living situation arouses his suspicion. As the hero examines her more closely, he wonders whether his charming and gracious hostess is in fact a fallen woman:

> Quelquefois il croyait se remettre son visage; et comparant surtout le temps qu'elle avait passé avec le souvenir de ce qui était arrivé trois ans auparavant à la fille de M . . . qui avait disparu de Londres avec le maître d'hôtel de son père, il ne doutait pas que ce ne fût cette dame, qui avait préféré la satisfaction de son cœur à son honneur et sa fortune, [mais comme . . .] il ne l'avait jamais vue d'assez près pour la reconnaître parfaitement, il craignait de faire outrage à celle qui le traitait avec tant de bonté, par une conjecture qui ne pouvait s'accorder avec l'élévation de son esprit et de ses sentiments. (*CS*, 191–92)

> [Sometimes he thought he recognized her face; and especially by comparing the time she had been away with the memory of what had happened three years before to the daughter of Mr . . . who had disappeared from London with her father's butler, he did not doubt that she was that lady who had preferred the satisfaction of her heart to her honor and her fortune, (but as . . .) he had never seen that lady close enough to recognize her for sure, he was afraid of outraging a person who had treated him with so much kindness with a conjecture that could not correspond to the superiority of her mind and her sentiments.]

The ambiguity of her identity—whore or lady—only intensifies Anna's allure and the hero's (and reader's) interest. Tzvetan Todorov has written that "the story is formed around a character or a phenomenon, enveloped in a certain mystery which will be solved at the end;"[8] however, when Mylord L returns the next day to continue his conversation with her—turning in circles for hours before a local peasant leads him to the cottage—he finds the house empty and abandoned as if Anna had vanished into thin air. The mystery surrounding her does not dissipate and instead lingers after the story's inconclusive ending. Here, the labyrinth structure contributes to the construction of a puzzle, an intellectual architecture that invites the reader's critical reflection.

While the presence of these labyrinthine passages may be explained as the external manifestation of the unconscious connections between Prévost's various works, it must also be recognized that Prévost was quite conscious of his use of this "underground" structure. When Crébillon *fils* criticized old-fashioned novels for their use of unlikely elements, this evocation of subterranean settings was so easily identified as an attack on Prévost that the author felt compelled to respond by defending the success of his trademark "souterrains" [underground caves] (*PC* 105, 355). Prévost's rejoinder shows that he recognized the reception of his various works and consciously reused elements that contribute to readers' enjoyment. When, in "Aventure intéressante des mines de Suède" [Interesting Adventure in a Swedish Mine], he sets the story of a beautiful criminal in an underground location, Prévost is exploiting two *valeurs sûres*. When Prévost describes the English explorer's attraction to the abyss and to the gorgeous girl condemned to bury her youth in a tomb, he is offering a model for the reader's interest in this setting and character. Prévost thus evokes the English mineralogist's desire to descend into the Swedish mine—"La curiosité fit souhaiter au voyageur anglais de connaître par ses propres yeux ces demeures souterraines" [Curiosity made the English traveler desire to see with his own eyes these subterranean places] (*CS*, 185)—and his attraction to the stunning beauty he finds there:

> Une femme entra dans la loge, les yeux en larmes, et s'étant jetée aux pieds du ministre, elle lui parla quelque temps avec toutes les marques d'une vive douleur. L'Anglais ne comprit rien à son langage; mais il lui trouva tant de beauté et de jeunesse qu'étant surpris de voir une personne si aimable dans ce lieu d'horreur, il attendit à peine qu'elle eût fini son discours pour en marquer de l'étonnement au ministre. (*CS*, 185)

> [A woman entered the office, tears in her eyes, and throwing herself at the feet of the minister, she spoke to him for a time with all of the marks of a deep sorrow. The Englishman did not understand her language; but he saw in her so much youth and beauty that, surprised to see such an admirable person in such a horrible place, he hardly waited for her to finish speaking before he expressed his surprise to the minister.]

Much like in *Manon Lescaut* where Renoncour admires Manon despite her situation—seeing in her a princess among prostitutes—the hero of the *conte* is immediately intrigued by the Swedish girl. While Prévost's novels often revolve around the question of the heroine's innocence or guilt, this *conte* literally shows the heroine on trial for the crimes of her husband, a thief who is sentenced to hard labor in the mine. Because of her high birth, the Swedish girl is not convicted, but once her husband is imprisoned, she bravely begs to share his fate. Having married below her station, the young woman is a target for public condemnation, but her loyalty to her husband in his time of need invites approval as well. In this story, Prévost returns to a familiar setting and character in order to set up the paradigm of judgment that is characteristic of his work in both fact and fiction. The irrational attraction to the abyss and the problematic fascination with the fallen woman are combined with an appeal to the reader's conscious critical faculties.

While the fast pace of news propels the reader of *Le Pour et contre*, the *contes* stop this forward movement. In one of the longest *contes*, "Histoire intéressante d'Amsterdam" [Interesting Story from Amsterdam], the story's setting in an Amsterdam inn represents a halt in the narrative journey to signal a move from fact to fiction. From his first novel, in which French travelers are regaled with ghost stories at a Spanish inn, Prévost has borrowed this traditional topos of pilgrimage stories and picaresque novels. Here the setting of the inn is not just a sign that the story is fictional, but the treatment of this setting recalls the particular use of this place in Prévostian fiction as the sanctuary for secret lovers. In Prévost's novels, the inn is the place where identities are adrift, where Manon can be first innocent then guilty, where Mme de Gien is at first virtuous then impetuous in her attachment to Montcal, where Théophé rebuffs Ferriol and embraces her young admirer. Prévost's "Histoire intéressante d'Amsterdam" presents another questionable coupling, for while the pair go by the names "le baron" and "la baronne," the baroness is "une dame dont la figure autant que l'équipage annonce une personne de distinction" [a lady whose face as well as her carriage announce a person of distinction], but her companion is obviously not her equal, "un homme assez bien mis mais qu'on ne prend à la physiognomie que pour son premier domestique" [a man who was dressed well enough but whose physiognomy seemed to be only that of a servant] (*CS*, 256).

The story of this mysterious couple does not just echo episodes in Prévost's novels but also episodes of the author's own life, since he, too, has taken refuge in Amsterdam inns. "[O]n ne peut y être porté à s'y retirer que pour se dérober au monde, et s'en faire une espèce de sépulture" [One only retires there to hide from the world and to make for oneself a kind of sepulcher] (*CS*, 256) he writes, describing Amsterdam as a place to bury past pains or present secrets. One of the solutions offered to explain the presence of the story's mysterious couple is also an admission by Prévost of his own questionable conduct in Amsterdam: "[U]n autre bruit le fit passer pour un prélat romain qui était venu se réfugier avec sa maîtresse dans le pays de la liberté" [(A)nother rumor characterized him as a Roman prelate who had come to seek refuge with his mistress in the land of liberty] (*CS*, 257). This conjecture recalls Prévost's novels (*Le Monde moral* most specifically) but also his own life story as a runaway priest living in an Amsterdam inn with his mistress. Not only is this story remarkable for its autobiographical resonances but also for the actual presence of Prévost as a character in the plot, as one of the guests who participates in the gathering of information and invention of rumors about the mysterious couple at the Amsterdam inn. By echoing Prévost's fiction and his life, this story invites the reader to look for the author's reflection in the text's game of mirrors and requires recognition of his authorial agency in creating this complex, self-referential structure.[9]

PRÉVOSTIAN SELF-PARODY
IN THE *CONTES SINGULIERS*

While the repetition of certain essential structures in Prévost's writing contributes to the aesthetic unity of his work, the reuse of settings, characters, and plots in the *contes* may also weaken their strength, turning once powerful images into laughable clichés. Prévost's overreliance on certain elements was much mocked by his critics like the Jesuit Bougeant who in his *Voyage merveilleux du Prince Fan-Férédin en Romancie* (1735) attacked the novel genre by parodying Prévost's overuse of exaggerated emotions and extravagant adventures through Fan Férédin's comical encounters with moody lovers in subterranean lairs.[10] Prefacers of a recent edition of this text explain: "In the eyes of Bougeant, Prévost represents all of the vices of the novel: the banality and the unlikelihood of the plots, the maudlin sentiments, the unrealistic aspirations—which make these works resemble the heroic novels of High Novelland [*Haute Romancie*]—but also the coarseness of the situations takes us back to Low Novelland [*Basse Romancie.*]"[11] Since Prévost was aware of his critics[12] but persisted in repeating himself from novel to novel, his refusal to change his ways may be seen as laziness or stubbornness. However, the transfer of traits of his novels to newspaper stories may instead be viewed as an act of conscious self-parody. When Prévost shrinks a series of strange events from several hundred pages into a few short paragraphs, the effect is similar to that of Bougeant's satire: Prévost's closer look at some familiar features of his own novels invites the reader of his newspaper to recognize their ridiculousness. Reading Prévost's *contes* is like looking at his novels through a lens that both magnifies and distorts the original. Seen in this way, the *Contes singuliers* are not just miniatures of the novels but often caricatures of them. In many cases, the self-reflexivity of these stories shows Prévost to be capable of a sophisticated sense of irony and an artistic self-consciousness that many of his critics seem not to suspect.

For some admirers of Prévost's fiction, the *contes* are just failed novels. Pierre Berthiaume has written: "In the context of Prévost's literary production they constitute, it must be recognized, a failure."[13] Berthiuame complains that these stories lack psychological depth: "The narrator's gaze skims over the surface of the characters; he never penetrates the 'labyrinth,' the obscure meanderings of the heart, and he does not give an account of the hero's inner life nor of Prévost's 'metaphysics of sentiment.'"[14] For Berthiaume, Prévost's stories are superficial: the narrator of the *contes* cannot achieve in a brief text the intimate relationship with the narratee that is the essence of the pact of Prévostian fiction. In fact, this change in affect is the effect of a particular narratological choice on Prévost's part. While the first-person narration perfected in the Prévostian novel appeals to the reader's emotions and draws him into the fiction, the third-person narrator of the *contes* prevents communion between readers and characters and instead creates a critical distance that allows the reader to more consciously judge the *contes'* contents as well as their form.

In "Etrange accident arrivé à une jeune anglaise" [Strange Accident of a young Englishwoman], Prévost avoids long descriptions and extravagant emotions by reducing the couple's trials and tribulations to a trite line about love: "Leur tendresse avait passé par mille obstacles, et la constance avec laquelle ils étaient parvenus à les surmonter passait pour un miracle de l'amour" [Their tenderness had vanquished a thousand obstacles, and the constancy with which they surmounted them was explained as a miracle of love] (*CS*, 170). When an ultimate accident prevents the lovers' union, the sentimental is replaced with the slapstick: the bride collapses at the altar having suddenly lost control of her legs. Prévost compares this contemporary anecdote to a classical tragedy, but the improbable juxtaposition of a mythic heroine and a middle-class Englishwoman makes Prévost's story comical. He notes:

> C'est précisément ce qui arriva à la reine Phèdre si on en croit monsieur Racine. 'N'allons pas plus avant, demeurons chère Œnone, / Je ne me soutiens plus, ma force m'abandonne, / Mes yeux sont éblouis du jour que je revois, / Et mes genoux tremblants se dérobent sous moi. (*CS*, 170).

[This is precisely what happened to Queen Phaedra, at least if one believes Monsieur Racine. 'Let us not move forward, let us stay, dear Œnone / I can no longer stand, my strength abandons me, / My eyes are blinded by the daylight / And my knees tremble and give way beneath me.]

Racine's heroine is the plaything of the gods; Prévost's is a marionette whose strings are suddenly cut. Instead of dwelling on their despair as do the heroes of Prévost's novels, the couple in this *conte* finds a fast and simple solution to their problems:

L'amant, dont on doit se figurer le désespoir par l'idée que j'ai donnée de sa passion, n'a pu supporter, disent les mêmes nouvelles, que son bonheur fût retardé par un si cruel contretemps. Dans l'état où est sa belle, il a trouvé facilement le moyen de la vaincre; et pour elle, la faiblesse de ses jambes lui a servi d'excuse. On assure que les parents, après s'être aperçus que l'amour leur avait fait faire trop de chemin, ont pris le parti de les faire entrer du moins dans la voie légitime, en les mariant dans leur chambre. (*CS*, 171)

[The lover, whose despair one must imagine from the idea I have given of his passion, could not bear, the same stories say, that his happiness be delayed by such a cruel accident. In the state his beloved was in, he easily found a way to conquer her resistance; and for her part, the weakness of her legs served as an excuse. It is said that the parents, after having noticed that the lovers had gone too far, decided to lead them down the right path by marrying them in their bedroom.]

The narrator, too, approaches the problem of the bride's paralysis with pragmatism, turning this sad state of affairs into a joke at the expense of wandering wives:

Bien des gens plaignent le mari, qui se trouve forcé d'aimer constamment une femme sans jambes. D'autres qui pensent sans doute beaucoup mieux, estiment qu'un mari peut se passer de jambes dans une femme, pourvu qu'il y trouve une tête raisonnable et un cœur tendre. Quelques-uns prétendent même que le monde n'en irait pas plus mal et que la fidélité s'en trouverait fort bien dans les mariages, si toutes les femmes ressemblaient à l'épouse de Carnavan. (*CS*, 171)

[Many people pity the husband, who is forced to be faithful to a legless wife. Others, who doubtless think better, judge that the husband can do without a wife's legs as long as she has a reasonable mind and a tender heart. Some even say that the world would be a better place and that married couples would be more faithful if all women resembled the bride of Carnavan.]

In a novel, this same situation would have caused endless suffering over countless pages; in a *conte* the tragic event is related tersely, and the long lamentations of the hero are replaced with the quick-witted comment of the narrator.

In another *conte*, the "Aventure de M . . . ," Prévost pokes fun at the novelistic topos of the perfect lover who upon his mistress' death can think of nothing but his own. In this story, the young English hero finds a seemingly safe haven for himself and his mistress, but soon after their reunion the heroine falls from a window and dies. In a Prévostian novel, the heartbroken Englishman would immediately consider suicide, but in the *conte* this stereotypical reaction is the inspiration for satire. To mark the fateful moment, Prévost does evoke the register of high tragedy, quoting Racine again: "Il y vit, quel objet pour les yeux d'un amant " [He saw there, what an object for the eyes of a lover] (*CS*, 149). However, instead of acting like a character from a novel, the young lover steps back from the window ledge and decides to live on. Nevertheless, since Prévost's novels have established suicide as the standard end of unhappy Englishmen, the public requires an even more supernatural explanation to accept the antinovelistic outcome of M's story:

> Il allait la suivre et se précipiter volontairement, mais un génie favorable, qui veillait à son salut le tira rudement par le bras, le fit descendre malgré lui, et le conduisit dans un lieu de sûreté, où à force de prières et de bonnes raisons, il le fit consentir de souffrir la vie. C'est ainsi qu'une infinité de gens racontent la conclusion de cette aventure, et l'on ne réussirait point à leur persuader qu'un jeune Anglais, bien amoureux, pût être sauvé dans les mêmes circonstances par un autre secours que celui du ciel. (*CS*, 129)

[He was going to follow her and throw himself from the window, but a favorable genie, who was watching over him, pulled him roughly back, made him climb down against his will, and forced him to consent to continue living. This is how an infinite number of people recount the conclusion of this adventure, and it would be impossible to persuade them that a young Englishman in love could be saved in these circumstances by anything other than divine intervention.]

When the narrator suggests that the hero was not saved by a guardian angel but by his dutiful manservant, he reminds the reader of the distance between literature and life, acknowledging that few men — English or not — are truly willing to die of despair. He ends the story with an ironic line that uses a national and fictional stereotype as a source of humor, reducing to a mockery the figure of the melancholic Englishman made famous by his own *Cleveland*: "On doit sentir que s'il y a ici quelque difficulté, c'est uniquement parce qu'il est question d'un jeune Anglais; car il y a peu de Français dont on ne pût expliquer la patience et la résignation dans le même cas, sans en être obligé de recourir aux génies" [One must admit that if there is any difficulty here it is only because this story is about a young Englishman; for there are few Frenchmen whose patience and resignation in the same case need be explained by having recourse to genies] (*CS*, 129).

In "Exemple admirable de la générosité" [Admirable Example of Generosity], where adventures on the high seas end in the enslavement of European travelers by Oriental masters, setting and story remind the newspaper reader of similar episodes from *Histoire d'une Grecque moderne* or *La Jeunesse du Commandeur*. Here, however, the *conte* is not a simple copy but rather a caricature of the Prévostian novel. Pierre Berthiaume has noted that the round characters of the Prévostian novel are flattened in the *conte*, where the interruption of the narrator pierces the story's bubble and deflates the fullness of Prévost's longer fictions: "The story is frequently interrupted by the narrator who states maxims and takes away the characters' individuality by transforming them into paradigms of psychological laws."[15] In this story of the kidnapping of a young couple and their rich uncle, the narrator sacrifices scene for summary; instead of exploring the characters' emotions, he explains them rather dryly: "Mais tout cela se suppose sans peine dans un riche marchand de Venise, dans un jeune homme passionné, et dans une fille de dix-huit ans qui n'allait pas malgré elle à ses noces" [But all this is easily imagined of a rich Venetian merchant, a passionate young man, and a girl of eighteen who was not marrying against her will] (*CS*, 127). The protagonists' suffering is not presented to inspire sympathy but is instead analyzed cynically: the merchant is chagrined not by the loss of his freedom but by the loss of his fortune; the couple's regrets are caused not by the interruption of their wedding day but by the postponement of the wedding night. Motivated not by high ideals but by base drives (greed and lust in this case), the characters of the *conte* may be less developed than those of the novel, but they are at the same time more true to life, and their simplicity reveals the artifice of the very fictions which they imitate.

At the same time, this *conte* ("Exemple admirable de la générosité") performs a critique of the narrative system of Prévost's novels when the *conte*'s narrator attacks the initial account of these events for its overly emotional exaggerations. This narrator explains that his article is based on an episode from the journal of an English sea captain, and in editing the original for inclusion in *Le Pour et contre*, he complains of the Englishman's sentimental style: "Le capitaine qui a fait imprimer cette relation s'est efforcé de l'orner par l'image touchante de leur tristesse et de leurs pleurs" [The captain who had this relation printed worked hard to embellish it with the touching image of their sorrow and their tears] (*CS*, 126). The *conte*'s narrator, by contrast, eschews anything ornamental, seeing a long description of the characters' sadness as unnecessary in a situation that is so obviously upsetting. He interrupts his article to criticize its source, noting the captain's efforts to render his characters' emotions, and he indicates these effusions only to excise them from his final version: "Ici le capitaine renouvelle toutes ses forces pour exprimer la consternation de l'amant" [Here the captain renews all his powers to express the lover's consternation] (*CS*, 127). The captain has written the story not with his head but with his heart, identifying completely with his characters: "Les deux amants quittèrent l'Asie avec leur oncle, avant le départ du capitaine anglais, de sorte qu'ayant lui-même le cœur fort tendre, comme il le fait connaître dans plusieurs endroits de sa relation, il eut une joie infinie de les voir partir contents et chargés de bienfaits" [The two lovers left Asia with their uncle, before the departure of the English captain, so that being tenderhearted as he shows in many places of his relation, he had an infinite joy in watching them leave happy and loaded with good wishes] (*CS*, 128). The journalist cuts out the captain's expressions of empathy in order to keep his own reader from indulging in an emotional relationship with the story's characters. Instead, the reader remains at a critical distance from which he can examine the original and understand the manipulation of a narration that appeals to the heart in order to trick the head. In denouncing sentimentality, Prévost's *conte* deconstructs itself and at the same time critiques the essence of Prévost's novels.

One of the longest *contes*, "Mémoires d'une dame turque" [Memoirs of a Turkish Lady,] is again both a caricature and a critique of the Prévostian novel. Modeled on the Oriental episode of book 4 of the novel *Mémoires d'un homme de qualité*, "Mémoires d'une dame turque" recounts the imprisonment of a Western man in an Eastern harem, his friendship with his master and his betrayal of that friendship through his illicit love for the master's daughter, the couple's daring escape, and their eventual return to Europe where she is converted to Christianity. This sequence, presented as serious in Prévost's novel, is parodied not only by Bougeant in a chapter of *Le Voyage du Prince Fan-Férédin* entitled "Des grandes épreuves" but also by Prévost himself in *Le Pour et contre*'s "Mémoire d'une dame turque." While the tone of the original novel is serious and often pathetic, the *conte* is comical. While the novel elevates its heroes, the *conte* brings them down to earth: even the name of the heroine, Plomby, suggests a certain leadenness, and the narrator's description of her is not an idealized portrait but an exaggerated caricature: "En général elle serait une des plus belles personnes du monde, si elle n'avait pas la bouche un peu trop grande" [In general, she would be one of the most beautiful people in the world if her mouth were not a bit too big] (*CS*, 217). Whereas the actions of the novel's characters are attributed to noble motives, the characters of the *conte* are animated by vulgar drives so that instead of appreciating each other's qualities, they exploit each other's weaknesses. In the novel, the relationship between the slave and his master is described as one of mutual admiration, but in the *conte* it becomes one of cold calculation when Verdinitz realizes that the way to his master's heart is through his purse: "Verdinitz . . . s'étant aperçu que sa passion dominante était l'avarice, il s'appliquait à lui faire prendre une bonne idée de son économie" [Verdinitz . . . having noticed that his dominant passion was greed, strove to give him a good impression of his own frugality] (*CS*, 208). While the novel's Salem and Selima struggle virtuously against their forbidden desire, Verdinitz and Plomby simply pursue their pleasures: "Le jeune homme, qu'on produit sous le nom de Verdinitz, était depuis plusieurs années dans l'esclavage, et se consolait par le bonheur de plaire à la fille de son maître qui ne lui avait pas fait acheter trop cher la conquête de son cœur" [The young man, who is called Verdinitz in the story, had been living as a slave for several years, and consoled himself with the good fortune of pleasing the master's daughter who did not make him work too hard to conquer her heart] (*CS*, 206).

While in the novels the heroes are placed in serious peril, the heroes of the *conte* find themselves in situations that are less dangerous than ridiculous. It is not some mysterious menace but rather a mundane fact of life that threatens to betray Verdinitz who, disguised as a woman, has been hiding in Plomby's husband's harem:

[M]ais il restait deux affreux sujets de crainte contre lesquels il semblait que le courage et l'adresse n'avaient aucune ressource. L'un était la difficulté de faire savoir au négociant par quel obstacle on se trouvait arrêté, et de l'avertir du jour où l'on serait parvenu à le surmonter. L'autre, incroyablement plus terrible, était la barbe de Verdinitz qui croissait à vue d'œil et qu'il était impossible de cacher. (*CS*, 212)

[(B)ut there remained two terrible reasons for fear, reasons which, it seemed, neither courage nor skill could combat. The first was the difficulty in informing the merchant of the obstacle which was stopping them and in indicating the day when they would be able to overcome it. The other, incredibly more terrible, was Verdinitz's beard which was growing before their very eyes and which was impossible to hide.]

The image of the hero dressed in drag, his safety threatened by his irrepressible hair growth, is hilarious here, since the source of danger is not the abstract force of destiny but a simple bodily function. This hero is not admirable but laughable since his life depends on finding a barber. In accordance with its comic setup, the scene ends not with Verdinitz's demise but with a surprise that eliminates his enemy. When Plomby's husband pursues Verdinitz, bent on having his way with the most aloof inhabitant of his harem, the shock of discovering a rough masculine beard in the place of the expected feminine face immediately causes the lovers' enemy to die of a heart attack:

Il entra dans sa chambre [de Verdinitz] sans l'avoir fait avertir, et le surprenant dans son lit, il fut extrêmement surpris lui-même de lui trouver une barbe prodigieuse, qui le rendait moins semblable à une femme qu'à une bête féroce. Soit frayeur, ou d'autres causes qui n'ont jamais été bien approfondies, le pauvre gouverneur fut attaqué sur le champ d'une apoplexie violente. Les esclaves, plus attentifs à son accident qu'à ce qui le pouvait causer, l'emportèrent mourant, et n'aperçurent pas même la barbe fatale que Verdinitz avait toujours eu l'adresse de leur cacher. (*CS*, 214)

[He entered (Verdinitz's) room without warning, and surprising him in his bed, he was extremely surprised himself to find that he had a prodigious beard, which rendered him less like a woman than like a wild animal. Either from fear or from other causes which have never been fully investigated, the poor governor suffered on the spot a violent attack of apoplexy. The slaves, more attentive to his accident than to its causes, carried him away dying and did not notice the fatal beard that Verdinitz had always skillfully concealed from them.]

Danger is defused in the *conte* and emotional exaggerations are undercut by the narrator's ironic incursions. The narrator notes the heroine's anxiety over the hero's fate but dismisses her worries as the result of an overactive imagination: "Elle s'était livrée d'abord à mille noirs soupçons, et plus ingénieuse à se faire des sujets d'inquiétude qu'à trouver des raisons de se rassurer, elle avait vécu pendant plusieurs jours dans des agitations mortelles" [She gave herself over at first to a thousand dark thoughts, and more ingenious at inventing worrisome ideas than at finding reassuring ones, she lived for several days in a state of mortal agitation] (*CS*, 207). The narrator sweeps aside the heroine's thousand dark thoughts with one disdainful remark, applying an editorial policy of eliminating objectionable exaggerations, amplifications, and repetitions in his rendition of the story. In publishing this story in *Le Pour et contre*, the narrator refers to the original manuscript of the heroine's memoirs much as the editor of the novels refers to the manuscript memoirs of heroes such as Renoncour or Cleveland to argue for their authenticity. However, unlike the prefacer of the novels who supposedly respects the first version of events and presents it uninterrupted, the editor-narrator of the *contes* eliminates the excesses of the original, noting: "[J'] abrège beaucoup cette relation" [I much abridge this relation] (*CS*, 209). He decries the useless digressions of the manuscript, remarking: "Ce que je viens de raconter en peu de lignes occupe . . . du moins vingt pages dans l'original" [What I have just told in a few lines . . . occupies at least twenty pages in the original] (*CS*, 209). This disrespectful disruptiveness not only shortens the story but curtails the reader's emotional attachment to its underdeveloped heroes, causing him even to question the idea of their existence.

Whereas Prévost's memoir-novels present themselves as true records of events, the *conte* questions its own trustworthiness from within. Instead of ignoring the strangeness of certain situations, the narrator of the *conte* characterizes the improbable as probably imagined, writing of the couple's extraordinarily complicated adventures: "[L]eur histoire commence à prendre ici l'apparence d'une fiction" [(T)heir story begins here to take on the appearance of fiction] (*CS*, 211). As reversals foil the lovers' plans to escape their enemies, leading them to see suicide as their only avenue, their desperation seems unrealistic in its exaggeration, a quality which the narrator emphasizes when he admits that "Verdinitz et Plomby m'ont paru des héros romanesques" [Verdinitz and Plomby seemed to me heroes of a novel] (*CS*, 215). When the narrator ends the tale with the rhetorical question, "Qui osera croire, après tant de circonstances, que Plomby ne soit qu'un fantôme d'imagination, et ses aventures un roman?" [Who will believe, after so many circumstances, that Plomby is only a phantom of the imagination and that her adventures are only a novel?] (*CS*, 217) the reader is tempted to answer that, after the narrator's repeated hints, he or she believes nothing so strongly as the story's novelistic nature.

While the content of Prévost's narratives in *Le Pour et contre* is so often highly novelistic, the treatment of these elements reveals a pointedly antinovelistic attitude in keeping with the newspaper's efforts to privilege fact over fiction. The suspension of disbelief upon which the novel depends is constantly questioned in the *contes*; the emotional connection between narrator and narratee of the novels is rarely made in the newspaper context. In *Le Pour et contre*, doubt is the new trust, as Shelly Charles explains: "Everything is thus founded on trust, a trust constructed from doubts and sincere confessions, the contrast of yesterday's lies with today's truths."[16] The pact of the novel is replaced by the contract of the newspaper by which the journalist admits that his stories seem false only to reassert that they are in fact true or at least true lies faithfully reported.[17] By cutting in to anticipate readers' doubts but also by cutting his stories down to size for inclusion in his newspaper, Prévost transforms the problem of truth from a question of philosophy to a matter of style. In an article entitled "Trait horrible" [Horrible tale] Prévost notes: "J'ai rendu ce récit fort laconique, pour n'être pas soupçonné d'ajouter quelque chose aux circonstances" [I have rendered this story quite laconic so as not to be suspected of having added anything to the circumstances] (*CS*, 252), thus equating a brief form with a true content.[18]

The laconic manner of the *contes*, the distance they establish between the narrator and the narrated, opens up a new interpretive perspective in Prévostian writing in which the reflexes of novel reading are recalled and then ironically dismissed. What Prévost has used to provoke tears in the novel, he rewrites in the newspaper to provoke laughter or at least a sardonic smirk, in a move that demonstrates an awareness of his personal style and an ability to laugh at himself. The final phrases of some of these stories almost function as punch lines. In "Relation qui n'ennuiera personne" the last lines prevent the reader from dwelling on the horror of the hero's death by alluding in a matter-of-fact way to the problem of the division of his wealth among his many wives: "Mais qui s'intéressera pour le pauvre Acmet? Chacune de ses filles, pour faire le calcul de leur devoir à l'anglaise, n'y est intéressée que pour un douzième" [But who will take an interest in poor Acmet? Each of his girl-friends, to calculate their duty by the English method, is only interested for a twelfth] (*CS*, 134). Sentimentality is thus replaced by practicality. Similarly in the article entitled "Fin funeste d'un homme d'esprit et de savoir" [Fateful end of a man of wit and wisdom], the story of the suicide of a ruined Protestant clergyman might normally provoke our sympathy for the pious yet desperate man, but the end of the anecdote does not invite emotion but reflection: "La prière [du suicidaire avant sa mort . . .] marque qu'il n'était point sans religion, mais on assure que ses idées étaient fort différentes des principes communs et qu'il était grand admirateur de Collins et de Tyndall. Il connaît à présent la valeur réelle de leur doctrine" [The prayer (of the suicidal man before his death . . .) shows that he was not without religion, but it is assured that his ideas were quite different from common principles and that he was a great admirer of Collins and Tyndall. He now knows the real value of their doctrine] (*CS*, 137). Here, death does not mark the beginning of a lengthy mourning process as it does in the novels but is presented instead as an elegant and ironic solution, the concise answer to an intellectual question.

In the last of the *Contes singuliers*, "Remarque historique" [Historical remark], Prévost satirizes the peaceful retreat idealized by his novels' heroes and even by the author himself. While the hero of the newspaper story does invite his mistress to accompany him to his retreat, his careful planning is the antithesis of the passionate folly of Des Grieux or the young commander. The hero of the *conte* is not governed by his emotions but instead chooses a mistress based on a "calcul" (*CS*, 262) or "système" (*CS*, 262) which assures their compatibility. The narrator of the story emphasizes the sacrifice of sentimentality for practicality when he adds: "Enfin il crut avoir réussit dans son choix. Il lui restait deux autres; celui d'un laquais et d'un chien. Il n'y apporta pas moins de précaution" [In the end he believed he had succeeded in his choice. Two others remained; that of a manservant and that of a dog. He brought no less precaution to these] (*CS*, 262). When his mistress dies, extravagance of emotion is obviated and dramatic scenes of mourning elided for a laconic summary: "On ne dit point jusqu'où il porta la violence de ses regrets; mais il reprit le chemin de la ville avec le corps de celle qu'il avait aimée, son laquais, son Homère et son chien" [No one has said how far he took his regrets; but he set out for the city with the body of the woman he had loved, his manservant, his Homer, and his dog] (*CS*, 262). If his beloved is dead, at least our hero still has his faithful and carefully chosen pet.[19] By evoking the most essential strutures of the Prévostian novel in order to deconstruct and ultimately parody them, the *contes* are literary texts that also function as literary criticism and as such are totally at home in the context of *Le Pour et contre*.

Moreover, Prévost's self-parody in the *contes* reframes the interpretation of repetition in the Prévostian novel, recasting it as intentional and ironic. The ideal of *otium* outlined by the Man of Quality in his preface to *Manon Lescaut* is parodied not only in tre *contes* but also from within the novel itself. Renoncour describes the happy life as a sort of leisurely solitude: "Les plus doux moments de leur vie sont ceux qu'ils passent, ou seuls ou avec un ami, à s'entretenir à cœur ouvert des charmes de la vertu" [The sweetest moments of their life are those spent either alone or with a friend, speaking with an open heart of the charms of virtue] (*MHQ*, 363), and nowhere does the Man of Quality mention the company of a mistress as key to the scholar's tranquility. Des Grieux's voluptuous retreat with Manon at Chaillot is then a caricature of Renoncour's philosophical retirement. Not only does this novel critique its own premise, but the rewriting of this episode in a later work, *La Jeunesse du Commandeur*, is another example of Prévost's ability for self-reflection and self-derision. The young commander, a reader of *Manon Lescaut* and imitator of its hero, reenacts that novel's retreat to equally comical results. When the commander and his mistress seek refuge in a country house, the hero of this novel ends up, like Des Grieux, dressed in drag and humiliated when discovered in this state. The philosophical and masculine ideal of scholarly retirement is rewritten as a frivolous, effeminate episode that reveals the essentially unheroic character of these novelistic heroes and the self-critical character of Prévost's writing or rather his ironic rewriting of his own work.

In the longest of the *contes*, "Histoire de Donna Maria" [Story of Donna Maria,] the scene in which the heroine meets danger in a dark wood when brigands attack her carriage seems to take its tone from the Prévostian novel: "On peut juger quelle fut la frayeur et la consternation de cette jeune personne lorsqu'elle se vit au milieu de trois voleurs, dans l'obscurité de la nuit, et sans espoir même que ses cris, qui étaient son unique ressource, pussent être entendus. La perte de son honneur et de sa vie lui parut inévitable" [One may judge the fear and consternation of this young person when she saw herself surrounded by three robbers, in the dark of night, and without even the hope that her cries, which were her only resource, could be heard. The loss of her honor and her life seemed to her inevitable] (*CS*, 114).[20] This scenario of the virgin ambushed in the forest has its source in an episode from the *Mémoires ∂'un homme ∂e qualité* in which Renoncour's sister is attacked and killed by bandits before the hero's very eyes. Its repetition in the *contes* could be read as the working out of some deep-seated fear,[21] but its recurrence in another of Prévost's novels seems to undermine this explanation. In *Le Doyen ∂e Killerine* the bandits' attack on M. de L's carriage has been prearranged by Patrice to allow him to demonstrate his valor and win approval for his marriage to the wealthy man's daughter. (*DK*, 67) This particular repetition of a recurrent nightmare may represent a psychic victory for the hero who finally asserts his control over threatening circumstances. However, just as the hero has removed any real danger from the scene, so has the author removed any real drama. Its recurrence in this novel makes the episode no longer a tragedy but a trick; its repetition reveals not a compulsion but a conscious and even ironic rewriting of this scenario by the author. "Qu'il est facile de faire des contes" [How easy it is to make up stories], remarks Diderot in *Jacques le fataliste* after he has just poked fun at the unrealistic coincidences of Prévost's *Cleveland*,[22] but Prévost's famous facility does not make him any less than Diderot a self-conscious and sophisticated novelist able to caricature and critique his own signature style.[23]

Conclusion

BETWEEN NOVELISTIC AND JOURNALISTIC, THE *CONTES SINGULIERS* represent a complex paradigm for readers' reactions. Shelly Charles has analyzed the construction of verisimilitude in these stories, but I would add that the *contes'* complexity plays out both in the texts' relationship to reality and also in their relation to the rest of the Prévostian *œuvre.* In his essay, "Le Secret du récit," Todorov has said of Henry James's short stories that they pose the fundamental problems of that author's novels,[1] and I would argue that the same analogy may be made between the *Contes singuliers* and Prévost's *œuvre romanesque.* With the *Contes,* Prévost satisfies the reader of his novels who turns to his newspaper looking for the same sort of stories found in the author's fiction. At the same time, Prévost reverses the readerly paradigm for his novels in these newspaper stories, when he uses the *contes* to abbreviate exploration into psychology, to cut short any outpouring of sympathy for the characters, and to criticize essential structures of the *romanesque.* Ironically, the sarcasm that characterizes the narration of many of the *contes* only achieves its full force for readers familiar with Prévost's longer fictions and thus able to appreciate to what extent this stance in the newspaper stories represents a departure from the narrator's position in the novels.

Just as knowledge of Prévost's novels enriches the understanding of his newspaper, Prévost's newspaper also provides new perspectives on the author's novels. The reader who sees the *contes* as a critique of the *romanesque* more easily recognizes the availability of this same self-critical position in the novels themselves. If the novels prescribe a sympathetic reading, they also imply a suspicious one; they encourage at the same time an identification with the hero and a rejection of him, a belief in his truth and an incredulousness toward his honesty. Where, in the *contes,* this dual attitude is made possible by the situation of third-person narration in which the narrator can comment on the actions of the heroes, the novels at first seem to render this distance impossible with the first-person narrative system precluding any difference between the narrator and the hero. Nonetheless, the memoir-novel genre implies not a personal difference but rather a temporal one, since the narrator has a certain distance from which to regard his past actions. Although the self-criticism that this perspective could afford does not often occur — unlike the narrator of the *conte* who points out the ridiculousness of his heroes, the narrator of the novel rarely laughs at his own errors — the memoirist's refusal to recognize his faults provokes the reader to enter this breach and to examine the character and his story more critically.

While Shelly Charles has established that the debate about the truth of various articles in *Le Pour et contre* creates a dialogue between author and public, I have recognized this same dialogism in the presentation of both narrative honesty and personal *honnêteté* in Prévost's novels. What is at stake in the novels is not only their truth status but rather the social and moral status of their protagonists, and as a result, questions about the hero's quality create an ongoing conversation between the protagonist and his public. Although R. A. Francis has noted that the aristocracy of Prévost's heroes seems a given in titles like *Mémoires d'un homme de qualité* or *Mémoires d'un honnête homme*, Prévost's works themselves show that these qualities are not natural but negotiated, the product of a self-construction through which an identity is established in concert with others. For Prévost, nobility is not an unquestionable value but an essential fiction and even a performance, as an early episode in the *Mémoires d'un homme de qualité* illustrates. In this anecdote, a master and servant switch places, and the first says of the second: "On ne l'eût pas pris d'ailleurs pour un fripon ni pour un valet, tant il copiait naturellement l'homme d'honneur et de distinction" [One would not have taken him for a rascal or a servant, as he copied most naturally the manner of a man of honor and distinction] (*MHQ*, 274). Honor and distinction are easily imitated, not innate but enacted. By extension, the memoirs of men of quality are a means of establishing their status as such, for despite the hero's initial aloofness toward his readers, he is in fact writing for their approval, performing his identity in order to persuade the public of it.[2] In this way, Prévost's novels anticipate the postmodern idea that identity is manufactured, as Mark Currie explains in *Postmodern Narrative Theory:* "Most of the perspectives presented in this book are implicitly dedicated to the proposition that personal identity is not inside us."[3] Even if Prévost's novels seem to be so much about expressing the self, they are also deeply concerned with producing and ultimately selling it. Despite their declared independence from the public sphere, the heroes of Prévost's novels rely on their readers' complicity in order to exist.

While the novels' narrators depend on the narratee to affirm their status as men of quality and to admire them as heroes, Prévost addresses the public of *Le Pour et contre* in order to gain acceptance and garner respect for the new figure of the professional man of letters. If Prévost's "Apologie" in *Le Pour et contre* resembles the narratives of his fictional heroes, it is because the author's strategy of self-presentation mirrors the strategy of his characters. In his essay "Qu'est-ce qu'un auteur?" Foucault marks the beginning of the institution of authorship from the moment when "we began to tell the story not of characters but of authors."[4] Prévost's position as one of the first French authors, in the modern sense of the term, is affirmed not only by the way in which he conducted his professional career but also in the way he artfully constructed his authorial image so that the story of the man of letters is no less compelling than the story of his Man of Quality. Moreover, in the Prévostian *œuvre* the constructions of hero and author are not competing but rather complementary, since Prévost uses both his fiction and nonfiction to establish his authorial persona and to recount his literary life both by disseminating partial images of himself in his novels and his newspaper and by challenging the reader to catch his reflection in these fragments of a broken mirror. By searching for Prévost in his work, the reader is involved in the writing of the Prévostian *œuvre*; by verifying truths or rejecting rumors, he participates in the construction of the author's character just as he has the hero's.

Prévost's entire novelistic enterprise and indeed his entire professional gambit is based on this idea that a hero or an author's "quality" is not only inherent but can also be imposed through language. This proposition is perhaps most clearly demonstrated in *Le Pour et contre* with the "Histoire d'un illustre bâtard" [Story of an Illustrious Bastard], a story whose protagonist cannot make legal claims to his quality but can use language to convince the public of his worth. The story employs the typical Prévostian paradigm of the hero as accused and the narrative as a discourse of exculpation that ends in heroization. The hero's guilt is established at the outset, as Prévost writes: "Un jeune homme nommé Savage, bâtard de mylord Rivers, eut le malheur de tuer un homme dans une partie de débauche. . . . Il fut arrêté par la justice, et les procédures qui regardent le meurtre étant fort promptes chez les Anglais, il se vit condamné en peu de jours à perdre sa vie par le supplice ordinaire" [A young man named Savage, bastard son of Mylord Rivers, had the misfortune of killing a man in the course of a night of debauchery. . . . He was arrested, and since murder trials are quite quick in England, he was condemned to death by the ordinary method of execution after only a few days] (*PC* 102, 272). Despite the court's condemnation, the reader's sympathy is engaged almost from the beginning for this poor youth abandoned even by his own parents: "Son père et sa mère . . . parurent s'intéresser peu à sa disgrâce" [His father and mother . . . seemed little interested in his disgrace] (*PC* 102, 272). Not only do circumstances make Savage sympathetic, but he is also presented as undaunted by death and thus superior to most men: "L'approche de la mort, qui éteint le courage et l'esprit dans la plupart des hommes, lui fit naître, ou plutôt servit à lui découvrir dans lui-même un talent qu'il avait toujours ignoré. Il devint poète" [The approach of death, which extinguishes courage and reason in most men, inspired in him or rather made him discover in himself, a talent which he had always ignored. He became a poet.] (*PC* 102, 272). When things are at their worst, the Prévostian hero, like Prévost himself, will write his way out of a bad situation.

The "illustre bâtard" discovers in prison his gift for poetry, and his rhymed request for clemency convinces the king to grant his pardon. The talent of the writer—in the case of Prévost and of his heroes—is not employed in pure self-expression but rather in the service of some interest and is thus aimed at affecting an audience and moving a public in favor of the author: "Il s'efforça si heureusement de le toucher en faveur de son âge et de son repentir que ce prince suspendit en effet l'exécution de la sentence et lui fit grâce quelques jours après" [(H)e tried with so much success to move him to compassion because of his age and his repentance that the prince suspended the execution of the sentence and pardoned him a few days after]. When, after his pardon, Savage is attacked by critics who envy his newfound social and literary success, the bastard-murderer-poet writes another piece which definitively wins the public's favor:

Le public se porte de lui-même à mettre une juste différence entre les crimes volontaires, et ceux qu'une fureur aveugle produit dans la chaleur du vin. Le récit même que le jeune poète publia des circonstances de son action et le tour qu'il donna à ses regrets fit prendre une idée extrêmement avantageuse de son caractère. Rien n'était si tendrement et si naturellement exprimé que son repentir. Sa pièce fit verser des larmes à ses plus cruels ennemis, et les parents mêmes de celui qui était mort de sa main avaient consenti à le voir, et à se réconcilier avec lui, depuis l'opinion qu'elle leur avait fait prendre de ses sentiments. (*PC* 102, 274)

[The public judges on its own the difference between voluntary crimes and those which a blind fury produces in a drunken state. The story that the young poet published on the circumstances of his action and the turn that he gave to his regrets offered an extremely advantageous idea of his character. Nothing was so tenderly and so naturally expressed as his repentance. His piece brought his cruelest enemies to tears, and even the relatives of the man he had killed agreed to see him and to reconcile with him after his story had given them a new opinion of his sentiments.]

This story describes more directly than almost anywhere else in the Prévostian *œuvre* the hero's and author's motivation for writing while at the same time prescribing the right reaction for readers. Like Savage's, Prévost's apologetic writing—whether fictional or more explicitly autobiographical—strives to win the sympathy of a skeptical public. Prévost's writing is his best defense against the stories written about him and circulated in the ever-expanding press and through a newly emerging culture of celebrity where rumors are constantly being fabricated and must be faced by an author interested in maintaining his mass appeal.

However, as I have already noted, Prévost is not only interested in countering rumors about himself but also sometimes in encouraging their persistence, both polishing his image and drawing his reader to the dark side of his character. Sympathy is obviously important to Prévost and marketable to a point, but as we have seen, Prévost is not above encouraging suspicion about his irreligion, libertinism, and even his dishonesty, since, as he well knows, scandal sells. The rumor, for example, that Prévost was not attached to his religion and easily converted to Protestantism to please Dutch and English patrons is echoed in stories of conversion to Islam in the Oriental adventures of his novelistic heroes. In the *Mémoires d'un homme de qualité*, Renoncour refuses to convert while other Christians do. In *La Jeunesse du Commandeur*, the young commander stands firm while the villain Antonio becomes a Muslim in order to reap rewards from the Moroccan king. In these novels, the heroes resist betraying their religion, while secondary characters convert not out of deep conviction but instead to further personal ambitions. In *Histoire d'une Grecque moderne*, these two attitudes merge in the strategy of Ferriol, who allows his Oriental friends to assume that he has converted without really abandoning his Christian convictions. These various versions of religious conversion represent an ambivalent response by Prévost to his critics.[5] In *Le Pour et contre*, the story of the Duc de Riperda (*PC* 8) is a mocking rebuttal to these rumors, a story even more scandalous than the ones told about its author, for Prévost's hero converts from Protestantism to Catholicism, back to Protestantism, and then to Islam when it suits him and ends by inventing his own religion.

Likewise, Prévost engages accounts of his own supposed libertinism in his writing in a way that both explains and exploits it. If he rejects Lenglet's description of him as a ladies' man by refusing to be identified as "ce Médor si chéri des belles"(*PC* 47) and by insisting on his almost ascetic lifestyle, his stories' heroes are nonetheless seducers. Despite their stern and sober character, almost all of Prévost's protagonists have women falling at their feet, and while Renoncour and Cleveland most often refuse the advances of their female admirers, others cannot resist similar temptations. The figure of the cleric converted by love is not infrequent in Prévost's writing: Des Grieux and the young commander are both knights of Malta who violate their vow of chastity to pursue their passions in circumstances that recall Prévost's own dereliction of religious duties in favor of amorous pursuits. In *Le Monde moral*, the story of the abbé Brenner who falls in love with his comely pupil, the princess Tekely, reads almost like a retelling of a rumor about the abbé Prévost's own adventures in England. As tutor to the children of the director of the Bank of England, Prevost supposedly seduced one of his charges, the young Mary Eyles in an episode which Frédéric Deloffre has termed Prévost's *fiançailles anglaises*.[6] This scenario of the subaltern man and socially superior young woman repeats itself throughout Prévost's work (in the harem sequences of the *Mémoires d'un homme de qualité* and "Mémoires d'une dame turque," for example), admitting the hero's guilt but also mitigating it by showing his disinterestedness in his mistress' fortune. Whether fact or fiction, this narrative sequence reflects a desire for social promotion made sympathetic by the seducer's characterization as the innocent victim of his own passionate nature.

Prévost's self-presentation as sympathetic criminal recurs throughout his work where many of his heroes find themselves behind prison bars. If Brenner is first seen in the Bastille where he is being held for mishandling the fortunes of his master, his circumstances may mirror another sequence in the life of his creator. As Mysie Robertson has discovered, Prévost himself was imprisoned for mishandling his master's money, specifically for forging the name of his pupil, Francis Eyles, on a letter of credit.[7] The particular crime for which Prévost was punished seems characteristic of him, since forgery is both a crime of writing and a crime of identity. Prévost, who often suppressed his own signature in favor of a pseudonym, seems to easily borrow the identity and then the money of another. Just as he signed the name of a gentleman to his novels (using the pseudonym "par l'auteur des *Mémoires d'un homme de qualité*"), so then did he use the name of a gentleman, Francis Eyles, to pay his bills. However, just as writing was central to the commission of Prévost's crime, it was also central to his exoneration: he used it to establish himself not as a petty thief but as an important author.

In the ambivalent portrayals of his heroes as religious men and renegades, as preceptors and seducers, as gentlemen and scoundrels, Prévost examines the problematic position of the individual with the talents of the Man of Quality but without the fortune. Prévost describes the situation of such men in a telling passage of *Manon Lescaut*: "Les qualités du corps et de l'âme sont accordées à ceux-ci, comme des moyens pour se tirer de la misère et de la pauvreté. Les uns prennent part aux richesses des grands en servant à leurs plaisirs: ils en font des dupes; d'autres servent à leur instruction: ils tâchent d'en faire d'honnêtes gens" [The best qualities of the body and soul are accorded to those people to be a means of extracting them from their misery and their poverty. Some take part in the wealth of nobles by serving their pleasures: they make of them their dupes; others work for their instruction and try to make *honnêtes gens* out of them] (*MHQ*, 402). The personally meritorious but socially marginal hero is faced with two choices: he can be a teacher or he can be a trickster. The author faces the same dilemma in relation to his reader, often characterized as the alternative between instruction and amusement, and while Prévost himself presents his stories as instructive, they are often a less than moral means of making a profit from his reader's pleasure.[8]

Although Prévost tried to establish his resemblance to Renoncour, his readers often saw him as Des Grieux. However, an early German translation of *Manon Lescaut* identifies its author neither as gentleman nor adventurer but rather as the *opérateur*, Miraculoso Florisonti, a charlatan figure from the early pages of the *Mémoires d'un homme de qualité*. This equation of author and sideshow entertainer is borne out in *Le Pour et contre* where Prévost exhibits a constant parade of oddities: from doctors offering miracle cures to deaf mutes performing remarkable feats. While in the newspaper, each issue may boast several articles about these cheap tricks, each of Prévost's novels may be read as one long performance of a con-man playing his audience. When in his last novel Prévost revisits the scene of the sideshow, describing a family who crippled their child in order to expose him as a freak (*MM*, 302), he both condemns this immoral act and profits from it as he rivets readers with his retelling.

If the author may be condemned as a trickster, Prévost nonetheless justifies his actions by characterizing his reader as a willing dupe. Prévost makes this case in *Le Pour et contre* at the end of the story of Molly Siblis when he simultaneously censures and exploits the public's salacious desire for news of this monstrous murderess. He argues this point even more clearly in another newspaper article about a charlatan doctor who panders to the debauchery of his patients by curing their venereal diseases with diets rich in vice. Prévost tells his patients/clients/readers that what he writes is good for them, when in fact what he writes is really just what they want to read. He promises moral instruction and delivers amorality in *Manon Lescaut;* in *Histoire d'une Grecque moderne* the "Avertissement" describes the story as pure and virtuous only to engage us to read a text that is sexually and psychologically perverse. Prévost's prefaces and *Le Pour et contre* all characterize the reader as a *lecteur incrédule,* but the success of his works shows what he already knows: that the reader wants to suspend not only his disbelief but also his supposed indignation at immoral incidents in order to indulge in the enjoyment that the Prévostian narration promises. Even if he realizes that Prévost's novels and stories are neither factual nor moral, the reader is only too eager to agree that the author's writing is innocent in order to allow himself the guilty pleasure of it.

In the end, the long identification of Prévost with Des Grieux draws not only on the idea that they were passionate young men who broke their vows for love, only to end with broken hearts, but this analogy is just as strongly sustained by the argument that the two were tricksters who used language to obtain both recognition and remuneration. Nonetheless, if Prévost does encourage readers to equate him with Des Grieux, so much so that one biographer wrote of the author "Des Grieux, c'est lui" [He was Des Grieux],[9] there is yet another equation to be made between one of his characters and the character of the author. Prévost has much in common with the narrator and the narratee of *Manon Lescaut* —with Des Grieux and with Renoncour —but surprisingly, he is not only like the lover in this tale but also like his beloved Manon. I would suggest here that the importance of *Manon Lescaut* in the Prévostian œuvre takes on its full meaning when we see in the enigmatic character of the heroine yet another self-portrait of the author, a self-representation of Prévost as prostitute. If Prévost as productive author is accused by his critics of prostituting his talents, he reflects this accusation in the reappearance of the figure of the prostitute in his works: from the concubines of the Orient to the fallen women of Europe. These women are blamed for turning something that should be outside of economics into a profitable business, and in a way their transgression mirrors Prévost's move from the status of *amateur* (one who does something for the love of it) to professional. Indeed, the accusation of professionalism—of selling out—is made with as much righteous indignation against the heroines of the novels (Sergie in the *Mémoires d'un homme de qualité*, Helena in *La Jeunesse du commandeur* to name a few others) as it is against their creator, Prévost. Like the courtesan, Prévost is both passionate and practical. Like Manon, he can act with an aristocratic aloofness toward money, but only when he knows where the next day's bread is coming from.[10] If Manon wants to be both loved and paid, so does Prévost.

In my view, the inside of Prévost's novels is not divorced from the outside, the adventure of the story is in no way removed from that of the writing. Moreover, the rhetorical operations of seduction, persuasion, extortion, and exculpation that go on inside of Prévost's novels are not just inherent to the strategies of the narrator but to the strategies of the author in the overall dynamic of his career. Aurelio Principato has analyzed the operation of rhetoric in Prévost's fiction on the three levels of *histoire*, *récit* and *narration*, writing: "This distinction between different narrative levels will now allow me to analyze the functioning of the art of persuasion and to exclude a relationship which is not relevant here, that existing between the author and his public which aims to convince it of the authenticity and the moral utility of the story told."[11] My analysis of Prévost has diverged from Principato's model to look at the internal rhetoric of Prévost's writing as a mirror for the external rhetoric that operates between author and public. However, I have examined the author's persuasion of the public not strictly in terms of a negotiation about authenticity or morality, but rather I have tried to present Prévost's overall professional program by which he persuades his public to take an interest in himself and in his work.

If the hero-narrator is intent on proving that he is a man of quality, these assurances are doubled by the author's efforts to convince the public of the quality of his work. This is especially evident in the cross-over abilities of Renoncour in his movement from the insider position of Man of Quality to the outsider role of Man of Letters. In his own memoir, Renoncour affirms his quality, and in prefacing the memoirs of other men he goes on to assure the reader of their resemblance to himself. In this assurance of the characters' quality—a rhetorical act internal to the text—there is also couched an assurance of the quality of the writing—a rhetorical act external to it—which acts as an encouragement to readers to buy the author's next work. With Renoncour's signature serving as a quality seal, his recommendation of a text is the ultimate advertisement: this character who so emphatically refuses the spotlight is the one most actively engaged in Prévost's marketing campaign. While Prévost's ideas about the writer's role in the public sphere are most explicitly exposed in *Le Pour et contre,* I have been able to see these same problems posed in his novels in the paradoxically reluctant performance of the hero-narrators who act as both Men of Quality and Men of Letters. While for a long time critics have looked at *Manon Lescaut* in terms of its realistic presentation of its characters' socioeconomic condition, few have seen its concern with money as a manifestation of Prévost's larger exploration of changes in the literary field. My interpretation of Prévost's novels after my examination of his newspaper has allowed me to see that each of these forms operates dialogically to establish a constant conversation between author and public and that they are in dialogue with each other to negotiate the value of his work in a modern literary marketplace.

Notes

INTRODUCTION

1. Prévost refers specifically to "les Clélies, les Cyrus, les Polexandres . . . qui firent gémir les presses sous un amas de volumes" [the *Clélies*, the *Cyrus*es, the *Polexandres* . . . whose heavy volumes made the presses groan]. All translations are my own unless otherwise indicated.

2. Prévost, *Le Pour et contre* 17, 46–47; hereafter cited in text as *PC*.

3. The overwhelming critical interest in *Manon Lescaut* and the relative neglect of the rest of Prévost's œuvre is demonstrated quantitatively in Leborgne's 1996 *Bibliographie de Prévost d'Exiles*, which lists 308 studies on *Manon* followed by 56 on *Cleveland* (the next most studied novel) and 46 on all of Prévost's journalism together. Moreover, while Prévost wrote as much as Marivaux, Rousseau, or Diderot, scholars have written much less on Prévost than on many of his contemporaries.

4. In the conclusion to his study of Prévost's novels, R. A. Francis notes that Prévost "falls uncomfortably between generations and schools" (*First-Person Narrators*, 322).

5. Walter, "Les Auteurs et le champ littéraire," in *Histoire de l'édition française*, ed. Chartier and Martin, 2: 500.

6. Prévost writes: "Je suis bien aise . . . de pouvoir déclarer de nouveau ce que j'ai déjà répété plus d'une fois: les *Mémoires et aventures d'un homme de qualité*, leur suite, l'histoire de Cleveland et celle du Doyen de Killerine sont des ouvrages de pur amusement. Ma vue dans une confession si simple et si ingénue est de disposer le public à juger autrement de quelques ouvrages plus sérieux dont je fais actuellement mon occupation et surtout de *l'Histoire des grands hommes de la monarchie française*" [I am happy . . . to be able to declare yet again that which I have already repeated more than once: the Memoirs and Adventures of a Man of Quality, their continuation, the story of Cleveland, and that of the Doyen de Killerine are merely works of entertainment. My aim in such a simple and ingenuous confession is to dispose the public to judge differently the more serious works which I am currently undertaking, especially the *History of the Great Men of the French Monarchy*] (*PC* 135, 342).

7. Prévost declares early on: "Le *Pour et contre* n'est point un ouvrage d'imagination" [The *Pour et contre* is not a work of fiction] (*PC* 4, 313).

8. Crébillon, *Œuvres complètes* 2:69.

9. Diderot, *Œuvres complètes* 23:56.

10. Ibid., 25.

11. For a more complete treatment of Prévost and Diderot see Gilot, "*Cleveland* et

185

Jacques le fataliste" and Sermain, *"L'Eloge de Richardson* et *L'Avis* de Renoncour en tête de *l'Histoire du Chevalier des Grieux et de Manon Lescaut,"* *Cahiers Prévost d'Exiles* 1 (1984).

12. For more on Prévost's baroque sources see Virolle, "Quelques sources possibles de Prévost: les romans de Gerzan et les *Histoires tragiques* de Rosset," in *L'Abbé Prévost: Colloque d'Aix-en Provence,* 31–39.

13. Sgard, *Labyrinthes de la mémoire,* 47.

14. Sgard, *Prévost romancier,* 12.

15. May, *Dilemme du roman au XVIIIe siècle,* 14.

16. Francis, *First-Person Narrators,* 239.

17. Sgard, *Labyrinthes de la mémoire.*

18. Censer, *French Press in the Age of Enlightenment,* 12.

19. Labrosse and Rétat, *L'Instrument périodique,* 43.

20. Sgard, ed., *Le* Pour et contre *de Prévost: Introduction,* 43.

21. Chartier, *Origines culturelles,* 32.

22. Contemporary with Voltaire's *Lettres anglaises,* Prévost's *Pour et contre* both critiques and complements Voltaire's views on England. Prévost's interest in English culture precedes that of Diderot and Rousseau and predates the phenomenon that Josephine Grieder has situated in the second half of the century and named "anglomania." See Grieder, *Anglomania in France 1740–1789.*

23. Prévost, *Mémoires et aventures d'un homme de qualité* in *Œuvres de Prévost* 1: 247; hereafter cited in text as *MHQ.*

24. Mackie, *Commerce of Everyday Life: Selections from* The Tatler *and* The Spectator, 26.

25. Sgard, *Prévost romancier,* 11.

26. Houssaye, "Manon Lescaut a-t-elle existé?" in *Suite de Manon Lescaut* by Courcelles, 143.

27. Anonymous, Avant-Propos, in *Suite de Manon Lescaut,* 7.

28. Lebreton, *Le Roman au XVIIIe siècle,* 92.

29. Sgard, *Prévost romancier,* 23.

30. Sgard, *Vie de Prévost,* 279.

31. Houssaye, "Manon Lescaut?" 143.

32. Sainte-Beuve, "Sur Manon Lescaut," in *Suite de Manon Lescaut,* 9.

33. Janin, Preface, in *Suite de Manon Lescaut,* 10.

34. For more on the reception of Prévost during the nineteenth century, see Gilroy, *The Romantic Manon and des Grieux.*

35. Sgard, *Prévost romancier,* 9.

36. Ibid., 22.

37. In the first chapter of *Prévost romancier,* Sgard cites Charles Mauron's work, *Des métaphores obsédantes au mythe personnel. Introduction à la psychocritique,* as an important influence (27). In the title of his doctoral dissertation, *Saturne libertin: Libertinage et fantasmes chez Prévost,* Leborgne announces his psycho-critical approach.

38. Démoris, *Roman à la première personne,* 431.

39. Sermain, *Rhétorique et roman,* 34.

40. Ibid., 2.

41. See note 20.

42. Larkin, *Le* Pour et contre *nombres 1–60.*

43. Charles, *Récit et réflexion.*

44. Foucault, *Dits et Ecrits (1954–1988)*, 811.

45. Ibid., 799. Foucault pinpoints this moment at the end of the eighteenth and the beginning of the nineteenth centuries, but I will propose that Prévost's works indicate that the interest in authorial identity comes earlier.

46. Chartier, *Ordre des livres*, 46–47.

47. Viala, *Naissance de l'écrivain: sociologie de la littérature à l'âge classique*, 178.

48. Ibid., 113.

49. Robert Darnton, *Literary Underground*, 16.

50. Ibid., 19–20.

51. Ibid., 20.

52. Pierre Bourdieu, *Règles de l'art*, 235.

53. Mackie, *Commerce*, 3.

54. Ibid., 30.

55. Simon, *Mass Enlightenment*.

56. See Habermas, *Structural Transformation*, chapters 7 and 8.

57. Sgard, "La Multiplication des périodiques," in *Histoire de l'édition française* 2:257.

58. Ibid., 255.

59. Rétat and Sgard, *Presse et histoire*, 26.

CHAPTER 1. AUTHORSHIP IN PRÉVOST'S NOVELS

1. Collé, Rubrique nécrologique de Prévost, in *Journal et mémoires de Charles Collé* quoted in Sgard, "Vies de Prévost," *Cahiers Prévost d'Exiles* 7:47.

2. The Man of Quality supposedly serves as editor for *Cleveland*, *Le Doyen de Killerine*, *La Jeunesse du Commandeur*, *Campagnes philosophiques*, and *Le Pour et contre*, and it is his name that appears on the title pages of these works.

3. Prévost, *Le Doyen de Killerine* in *Œuvres de Prévost* 3:13; hereafter cited in text as *DK*.

4. Francis, *First-Person Narrators*, 225.

5. Prévost, *Mémoires d'un honnête homme* in *Œuvres de Prévost* 6:212; hereafter cited in text as *MHH*.

6. Prévost, *Le Monde moral* in *Œuvres de Prévost* 6:289; hereafter cited in text as *MM*.

7. For a full study of Prévost's evocation of the code of honor, see Francis's chapter 15.

8. Stanton, *Aristocrat as Art*, 2.

9. Montandon, *L'Honnête homme et le dandy*, 229.

10. Stanton, *Aristocrat as Art*, 53.

11. Bury, *Littérature et politesse*, 104.

12. Prévost's heroes provide a missing link in the lineage between Molière and Rousseau, since Rousseau's admiration for Alceste (expressed in the *Lettre à d'Alembert*) was likely influenced by his affection for Prévost's Cleveland (expressed in his *Confessions* in *Œuvres complètes* 1:220]). See Sgard, "Rousseau et Prévost: rapports personnels et lectures" and Steve Larkin, "*Cleveland* et les *Confessions*."

13. Molière, *Le Misanthrope*, Act 2, scene 4.

14. Stanton, *Aristocrat as Art*, 22.

15. Prévost, *Cleveland* in *Œuvres de Prévost* 2:17; hereafter cited in text as *C*.

16. Elena Russo, "Virtuous Economies," 265.

17. Leborgne, *Saturne libertin*.

18. According to Russo, the idea of sacrifice is also key to Montesquieu's conception of virtue in which "the military nobility . . . by a self-immolating gesture, wastes its wealth and consumes its energies to serve the state" ("Virtuous Economies," 267).

19. Prévost, *Mémoires pour servir à l'histoire de Malte* ou *La Jeunesse du Commandeur* in *Œuvres de Prévost* 4:129; hereafter cited in text as *JC*.

20. Stanton has written that "as an aristocracy of merit, *honnêteté* rejects the archetypally bourgeois equation of money with inherent value" (*Aristocrat as Art*, 93). This argument about aristocratic anticapitalism is also central to Elena Russo's study of Montesquieu, where she notes that the philosopher "criticizes the power of money able to buy the symbolic capital of prestige" ("Virtuous Economies," 252). R. A. Francis also notes that "it is an important part of the noble image not to be too attached to money" (*First-Person Narrators*, 226).

21. Molière, act 4, scene 1, vv. 1141–48.

22. Molière, act 1, scene 3, vv. 363–72.

23. Jenny Mander writes that in texts where the narrator is reluctant to see himself as an author "the deliberate posture of anonymity is very clearly bound up with the code of *honnêteté*, developed in the seventeenth century, according to which public acts of self-revelation were considered to be immodest" (*Circles of Learning*, 81).

24. Viala, *Naissance de l'écrivain*, 104.

25. The opposition of discourse and story in the Prévostian novel has been well documented by Stewart, Démoris, Francis, Leborgne, and Sermain, and their analyses of the tension between rhetoric and action in the novels provides the foundation for my examination of the tension between Prévost's theory and practice of authorship.

26. Roth, *Les Aventuriers au XVIIIe siècle*, 12–13.

27. In *Les Aventuriers des Lumières*, Alexandre Stroev includes Prévost with Casanova, Castiglione, and the Chevalier d'Eon in his study of adventurers. Suzanne Roth also alludes to Prévost in her work.

28. Segal, *The Unintended Reader*, xii–xiii.

29. Despite his duel with Synnelet at the novel's end, Des Grieux is a lover not a fighter. He only kills a prison guard by mistake with Lescaut's loaded pistol; when Lescaut himself is attacked, Des Grieux flees the scene just as he abandons his efforts to fight for Manon when his hired guns abandon him.

30. Prévost, *Campagnes philosophiques* in *Œuvres de Prévost* 4:290–91; heareafter cited in text as *CP*.

31. Before undertaking his study of the degeneration of the Prévostian hero, R. A. Francis explains, "The world of Prévost's novels is a hard one where heroes no longer move effortlessly as in the seventeenth-century novel. More usually they are men of a modest fortune, clinging to their noble status while at the same time carving themselves a career by means which may be less than noble" (*First-Person Narrators*, 247).

32. In his study of Prévost's narrator-heroes, Démoris evokes their problematic concern with their own "promotion sociale" (*Le Roman à la première personne*, 432, 435).

33. See *PC* 276.

34. R. A. Francis sees the conflict between ideal and real codes as central to Prévost's mid-career novel, *Le Doyen de Killerine* (Francis, *First-Person Narrators*, 259).

35. Prévost, *Voyages du capitaine Robert Lade* in *Œuvres de Prévost* 4:17; hereafter cited in text as *RL*.

36. Prévost will emulate the English as authors of treatises useful to national commerce when he publishes the multivolume *Histoire générale des voyages*.

37. This happens to be one of the definitions of "mémoire" listed in the *Encyclopédie*: "*Mémoire en termes de commerce,* . . . on appelle aussi quelquefois mémoire chez les marchands et chez les artisans, les parties qu'ils fournissent à ceux à qui ils ont vendu de la marchandise ou livré de l'ouvrage" [*Memoir in business,* . . . we also sometimes call memoir in the case of merchants and artisans the bills which they furnish to those to whom they have sold merchandise or delivered work] (*Encyclopédie* 10:330).

38. In "Prévost, Neaulme et les femmes," Steve Larkin provides a detailed overview of Prévost's complicated relationship with Jean and Etienne Neaulme (in *L'Abbé Prévost au tournant du siècle*, ed. Francis and Mainil, 23–32).

39. Prévost, Correspondance in *Œuvres de Prévost* 7:540; hereafter cited in text as *CDP*.

40. Prévost writes to Neaulme: "Il n'est pas nécessaire, par exemple, que vous en parliez à M. votre frère" [It is not necessary, for example, that you speak of this with your brother] (*CDP*, 537).

CHAPTER 2. AUTHORSHIP IN PRÉVOST'S NEWSPAPER

1. Bourdieu, *Règles de l'art*, 90.

2. Darnton, *Literary Underground*.

3. Voltaire, "Gazette" in *Encyclopédie* 7:534.

4. Darnton, *Literary Underground*, chapter 1.

5. Voltaire, "Auteurs" in *Dictionnaire Philosophique*, cited in Chartier, *Origines culturelles*, 88.

6. Viala, *Naissance de l'écrivain*, 222.

7. Russo, "Virtuous Economies," 258.

8. In "Les Figures de l'auteur chez Prévost," Mami Fujiwara sees Prévost's claims to copyright as relatively weak because of Prévost's refusal to sign his work (*L'Abbé Prévost au tournant du siècle*, 97, 99). In my view, Prévost does sign his work (via his well-known pseudonym and other highly identifiable indicators of his authorial agency) and thus has a strong argument for his right to profit from it.

9. An early image of the buried yet burning heart appears in Book 5 of the *Mémoires d'un homme de qualité* when Renoncour retreats to an underground cave to worship by torchlight the embalmed heart of his late wife.

10. Jean Sgard notes that *PC* 33 was in fact written not in London but upon Prévost's return to Paris (*Vie de Prévost*, 94), but he also observes that this reference to the English character of its content is Prévost's "own personal mark, that English touch which had made him successful" (n.18).

11. In his final chapter on Prévost's life, entitled "Living from his pen," Sgard attempts to distinguish between the implications of this new professional situation for an "écrivain" [writer] and a "professionnel du livre" [literary professional], writing:

"For a writer, it represents the ambition to live from the revenues of his art, to earn from the published work recognition and remuneration. For a literary professional, it simply means participation in the market, providing a supply in response to society's demand which is then ratified by a revenue; it is the simple salary of the intellectual worker." (*Vie de Prévost*, 261). This view seems to accept almost unquestioningly Prévost's distinction between the nobility of his own activity as opposed to the ignominy of his publisher's profiteering and ignores the author's ambiguous attitude toward writing as both the pursuit of a gentleman and the work of a skilled laborer.

12. Viala, *Naissance de l'écrivain*, 85.

13. Ibid., 94.

14. Ibid., 92.

15. Chartier, *Ordre des livres*, 57.

16. Sgard and Fujiwara both emphasize Prévost's interest in symbolic as opposed to financial rights. Sgard writes: "In fact, he was much more attached to symbolic than to financial rights [*il s'attache beaucoup plus au droit moral qu'au droit de propriété*]; without a doubt he preferred, just as Voltaire did, to deal high-handedly with his publishers and to avoid talking money while at the same time extracting from them the most money possible, as was only fair" (*Vie de Prévost*, 264). Fujiwara notes: "If the concept of copyright [*droits d'auteur*] includes a distinction between financial and symbolic rights [*un droit pécuniaire et un droit moral*], we see in *Le Pour et contre* only references to symbolic rights. . . . [I]n his literary works, Prévost never mentions the right to financial profit" ("Les Figures de l'auteur," in *L'Abbé Prévost au tournant du siècle*, 100–101). These critics' contentions seem to me a rather literal interpretation of Prévost's self-presentation as a pseudoaristocrat, unconcerned with earning money. In my view, Prévost's celebration of the English economy in *Le Pour et contre* is a strong indication of his interest in financial success for craftsmen, merchants, and even authors.

17. C. E. Engel evokes a possible parallel between Prévost's Manon Lescaut and Lillo's Millwood in order to argue for an even stronger connection between Prévost's Molly Siblis and Defoe's Moll Flanders (*Figures et Aventures du XVIIIe siècle*, 154).

18. See "Sur la considération qu'on doit aux gens de lettres" in Voltaire, *Lettres philosophiques* in *Œuvres complètes*, Vol. 25.

19. See Lenglet-Dufrenoy, *De l'Usage des romans*, 173–74 and *Bibliothèque des romans*, 103.

CHAPTER 3. THE PUBLIC AS HERO
OF *LE POUR ET CONTRE*

1. Habermas, *Structural Transformation*, 41–42.

2. Chartier, *Origines culturelles*, 32.

3. Labrosse and Rétat, "Les Périodiques de 1734," in *Presse et histoire*, ed. Rétat and Sgard, 26.

4. Habermas, 57.

5. Ibid., 42.

6. Charles, *Récit et Réflexion*, 201.

7. *PC* 2 and *PC* 95.

8. See ch. 2 n. 17.

9. The rest of this passage is telling: "Cependant un ouvrage sur des matières qui sont à la portée de peu de personnes peut être excellent sans être beaucoup lu. Tels sont les ouvrages remplis d'une profonde érudition. . . . Ces sortes de livres ne font pas aujourd'hui la fortune des libraires" [However, a work on subjects that are not understood by many may be excellent without being very widely read. Such is the case of works filled with a profound erudition. . . . These sorts of books do not at present make a fortune for their publishers.]

10. While Prévost pays lip service to public opinion he nonetheless expresses his own reservations about Mme de Tencin's novel and criticizes key scenes (dealing with doomed love buried in a monastic retreat) which, he implies, have been borrowed from his own.

11. Crébillon had evoked this favorite Prévostian motif as a mark of the author's old-fashioned style.

12. Prévost refers here to Crébillon's penchant for the marvelous.

13. Sgard, "La Multiplication des périodiques," in *Histoire de l'édition française* 2: 205.

14. *PC* 90, 353–58.

15. See *PC* 30, 354–56.

16. See *PC* 36, 137–39.

17. Chartier, *Origines culturelles*, 40.

18. Maza, *Private Lives and Public Affairs*, 2–3.

19. Chartier, *Origines culturelles*, 58.

Chapter 4. The Role of the Reader in Prévost's Novels

1. In his analysis of Prévost's first-person narratives, René Démoris argues that the Prévostian hero does not merely suffer his difference but strives to perpetuate it, writing of Renoncour: "The tragedies that he provokes permit him to keep, without risk to himself, his reputation as an illustrious unfortunate, as well as his sentiment of his difference and superiority" (*Le Roman à la première personne*, 431–32).

2. The structure of the confidant as double is repeated in the pairs of Cleveland and Bridge, Des Grieux and Tiberge, and the Jeune Commandeur and Peres.

3. Jean-Paul Sermain confirms a connection between similarity and sympathy but in reverse: "By letting himself be touched, the listener [Renoncour] recognizes his membership in the same emotional community as the speaker [Des Grieux]; can he then condemn one who is of the same nature as himself?" (*Rhétorique et roman*, 45).

4. Mlle Aïssé, *Lettres*, 271.

5. Leborgne discusses the problem of the amorous hero's conversion to stern Mentor in a section entitled "La censure du libertin: Renoncour philosophe ou le narcissisme triomphant" (*Saturne libertin*).

6. The judicial paradigm of *Histoire d'une Grecque moderne* has been noted by several critics including Sgard, who compares the novel to a "procès" (*Prévost romancier*, 457) and Sermain, who sees a parallel between the novel and *Les Causes célèbres* (*Rhétorique et roman*, 131).

7. This reversal of the judicial paradigm whereby the judge becomes the accused is at the origin of Jonathan Walsh's interpretation of *Histoire d'une Grecque moderne*, which he subtitles *Figures of Authority on Trial*.

8. Sermain, *Rhétorique et roman*, 43.

9. Ibid., 42.

10. In his reading of the same passage, Sermain explains the difference between the *scène de reconnaissance*, which is characterized by a natural and spontaneous outpouring of sentiment and the *scène rhétorique*, where artful rhetoric is necessary to mediate a reconciliation (*Rhétorique et roman*, 34).

11. Ibid., 44.

12. Lejeune, *Le Pacte autobiographique*, 42.

13. Although the story of Brenner has been considered part of Prévost's novel by most scholars (including the editors of the Presses Universitaires de Grenoble edition), Alexandre Duquaire has noted that the Brenner episode may be an apocryphal "suite" to *Le Monde moral*, due to its publication after Prévost's death (*Les Illusions perdues du roman*, 15). If this is true, the inclusion of a story so similar to the circumstances of Prévost's life shows that his contemporaries knew the author's lifestory and were eager to profit from the public's interest in it, affirming my argument that Prévost's public image was an important factor in the marketability of his work.

14. In *Vie de Prévost*, Jean Sgard studies the various versions of Prévost's lifestory composed by the "nouvellistes" of his time, and remarks that "Prévost knew how to use them in his work for his own profit" (5).

15. While Sermain limits himself to "internal rhetoric alone" (*Rhétorique et roman*, 2), the inclusion of pseudoautobiographical epsidodes in Prévost novels seems to invite a comparison of the internal rhetoric of the narrator and the external rhetoric of the author.

16. Sgard, *Vie de Prévost*, 80.

17. Simon, *Mass Englightenment*, 77.

18. See Larkin, "J-J Rousseau, the *Histoire de Cleveland* and the *Confessions*," 1295–97.

19. Simon, 77.

20. Ibid., 83.

Chapter 5. From Private to Public

1. Genette, *Seuils*.

2. Théophraste Renaudot, founder of the *Gazette*, began by publishing a sort of classifieds section called the "Feuille du Bureau d'Adresses," and the "bureau" itself was a center for the exchange of information and news (See Bellanger, *Histoire générale de la presse française* 1:85).

3. See e.g., *PC* 1, 2, 5, 11.

4. The description of the English in the novel's preface stresses their strangeness and amplifies their exoticism by comparing them to Chinamen and characterizing them as creatures almost amphibious in nature: "L'Angleterre a presque autant de vaisseaux que de maisons, et l'on peut dire de l'île entière ce que les historiens de la Chine rapportent de Nankin: qu'une grande partie d'un peuple si nombreux demeure habituellement sur l'eau" [England has almost as many ships as houses, and one may say of the entire isle that which the historians of China write of Nanking: that a large number of such a large population make their home on the water] (*RL*, 13).

5. Alan Singerman underlines the status of the denial as an affirmation of this scandalous identification in his note on the "Avertissement," writing: "It is not surprising that Didot did not think it advisable to print the extra line which Prévost proposed to him since it only draws more attention to the parallel one could establish between Mlle Aïssé, 'the admirable Circassian,' and the heroine of Prévost's novel." (Introduction to *Histoire d'une Grecque moderne*, 52).

6. Jenny Mander sees the "private framework" established by the prefaces to eighteenth-century memoir-novels as essential to the "illusion of veracity" and as important in attracting a reading public interested in uncovering "scandalous secrets" (*Circles of Learning*, 85).

7. Georges May affirms that "innumerable prefaces of the period warn the reader that the book he is about to read is not a novel but the relation of true events" (*Le Dilemme du roman*, 144).

8. Prévost himself occupied such a role in relation to the wealthy young Englishman Francis Eyles. (See Engel, *Le Véritable Abbé Prévost*, 38).

9. Carole Dornier, "Préface et intentions d'auteur," in *Le Roman des années trente*, 90.

10. Prévost's knowledge of English is essential to *Le Pour et contre* and to the first volumes of the *Histoire générale des voyages*, and while a successful novelist in his own right, Prévost was just as well known by his contemporaries as the translator of Richardson's *Clarissa* among other English novels.

11. Jan Herman argues that for the generation of Prévost and Marivaux the prefatory declaration that the text is a translation is tantamount to an announcement that the text is a novel: "'I found this manuscript' resembles a performative utterance by which the author assigns his work to a genre [i.e., the novel]" (*Le Roman des années trente*, 109).

12. This interpretation is suggested by Frédéric Deloffre in his Introduction to *Manon Lescaut*, cxlix, cliv, 8.

13. Foucault, "Qu'est-ce qu'un auteur?" 799.

Chapter 6. Prévost's *Contes singuliers*

1. Prévost, *Contes, avantures et faits singuliers* (1764).

2. Prévost, *Contes singuliers* (1767).

3. Prévost, *Contes singuliers* (1852).

4. Charles, *Récit et réflexion*, 5.

5. Todorov, "Catégories du récit littéraire," 131.

6. Sgard, *Prévost romancier*, 27.

7. Sgard, *Labyrinthes*, 21.

8. Todorov, "Le Secret du récit," 154.

9. In his discussion of this story, Paul Pelckmans notes that Prévost uses his own scandalous life as a lure without ever revealing any of his secrets: "Lovers of scandalous stories remembered that Prévost had lived one of the most scandalous epiosodes of his exile there. Those readers, at the start, must have felt disappointed: Prévost does not play a role in the 'Story' except for the role of witness" ("Histoire intéressante ou la tragédie ignorée" in *Prévost et le récit bref*, 153).

10. Interestingly, Bougeant's attack on the genre as a whole often boils down to an attack on the novels of Prévost, and paradoxically this effort to defame Prévost results in the canonization of the novelist as the genre's most important practitioner.

11. Sgard, Introduction, *Voyage du Prince Fan-Férédin*, 15.

12. Prévost responds by publishing ironic reviews of Crébillon's preface to *Les Egarements* and of Bougeant's parodic *Fan Férédin* in *Le Pour et contre*. See "Critique du roman," in *Œuvres de Prévost* 7:500 and 490–91).

13. Berthiaume, "Esthétique des *Contes singuliers*," 387.

14. Ibid., 401.

15. Ibid., 399.

16. Charles, *Récit et réflexion*, 101.

17. Charles explains: "We are far here from the gratuitousness of fiction: if the difference between the false and the fictional be determined by the author's intent, there is no doubt that the Beautiful Muslim's lies do not take away the text's referential status" (*Récit et réflexion*, 109).

18. The article's relation of an adulterous affair followed by a violent revenge recalls the "Père célérier" episode, which takes up an entire volume of *Le Monde moral*.

19. In *Vie de Prévost*, Sgard cites a 1746 letter where Prévost describes his carefully planned retirement to Chaillot in terms that echo the description of the retreat in "Remarque historique": "C'est là que j'ai fixé ma demeure pour trois ans, par un bail en bonne forme, avec la gentille veuve ma gouvernante [Claude-Catherine Robin], Loulou, une cuisinière, et mon laquais" [It is there that I established my home for three years, by a lease in good form, with the good widow my housekeeper (Claude-Catherine Robin), Loulou, a cook, and my manservant] (210). Sgard suggests that Loulou may be a servant, but the close parallel with the text from *Le Pour et contre* persuades me that Loulou was the name of Prévost's dog, a necessary companion in real and imagined solitude.

20. This "signature scene" is also part of a work in which Prévost fights for recognition as an author by challenging the apocryphal conclusion of this story as imagined by his unauthorized replacement. Prévost announces his return to *Le Pour et contre* with the "authentic" end of the tale.

21. In *Le Pour et contre,* where the movement from journalistic to novelistic is often marked by a movement from clarity to obscurity, the passage into a darkened dreamscape is often announced when the author leads the reader into a dangerous forest. In "Histoire récente"(*CS*, 135) an Englishman leaves the city for the country, and while wandering in "un grand bois" he is attacked by a band of thieves. In another article, a man rides through a forest only to find a priest offering his final prayer before hanging himself from the nearest branch (*CS*, 137).

22. Diderot, *Œuvres complètes:* 23:25.

23. This ironic turn in Prévost's writing has been noted by other critics, albeit usually as an occasional phenomenon and not as a characteristic of the Prévostian text. Démoris sees the second half of Renoncour's adventures as an ironic comment on the first and finds a certain black humor in the misadventures of the Doyen (Démoris, *Le Roman à la première personne*, 431–32). Several critics see *La Jeunesse du Commandeur* as an ironic rewriting of *Manon Lescaut* (J-P Schneider in "*Les Mémoires de Malte*, une invitation à relire *Manon Lescaut*?" in *Les Expériences romanesques de Prévost après* 1740, eds. Leborgne and Sermain; Sgard in *Vie de Prévost*, 189). A. Duquaire and F. Gal-

tayries-Capdetrey see irony as a general tendency in Prévost's mid-career novels (see *Les Illusions perdues du roman*, ch. 3, and "Formes et enjeux de l'ironie dans trois romans des années 40 de Prévost" in *L'Abbé Prévost au tournant du siècle*). Francis (in the conclusion to *First-Person Narrators*) and Sermain (in "L'Humour de Prévost" in *L'Abbé Prévost au tournant du siècle*) are among the few who see this ironic dimension as fundamental to all of Prévost's fiction.

CONCLUSION

1. Todorov, "Le Secret du récit."

2. Interestingly enough, the final act of the young commander in his memoirs is to imagine himself an actor taking a bow onstage before his public.

3. Mark Currie, *Postmodern Narrative Theory*, 17.

4. Foucault, "Qu'est-ce qu'un auteur?," 792.

5. See *De l'usage des romans* Vol. 2, where Lenglet-Dufrenoy writes in a reference to *Mémoires d'un homme de qualité*: "The novel, which is written well enough, is by Father Prévost, a onetime Benedictine and after that a convert in England, in Holland, and in Basel, and everywhere else where he performs his tricks" (103) and *La Relation de Parnasse* in an episode attributed to Lenglet where he describes Prévost in these terms: "Bored with his life among the Protestants, he sought a way to return to the Catholic Church. After having been a soldier, then a Jesuit, a soldier again, . . . Protestant or Anglican, now he would like to be a Benedictine at Cluny in order to go from there to Constantinople to preach the Koran, to become a mufti if possible, and then to establish himself as a priest in Japan" (84).

6. Deloffre, Introduction, *Manon Lescaut*, lvii–lviv.

7. Robertson, Introduction, *Mémoires d'un homme de qualité*, Vol. 5.

8. The "Avis de l'auteur" of *Manon Lescaut* famously states its ambition to combine these qualities: "Outre le plaisir d'une lecture agréable, on y trouvera peu d'événements qui ne puissent servir à l'instruction des mœurs; et c'est, à mon avis, un service considérable au public, que de l'instruire en l'amusant" [In addition to the pleasure of an agreeable reading, one will find in it few events which cannot provide moral instruction; and that is, in my opinion, a considerable service to the public to instruct and amuse it at the same time] (*MHQ*, 363).

9. Anonymous, "Preface," *Suite de l'histoire de Manon Lescaut, 7*.

10. Des Grieux explains: "Manon était une créature d'un caractère extraordinaire. Jamais fille n'eut moins d'attachement pour l'argent, mais elle ne pouvait être tranquille un moment avec la crainte d'en manquer" [Manon was a creature of an extraordinary character. Never was a girl less attached to money, but she could not be tranquil for a moment if she feared the lack of it] (*MHQ*, 384). In a justification of her return to prostitution, Manon's letter reaffirms the tension between love and money: "Crois-tu qu'on puisse être bien tendre lorsqu'on manque de pain?" [Do you think one can be very tender when one has no bread?] (*MHQ*, 387).

11. Principato, "Rhétorique et technique narrative chez l'abbé Prevost," 1354. Principato delineates his own system of rhetorical activity in Prévost's fiction as that of the *histoire* on the level of Des Griex's interaction with other characters such as Tiberge, the *récit* on the level of his storytelling to the listener Renoncour, and the *narration* as the transmission of the narrative to the reader.

Bibliography

L'Abbé Prévost: Actes du Colloque d'Aix-en-Provence, 20–21 décembre 1963. Gap: Ophrys, 1965.

Aïssé, Charlotte. *Lettres*. 1787. Paris: Hatier, 1995.

Anonymous. *Le Philosophe anglais ou l'histoire de M.Cleveland. tome cinquième*. (apocryphal sequel to Prévost's *Cleveland*). Utrecht: E. Neaulme, 1734.

Bellanger, Claude, ed. *Histoire générale de la presse française*. Paris: Presses Universitaires de France, 1969.

Berthiaume, Pierre. "Esthétique des *Contes singuliers*." *Cahiers de l'association internationale des études françaises* 46 (1994): 387–402.

Bougeant, Guillaume-Hyacinthe. *Voyage merveilleux du Prince Fan Férédin en Romancie*. 1735. Edited by Jean Sgard. Saint-Etienne: Publications de l'Université de Saint-Etienne, 1992.

Bourdieu, Pierre, *Les Règles de l'art*. Paris: Seuil, 1992.

Bury, Emmanuel. *Littérature et politesse: L'Invention de l'honnête homme (1580–1750)*. Paris: Presses Universitaires de France, 1996.

Censer, Jack, *The French Press in the Age of Enlightenment*. London: Routledge, 1994.

Censer, Jack and Jeremy Popkin, eds. *Press and Politics in Pre-Revolutionary France*. Berkeley: University of California Press, 1987.

Charles, Shelly. *Récit et réflexion: poétique de l'hétérogène dans* Le Pour et contre *de Prévost*. Oxford: Voltaire Foundation, 1992.

Chartier, Roger. "Figures de l'auteur." Chap. 2 in *L'Ordre des livres*. Aix en Provence: Alinéa, 1992.

———. *Les Origines culturelles de la Révolution française*. 2d ed. Paris: Editions du Seuil, 2000.

Chartier, Roger, and Henri-Jean Martin, eds. *Histoire de l'édition française*. 2d ed. Paris: Fayard, 1990.

Courcelles. *Suite de Manon Lescaut*. 1847. Paris: Hatier, 1995.

Crébillon *fils*, Claude Prosper Jolyot. *Les Egarements du cœur et de l'esprit*. 1736. In *Œuvres complètes*. Vol. 2. Edited by Jean Sgard. Paris: Garnier, 2000.

Currie, Mark. *Postmodern Narrative Theory*. New York: St. Martin's Press, 1998.

Darnton, Robert. *The Literary Underground of The Old Regime*. Cambridge, MA: Harvard University Press, 1982.

Deloffre, Frédéric. Introduction. *Manon Lescaut*. Paris: Garnier, 1965.

Démoris, René. *Le Roman à la première personne.* Paris: Armand Colin, 1975.

Desfontaines, *Nouvelliste du Parnasse ou Réflexions sur les ouvrages nouveaux.* Paris: Chaubert, 1731.

Diderot, Denis. *Jacques le fataliste.* 1796. In *Œuvres complètes.* Vol. 23. Edited by J. Proust and J. Undank. Paris: Hermann, 1981.

Diderot, Denis, and Jean Le Rond d'Alembert. *Encyclopédie.* Paris: Briasson, 1751–65.

Duquaire, Alexandre. *Les Illusions perdues du roman: L'abbé Prévost à l'épreuve du romanesque.* Amsterdam: Rodopi, 2006.

Engel, Claire-Eliane. *Figures et aventures du XVIIIe siècle.* Paris: Je sers, 1939.

— — —. *Le Véritable Abbé Prévost.* Monaco: Editions du Rocher, 1957.

Foucault, Michel. "Qu'est-ce qu'un auteur?" *Dits et écrits (1954–1988),* Vol.1. Paris: Gallimard, 1994.

Francis, R. A. *The Abbé Prévost's First Person Narrators.* Oxford: Voltaire Foundation, 1993.

Francis, R. A., and Jean Mainil, eds. *L'Abbé Prévost au tournant du siècle.* Oxford: Voltaire Foundation, 2000.

Genette, Gérard. *Seuils.* Paris: Editions du Seuil, 1986.

Gilot, Michel. "*Cleveland* et *Jacques le fataliste.*" *Cahiers Prévost d'Exiles* 1 (1984): 73–83.

Gilroy, James. *The Romantic Manon and des Grieux.* Sherbrooke: Editions Naaman, 1980.

Grieder, Joesphine. *Anglomania in France 1740–1789: Fact, Fiction, and Political Discourse.* Geneva: Droz, 1985.

Habermas, Jürgen. *The Structural Transformation of the Public Sphere: An Inquiry into a Category of Bourgeois Society.* Trans. Thomas Burger. Cambridge, MA: MIT Press, 1989.

Labrosse, Claude, and Pierre Rétat. *L'Instrument périodique: La fonction de la presse au XVIIIe siècle.* Lyon: Presses Universitaires de Lyon, 1985.

Larkin, Steve. "*Cleveland* et les *Confessions.*" *Cahiers Prévost d'Exiles* 3 (1986): 15–26.

— — —. Introduction. *Le Pour et contre nombres 1–60,* by Prévost. Oxford: Voltaire Foundation, 1993.

— — —. "J-J Rousseau, the *Histoire de Cleveland* and the *Confessions.*" In *Transactions of the Fifth International Conference on the Enlightenment.* Vol. 3. Oxford: Voltaire Foundation, 1980.

Leborgne, Erik. *Prévost d'Exiles : Bibliographie des écrivains français.* Paris: Memini, 1996.

— — —. *Saturne libertin: Libertinage et fantasmes chez Prévost.* Thèse de troisième cycle, Université de Paris III, 1996.

Leborgne, Erik, and Jean-Paul Sermain, eds. *Les Expériences romanesques de Prévost après 1740.* Leuwen: Edition Peeters, 2003.

Lebreton, André. *Le Roman au XVIIIe siècle.* 1898. Geneva: Slatkine, 1978.

Lejeune, Philippe. *Le Pacte autobiographique.* Paris: Editions du Seuil, 1975.

Lenglet-Dufrenoy, Nicolas. *De l'usage des romans* and *Bibliothèque des romans.* 1734. Geneva: Slatkine, 1970.

Mackie, Erin, ed. *The Commerce of Everyday Life: Selections from* The Tatler *and* The Spectator. Boston: Bedford/St. Martin's, 1998.

Mander, Jenny. *Circles of Learning: Narratology and the Eighteenth-Century French Novel.* Oxford: Voltaire Foundation, 1999.

May, Georges. *Le Dilemme du roman au XVIIIe siècle.* Paris: Presses Universitaires de France, 1963.

Maza, Sarah. *Private Lives and Public Affairs: The Causes Célèbres of Pre-revolutionary France.* Berkeley: University of California Press, 1993.

Molière. *Le Misanthrope.* 1666. In *Théâtre complet.* Vol. 3. Edited by Pierre Malandain. Paris: Imprimerie Nationale, 1997.

Montandon, Alain, ed. *L'Honnête homme et le dandy.* Tubingen: Etudes de littérature française, 1993.

Pelckmans, Paul, and Jan Herman, eds. *Prévost et le récit bref.* Amsterdam: Rodopi, 2006.

Prévost, Antoine-François: *Aventures et Anecdotes.* Paris: Glomeau, 1852.

———. *Contes, avantures et faits singuliers.* Paris: Veuve Duchesne 1764.

———. *Contes singuliers.* Paris: Veuve Duchesne, 1767.

———. *Histoire générale des voyages.* Paris: Didot, 1746–59.

———. *Manuel lexique.* Paris: Didot, 1750.

———. *Œuvres de Prévost.* Edited by Jean Sgard et al. Grenoble: Presses Universitaires de Grenoble, 1977–1986.

———. *Le Pour et contre, ouvrage périodique d'un goût nouveau. Dans lequel on s'explique librement sur tout ce qui peut intéresser la curiosité du public, en matière de sciences, d'art, de livres, d'auteurs, etc. sans prendre aucun parti, et sans offenser personne. Par l'auteur des Mémoires d'un homme de qualité.* Paris: Didot, 1733–40.

Principato, Aurelio. "Rhétorique et technique narratives chez l'abbé Prévost." In Transactions of the Fifth International Congress on the Enlightenment. Vol. 3. Oxford: Voltaire Foundation, 1980 .

Rétat, Pierre, and Jean Sgard, eds. *Presse et histoire au dix-huitième siècle: l'année 1734.* Lyon: Editions du C.N.R.S., 1978.

Robertson, Mysie. Introduction. *Mémoires et aventures d'un homme de qualité,* Vol. 5. Paris: Champion, 1927.

Le Roman des années trente: la génération de Prévost et de Marivaux. Saint-Etienne: Publications de l'Université de Saint-Etienne, 1996.

Roth, Suzanne. *Les Aventuriers au dix-huitième siècle.* Paris: Editions Galilée, 1980.

Rousseau, Jean-Jacques. *A M. d'Alembert.* 1758. In *Œuvres complètes.* Vol. 3. Edited by Bernard Gagnebin and Marcel Raymond. Paris: Gallimard, 1959.

———. *Les Confessions.* 1782. In *Œuvres complètes.* Vol. 1. Paris: Gallimard, 1959.

Russo, Elena. "Virtuous Economies: Modernity and Noble Expenditure from Montesquieu to Caillois." *Historical Reflections* 25 (Summer 1999): 251–78.

Segal, Naomi. *The Unintended Reader: Feminism and* Manon Lescaut. Cambridge: Cambridge University Press, 1986.

Sermain, Jean-Paul. "*L'Eloge de Richardson* et *L'Avis* de Renoncour en tête de *l'Histoire du Chevalier des Grieux et de Manon Lescaut.*" *Cahiers Prévost d'Exiles* 1 (1984): 85–98.

———. *Rhétorique et roman au dix-huitième siècle: L'Exemple de Prévost et de Marivaux (1728–1742).* Oxford: Voltaire Foundation,1985.

Sgard, Jean. *L'Abbé Prévost: Labyrinthes de la mémoire.* Paris: Presses Universitaires de France, 1986.

— — —. *Prévost romancier.* Paris: José Corti, 1968.

— — —. "Rousseau et Prévost. Rapports personnels et lectures." *Cahiers Prévost d'Exiles* 3 (1986): 5–14.

— — —. *Vie de Prévost (1697–1763).* Laval: Presses de l'Université Laval, 2006.

— — —. *Vingt Etudes sur Prévost.* Grenoble: ELLUG, 1995.

Sgard, Jean, ed. *Dictionnaire des Journalistes* 1600–1789. Oxford: Voltaire Foundation, 1999.

— — —. *Dictionnaire des Journaux* 1600–1789. Oxford: Voltaire Foundation, 1991.

— — —. Le Pour et Contre *de Prévost: Introduction, tables et index.* Nizet, Paris, 1969.

Simon, Julia. *Mass Enlightenment: Critical Studies in Rousseau and Diderot.* Albany: State University of New York Press, 1995.

Singerman, Alan J. Introduction. *Histoire d'une Grecque moderne.* Paris: Garnier-Flammarion, 1980.

Stanton, Domna. *The Aristocrat as Art: A Study of the* Honnête Homme *and the Dandy in Seventeenth- and Nineteenth-Century French Literature.* New York: Columbia University Press, 1980.

Stroev, Alexandre. *Les Aventuriers des Lumières.* Paris: Presses Universitaires de France, 1997.

Todorov, Tzvetan. "Les Catégories du récit littéraire." In *Analyse structurale des récits.* Paris: Editions du Seuil, 1981.

— — —. "Le Secret du récit." In *Poétique de la prose.* Paris: Editions du Seuil, 1971.

Viala, Alain. *La Naissance de l'écrivain: Sociologie de la littérature à l'âge classique.* Paris: Minuit, 1985.

Voltaire, *Lettres philosophiques.* 1734. In *Œuvres complètes.* Vol. 25. Paris: Hachette, 1915–17.

Walsh, Jonathan. *Histoire d'une Grecque moderne: Figures of Authority on Trial.* Birmingham: Summa, 2001.